The Civil War in Missouri

Century of Missouri History Scholarship Series

A series edited by Lynn Wolf Gentzler and Gary R. Kremer

The Civil War in Missouri:
Essays from the
Missouri Historical Review,
1906-2006

Edited with an introduction by William E. Parrish

The State Historical Society of Missouri
Columbia

Volume Editor: William E. Parrish is professor emeritus of history at Mississippi State University.

Series Editors: Lynn Wolf Gentzler is associate director of The State Historical Society of Missouri. Gary R. Kremer is executive director of The State Historical Society of Missouri.

The State Historical Society of Missouri
Columbia, Missouri 65201
© 2006 by The State Historical Society of Missouri

ISBN-13: 978-0-9622891-4-9
ISBN-10: 0-9622891-4-0

Contents

Preface

This book launches a new series of State Historical Society of Missouri publications to be known as the *Century of Missouri History Scholarship Series*. Each volume will contain a dozen or more articles drawn from the pages of the *Missouri Historical Review* during its first century of publication (1906-2006) and organized either by geographic region or by topic.

We chose the Civil War in Missouri as the first topic for the series because, despite the vast number of books and articles that have been written about that tragic event, the war remains among the most popular subjects for discussion, inquiry, research, and writing in the state. Civil War records, manuscripts, diaries, letters, and newspapers are the most frequently requested materials at The State Historical Society of Missouri.

We asked Professor William E. Parrish to select the twelve essays for *The Civil War in Missouri: Essays from the Missouri Historical Review, 1906-2006* because of his stellar reputation as a Civil War historian of long standing. Parrish completed his doctoral dissertation, a biography of Civil War-era Missouri politician David Rice Atchison, at the University of Missouri in Columbia in 1955 under the direction of eminent scholar Lewis Atherton. Dr. Parrish has been writing about the Civil War in Missouri ever since. Among his most important works on the subject, in addition to his dissertation, which was published as a book by the University of Missouri Press in 1961, are the following: *Turbulent Partnership: Missouri and the Union, 1861-1865* (1963), *Missouri Under Radical Rule, 1865-1870* (1965), *A History of Missouri, 1860-1875* (1973), and *Frank Blair: Lincoln's Conservative* (1998).

We hope that you enjoy Dr. Parrish's introduction to this collection, as well as the essays that he has selected. We hope, also, that you find future volumes in this series to be stimulating reading.

The editors have modernized and standardized punctuation, capitalization, and endnote style. First names in brackets have been supplied by the editors, and illustrations have been added to articles originally printed without them. Unless otherwise credited, all illustrations are from The State Historical Society of Missouri's collections.

Lynn Wolf Gentzler
Gary R. Kremer

Acknowledgments

The editors wish to thank Bill Parrish for selecting the articles to include in this volume and for his carefully crafted introduction, which placed the individual articles within the context of the evolving study of Missouri Civil War history. We also want to express our appreciation to the Christine Gempp Love Foundation, whose generous contribution helped fund the publishing of this book. The Society's executive committee, Richard Franklin, Bruce Beckett, H. Riley Bock, Charles Brown, Lawrence O. Christensen, Doug Crews, Virginia J. Laas, Stephen N. Limbaugh Jr., Albert M. Price, and Robert C. Smith, are to be acknowledged for their endorsement and support of this series. Members of the Society's editorial advisory board, Lawrence O. Christensen, William E. Foley, Alan R. Havig, Patrick Huber, Virginia J. Laas, Bonnie Stepenoff, and Arvarh Strickland, also provided input. We thank the scholars who read the introduction and commented on the article selection and express our appreciation to Blaire Leible Garwitz, Society information specialist, who designed the volume and helped in numerous other ways.

Introduction

The story of the State Historical Society of Missouri's founding in 1898 has been well told in several places, most particularly in the excellent study by Alan R. Havig, *A Centennial History of the State Historical Society of Missouri, 1898-1998*, published by the University of Missouri Press. Although the aegis for its establishment came from the Missouri Press Association, the state quickly endorsed the idea with legislation passed in May 1899, which made the Society eligible for state funding. That authorization, as well as the Society's constitution, set out essentially four goals for the new agency: collecting, preserving, exhibiting, and *publishing* (italics mine) historical materials.

Beginning in December 1901, the Society established the format of an annual meeting at which both academics and lay personalities presented papers dealing with various aspects of Missouri history. It was not until the second annual meeting in January 1903, however, that the Society found sufficient funds to publish its "first historical publication," an eighty-five-page bound booklet containing two pages detailing the business items of that meeting followed by four historical papers that had been presented there.

The following year the Society published *A Catalogue of Publications by Missouri Authors* in conjunction with its exhibit in the Missouri Building at the 1904 Louisiana Purchase Exposition in St. Louis. This elaborate project displayed some 1,800 books written by Missouri authors, including 216 volumes of poetry as well as 928 bound volumes of 726 newspapers and magazines that had been published within the state during 1903. As the thousands of visitors flowed through the beautiful Missouri Building with its golden dome surmounted by an eye-catching statue of the *Spirit of Missouri*, the exhibit could not help but draw attention to the Society and its work, thereby increasing public awareness of the need to preserve and disseminate Missouri history. The Society received a grand prize from the Fair Commission, which also awarded Secretary Francis Sampson a silver medal for his work in putting the exhibit together.

Greatly encouraged by the success of this effort and by an increase in the state's funding, the Society's Executive Committee began to hope that it might be possible to undertake a historical quarterly. To that end, in December 1904 it authorized its Finance Committee to move forward with the idea. A presentation to the Missouri State Teachers Association in June 1905 secured its endorsement and led to the establishment of a publications committee to bring the project to fruition.

Thus, in October 1906, Missourians welcomed a new publication titled simply *Missouri Historical Review*, which this year celebrates its centennial. The new journal contained five articles, a bibliography of various writings on Missouri history, and notes of historical interest. As it grew with subsequent volumes, edited original documents were included, as well as genealogical studies of important early families, together with lists of cemetery inscriptions. Reprinted newspaper articles dealing with historical issues found their way into the journal, and reports on historical landmarks were also included.

From the outset, the *Review* frequently visited the topic of the Civil War. Missouri had been dramatically impacted by that conflict, which divided it so drastically not only between 1861 and 1865 but for many years thereafter. With the momentous event only forty years distant, many of its participants, both military and political, were still living and actively involved throughout the state as the *Review* began its publication. Thus, their stories of the events surrounding that conflict would draw attention and create interest in the fledgling journal.

Many of the early articles were papers read at the annual meetings of the Society. These dealt with both political and military reminiscences, as, for instance, the reflections of William F. Switzler, the well-known editor of the *Columbia Missouri Statesman*, on his experiences in the constitutional conventions of 1865 and 1875 published in the January 1907 number and a fascinating account of "The Shelby Raid, 1863," appearing in the April 1912 issue, in which George S. Grover, who had been in the Union forces opposing those of the Confederate Jo Shelby, wrote glowingly of the prowess of his former enemy. Read initially at an 1894 reunion of the participants from both sides, the latter strikingly revealed the way in which the wounds of the conflict were healing among the war's veterans.

The first articles on the Civil War, which might be considered scholarly as opposed to remembrances, appeared in the January and April 1913 issues of the *Review* and came from the pen of the venerable Floyd C. Shoemaker, then serving as a research assistant within the Society and as the journal's assistant editor. Titled "The Story of the Civil War in Northeast Missouri," these relied on secondary printed accounts as well as original source materials. Two years later, Shoemaker would become the Society's secretary and executive director, a position he would hold from 1915 until his retirement in 1960. Under his editorship and that of his successors, the *Missouri Historical Review* would welcome a broad range of scholarly articles dealing with all aspects of the Civil War, a practice that continues to the present day. As new scholarship developed different ways of looking at old topics and as new historical fields emerged, the journal welcomed these, and the variety of subjects broadened considerably.

Given all this, the staff and the Executive Committee of the Society decided that it would be appropriate, as part of the *Review's* centennial celebration, to put together an anthology of Civil War articles that have appeared therein over the past one hundred years. When first approached about this by Dr. Gary Kremer, the Society's current executive director and editor of the *Review*, I contemplated taking a chronological approach, using articles from each of the various time periods, going back through the long development of the *Review*. This might have shown how the various patterns of historical interpretation have changed with time, but I believe that it would have left the reader with only a vague picture of the total scope of this momentous conflict on the lives of those whom it affected.

Rather, after I examined the many issues of the *Review*, it seemed best to take a topical approach, albeit following a generally chronological timetable within the war itself. Thus, the vast impact of the Civil War in Missouri, as seen by various writers in the *Review* through the years, could be appreciated. Hence, the anthology will embrace a broad spectrum of articles in an attempt to show how that conflict affected the many different Missourians who found themselves caught up in it. An attempt will be made to place each article within its appropriate historical framework, showing how the war developed in the state during those critical years of 1861 to 1865. Where feasible, there will also be an effort to indicate how some of these articles reflected changing emphases within the ongoing rush of historical interpretation over time. Only twelve articles can be reprinted in the anthology, but it is hoped that they will give the reader a flavor of the broad complexity of the event.

From the outset, Missouri found itself bitterly divided between those older elements within its population whose roots came from their Southern and French heritage, with an economic base firmly entrenched with slavery, and those newcomers, primarily German, who had migrated to the urban and eastern areas of the state seeking freedom from Old World oppressions. Although the vast majority of Missourians preferred some form of neutrality in the approaching conflict, this proved impossible as a strongly pro-Southern state government quickly came into conflict with equally staunch pro-Union forces, dominated initially by the Germans, determined to force the issue of loyalty.

Matters came to a head in May 1861 when Governor Claiborne F. Jackson ordered the state militia into weeklong encampments across the state. Pursuant to this call, General D. M. Frost established Camp Jackson in the western part of St. Louis. The pro-Southern Jackson had hoped that his militia might be able to capture the arms in the federal arsenal in south St. Louis, but this action was thwarted by General Nathaniel Lyon and Congressman Frank Blair, who had already answered President Lincoln's call for volunteers with their German supporters after Jackson refused to fill Missouri's requested quota in the wake of the attack on Fort Sumter. The story of these maneuvers and their aftermath is told in my article "General Nathaniel Lyon: A Portrait" in the October 1954 issue of the *Review*, which opens this anthology. By these events war came to Missouri as both sides prepared for military action.

Among the many previously mentioned early reminiscences that found their way into the pages of the *Review*, one that stood out, as I read it, was the account in the April 1912 issue titled "The Battle of Lexington as Seen by a Woman." In this memoir, Mrs. Susan A. Arnold McCausland, a young woman with strong pro-Southern sympathies at the time of the war, reveals her fascination with the arrival of competing forces in her small community in September 1861 and her utter devotion to what she and many of her later contemporaries considered the "Lost Cause." These devotees of the Confederacy looked back upon their heroes with fervent admiration and nostalgia by the early twentieth century. In reflecting on the event of some fifty years previous, Mrs. McCausland expresses her admiration for the way pro-Confederate General Sterling Price and his men conducted their operation and handled the surrender of the Union military under Colonel James Mulligan. Her reminiscence also reveals, so strikingly, the utter lack of reality on the part of many in those initial months concerning the horrors that would soon be visited upon them and their state.

Price's pro-Confederate Missouri State Guard had come to Lexington after their recent triumph at the Battle of Wilson's Creek near Springfield. That engagement had seen not only a Union defeat but the death of General Lyon. Had Susan McCausland been present at Springfield in the aftermath of that battle, she would have had a different perspective on the war and its horrors than the one she received at Lexington. In his July 1999 *Review* article, "'Springfield is a Vast Hospital': The Dead and Wounded at the Battle of Wilson's Creek," William Garrett Piston, professor of history at Missouri State University in Springfield, reveals the tragedy of battle. One of a group of recent historians emphasizing the impact of the war on soldiers in the ranks and their families back home, Piston reveals the tragedy of battle as he discusses the efforts of military surgeons on both sides to establish field hospitals to care for the wounded on the battlefield. He brings home the tragic aftermath of Missouri's first major battle as the dead and wounded from the battlefield were brought into the city to be cared for in makeshift hospitals by the community's physicians and by the women of the town who volunteered as nurses. Then he goes further to show the impact on the home communities of these recently enlisted volunteers, who had been sent off with giant celebrations in anticipation that their courageous valor would bring quick success. Therein, Piston reveals a fairly recent dimension of Civil War history: the effect of the conflict on the home front.

By the time of the Battle of Lexington, the new political divisions of the state had already been established. In the wake of the exodus of Missouri's regularly elected but pro-Southern government from its capital at Jefferson City because of the confrontations with General Lyon, the convention previously called in February to decide the issue of secession reconvened in July and established the pro-Union provisional government under Hamilton R. Gamble, who had been the leader of the neutrality forces during its earlier session. This administration would govern Missouri with the assistance of Union troops and state militia until replaced by a regularly elected government in January 1865. In her October 1940 article in the *Review*, Marguerite Potter, a history teacher at Riverview Gardens High School in St. Louis, discusses in great detail the early life of "Hamilton R. Gamble, Missouri's War Governor" and his wartime efforts to walk a tightrope between Union military commanders and the various conflicting groups, military and civilian, within the state itself. A staunch conservative, Gamble sought to maintain as much control over the state's internal affairs as he possibly could. That his course was not an easy one is clearly revealed by Potter. Although he had a direct connection to the Lincoln administration through his brother-in-law, Attorney General Edward Bates, Gamble (who died in early 1864) and his successor, Willard P. Hall, found themselves confronted by myriad problems, some of which will be discussed in more depth in later articles in the anthology. Yet, through it all, Gamble displayed remarkable staying power, to his great credit.

The Gamble regime's counterpart, "Missouri's Secessionist Government, 1861-1865," is covered by Arthur R. Kirkpatrick, at the time a doctoral student at the University of Missouri and later a history professor at Bethany College in West Virginia, in his June 1951 article in the *Review*. Headed by Governor Claiborne Fox Jackson and, after Jackson's death in late 1862, by Thomas C. Reynolds, this duly elected but pro-Confederate administration found refuge in Arkansas and Texas after being driven from Missouri by Union forces under General Samuel Curtis in early 1862. From there it cooperated with the Jefferson Davis administration in Richmond and the Confederate military officials in the Trans-Mississippi Department with regard to Missouri's pro-Southern volunteers while also working to select the state's representatives and senators in the Confederate congress. Kirkpatrick, who excerpted this article from his doctoral dissertation at the University of Missouri, ably demonstrates the frustrations that the Jackson-Reynolds regimes encountered as they sought to keep the faith with Missouri's pro-Southern citizens.

Even as the pro-Confederate forces of Sterling Price and the Jackson-Reynolds government were being driven out of the state in the winter of 1861-1862, a large number who sympathized with their cause remained behind. Many of these turned to guerrilla action while others expressed their sympathies in a variety of ways. William B. Hesseltine, at the outset of a long and distinguished career as professor of history at the University of Wisconsin, details the fate of many of these in his April 1929 *Review* article, "Military Prisons in St. Louis." Hastily arranged in a variety of makeshift quarters, these facilities housed both military and civilian prisoners, the latter suspected Confederate sympathizers whom local officials throughout the state believed could not be trusted. These quickly became overcrowded and, like their counterparts elsewhere, proved largely inadequate to the demands being placed upon them, leading to considerable suffering on the part of their inmates. Proponents of the "Lost Cause" had portrayed federal authorities at these type of places as high-handed in their management, but Hesseltine emphasizes that those at the St. Louis facilities, working with the Western Sanitary Commission, a philanthropic organization (of which more later), sought to alleviate the conditions as best they could.

The situation along the Kansas-Missouri border proved to be particularly turbulent throughout the war as Kansas Jayhawkers raided the western counties, thereby stirring up pro-Southern guerrilla bands such as that of William Quantrill and others. Albert Castel, a professor of history at Western Michigan University, has written much about this deteriorating situation, but his article, "Order No. 11 and the Civil War on the Border," in the July 1963 *Missouri Historical Review* deals specifically with the background and impact of one of the most controversial military measures taken to quell it. Issued by Union General Thomas Ewing in August 1863 following Quantrill's raid on Lawrence, Kansas, Order No. 11 required the evacuation of all residents living more than a mile from Union military posts within a four-county area on the ground that many of them had been harboring guerrillas. Castel notes particularly how this so angered the well-known Missouri artist George Caleb Bingham that he protested the order vigorously—most notably through his famous painting that hangs in the Society's gallery in Columbia, which shows a family being driven from their home by Kansas militia in ruthless fashion as they are sent into exile. Bingham argued that the order was unnecessary in its harshness and ineffectual in what it sought to achieve, namely quelling guerrilla activities. In both of these, Castel sees a certain amount of truth while also indicating that Bingham exaggerated the situation. In a revisionist mode, Castel maintains that the order was a military necessity if peace was to be maintained along the Kansas-Missouri border, and he further reveals that subsequent commanders effectively modified most of its harsher features as they sought to sort out the questions of loyalty. Whatever the case, this episode has come down in Missouri history as one of the more infamous moments of the war.

Prodded by the Lincoln administration's Emancipation Proclamation, the Missouri State Convention passed a gradual emancipation ordinance in June 1863. In its wake, many of Missouri's slaves arbitrarily took matters into their own hands and fled to free territory. Together with recently established federal policy, it also opened the floodgates for the enlistment of African American troops into the Union armies. John W. Blassingame, at the time a graduate student at Howard University but later a professor of history at Yale University, relates the black experience in his April 1964 *Review* article titled "The Recruitment of Negro Troops in Missouri During the Civil War." Blassingame would become a major figure in the reinterpretation of slavery and the black experience in the post-World War II era, and his article reflects a growing interest in the lives of African Americans generally. In it he points to the difficulties of securing large numbers of black troops because of some indecision on the part of both federal and state officials in how to effect it. Unsympathetic provost marshals who had the task of carrying out the policy often performed their duty reluctantly as they sought to determine loyal slaveowners, whose slaves could not be touched, and those who were disloyal. In the end, scarcely more than eight thousand African Americans were enlisted, with many of these being brought in through the draft, whereby they could help fill the state's quota. Still, those who did enlist came eagerly and served well.

Yet another concern for the new freedmen was education, as Lawrence Christensen, professor emeritus of history at the University of Missouri-Rolla, demonstrates in "Black Education in Civil War St. Louis" in the April 2001 issue of the *Review*. He reveals that various groups came together to undertake the establishment of freedmen's schools, including women's volunteer organizations working with the Western Sanitary Commission; the national American Missionary Association, which had been actively engaged in this kind of work long before the war; and African American ministers, who readily moved to the forefront of the effort. This cooperation resulted in a broad-based school board that coordinated the work of a variety of agencies and individuals to accomplish this important undertaking and provided an opportunity for whites and blacks to work together in a meaningful enterprise. Blassingame's article and Christensen's work on black Missourians in this and other venues were but part of a growing volume of efforts, including those of the Society's current director, Gary Kremer, to reinterpret Missouri's African Americans' experiences in light of the changing times.

One of the major players in the attempts to alleviate the plight of African Americans in Missouri and throughout the Mississippi Valley was the Western Sanitary Commission headed by James E. Yeatman of St. Louis. Established initially to aid in the hospitalization of the wounded evacuated into St. Louis from the Battle of Wilson's Creek, it broadened its humanitarian activities in the following years to include a wide variety of projects, from providing hospital trains and boats in the western and trans-Mississippi theaters and assisting in medical care of the wounded generally to caring for refugees, both black and white.

Yet another project of the Western Sanitary Commission and, particularly, its women's auxiliaries is described in Robert Patrick Bender's article, "'This Noble and Philanthropic Enterprise': The Mississippi Valley Sanitary Fair of 1864 and the Practice of Civil War Philanthropy," in the January 2001 *Missouri Historical Review*. An instructor in history at Lane College at the time, Bender places the St. Louis fair within the context of the national movement for such events. Promoted as a means of allowing citizens to "make a perceptible contribution to the war effort," the Mississippi Valley Sanitary Fair, which ran in the summer of 1864, contained numerous exhibits and displays intended to promote patriotism and secure financial support for the efforts of philanthropic groups involved in alleviating various health and other conditions among the troops in the field and the refugees pouring into St. Louis from the war areas. The fair's tremendous success aided its sponsors greatly in their efforts to address the needs of those less fortunate. Bender's article reflects another growing historical trend, the interest in women's roles in American life.

As the war ended, Missouri underwent a major political transformation that brought to power the Radical Union Party in the election of 1864. Over the previous two years, many residents had been growing dissatisfied with the conservatism of the Gamble administration and the increasing turbulence that had erupted across the state. Many saw slavery as a root cause of the state's problems and its continuation as a threat to Missouri's postwar prosperity. They resented the periodic incursions of Confederate forces from Arkansas, climaxed by Sterling Price's unsuccessful September 1864 invasion on the eve of the election. In that political contest, they turned to the new Radical Union Party, which had emerged out of the controversy over the state's emancipation policy. At the same time they ushered the Radicals into office, the voters authorized the calling of a new constitutional convention to deal with the realities of postwar Missouri.

The work of this body is described in "Charles D. Drake and the Constitutional Convention of 1865" by David D. March, professor emeritus of history at Truman State University, in the January 1953 issue of the *Review*. He reveals the dominant role played by Drake in pushing the Radical agenda through the convention, including provision for immediate emancipation and the proscription of any who had espoused the Confederate cause from participating in the political and other affairs of postwar Missouri. This set the stage for five years of Radical rule, whose excesses would ultimately lead to the return of the conservatives, including many ex-Confederates, to political power in the 1870s.

Missouri has often been the setting for novelists and other writers seeking to portray the everyday lives of the state's citizens during this turbulent period in its history. Such literary efforts began to appear even while the war raged, and have continued to the present, as Larry Olpin, a professor of English at Central Missouri State University, reveals in his article, "Missouri and the American Civil War Novel," in the October 1990 issue of the *Review*. Novelists have always had an interest in exploring human emotions during the difficult circumstances of wartime and other crises, and the war-torn Missouri scene provided ample material for their craft, as Professor Olpin demonstrates. These efforts have ranged from the grotesque, depicting the horrors of guerrilla warfare and family divisions, to more reasoned portrayals of the difficulties of wartime life. Many of the early works were of the pulp variety, designed for immediate popular consumption, while later novels sought a more sophisticated audience. Whatever the case, Missouri and its wartime experience have not lacked for the novelist's attention.

These are but a sampling of the many fine articles dealing with all aspects of the Civil War in Missouri that have appeared in the *Missouri Historical Review* over the past one hundred years. For those interested in pursuing further reading, I would suggest consulting the bibliography in my *History of Missouri, 1860-1875*, revised edition, published by the University of Missouri Press in 2001, which includes many of these and other articles as well as additional sources of a wide variety. We wish you continued good reading!

William E. Parrish

General Nathaniel Lyon: A Portrait

WILLIAM E. PARRISH

On February 6, 1861, a company of United States regular troops arrived in St. Louis from Fort Riley, Kansas, to reinforce the Federal arsenal near that city.[1] The importance of this event did not lie in the eighty men who were added to the strength of the arsenal but in their commander, Captain Nathaniel Lyon. Few of the citizens of St. Louis or Missouri realized what significance the arrival of this soldier was to hold for that city and state in the days ahead. In the short space of six months, from the time of his arrival until his death at Wilson's Creek the following August, Captain (later Brigadier General) Lyon was to play a major role in the struggle to keep Missouri in the Union. Although successful in this endeavor, Lyon, more than any other one man, was responsible for driving the regime of Governor Claiborne F. Jackson into exile and for bringing civil war to Missouri, with all its attendant strife and bloodshed. It is the purpose of this article to examine the background and the writings of General Lyon in order to get a clearer picture of the forces which motivated him in his actions as a responsible officer of the United States Army in Missouri during the fateful year of 1861.

Doctor William A. Hammond has left one of the best descriptions of Lyon. Doctor Hammond was a close friend of Lyon during their mutual period of service at Fort Riley, Kansas, in 1854 and 1855 and says of him:

> He was intolerant of opposition, unmindful of the many obligatory courtesies of life, prone to inject the most unpopular opinions at times and places when he knew they would be unwelcome, and enforcing them with all the bitterness and vehemence of which he was capable; easily

aroused to a degree of anger that was almost insane in its manifestations; narrow-minded; prejudiced, mentally unbalanced, and yet with all this, honest to the core, truthful under all circumstances, intelligent, generous to a fault with those he liked, well-read in science and literature and popular theology, absolutely moral, temperate in the pleasures of the table, kind and considerate with his friends, attentive to his duties, a strict disciplinarian . . . and altogether a man, one of the most remarkable of his day, who commanded the respect . . . of those who knew his virtues and his faults, and that he was one to trust in emergencies with absolute confidence that he would always do what he had said he would do, even though he gave up his life for his constancy.[2]

It is interesting to see these traits at work as Lyon moved through the Missouri scene in the first year of the Civil War.

Lyon had "from the first, devoted love of country . . . [as] a controlling motive."[3] Coming of a staunch New England background, there had early been implanted in him a deep sense of patriotism by his family and friends. This loyalty was to remain with him throughout his life.[4]

It was his childhood desire to attend West Point and thereby carve out an army career for himself. This wish was fulfilled in 1837 when he received an appointment to the military academy on the Hudson. Entering that school the same year, he soon became noted for his conscientiousness and graduated

Nathaniel Lyon hated the Missouri slaveocracy.

on June 30, 1841, eleventh in a class of fifty-two, receiving a commission as second lieutenant.[5] This was the beginning of a long army career which was to be ended only by his death in 1861.

When Lyon arrived in St. Louis in the early part of that year, he was already familiar with the situation there. This is evidenced by his call upon Francis P. Blair Jr. the same day. Blair was the leader of the Unconditional Unionists in the city, and through him, Lyon became acquainted with the Union Safety Committee which had been set up by the loyal citizens, and with these men he worked in close cooperation during the period that followed.[6]

The situation in St. Louis was tense as both Union and secessionist sympathizers had organized their own local drill companies. The principal object of interest was the Federal arsenal, which was in the southern section of the city. This contained 60,000 stand of arms and various other materials of war which the secessionists hoped to capture when the time came for Missouri to depart from the Union and join her sister slave states in the Confederacy.[7]

Lyon was determined to prevent this at all costs. He was a staunch opponent of slavery and detested all those who supported that institution.[8] He was firmly opposed to the secession of one state without the consent of the others and believed that any such attempt should be met by coercion. His opinions on this matter had been formulated as early as 1850. At that time he was on duty in California, and from there he wrote, "I foresee a great excitement this winter in Congress on the subject of slavery, and much deprecate the final resort threatened by the South. Yet should the crisis come, I stand ready to tender a cordial support to the measures necessary to re-establish our Union upon a basis of permanent prosperity."[9] He reiterated this stand in one of a series of newspaper articles which he wrote ten years later.[10] When the secession movement was under way in 1861, he wrote, "It is no longer useful to appeal to reason but to the sword, and trifle no longer in senseless wrangling. I shall not hesitate to rejoice at the triumph of my principles, though this triumph may involve an issue in which I certainly expect to expose and very likely lose my life. I would a thousand times rather incur this, than recall the result of our Presidential election."[11] It was with this feeling that Lyon came to St. Louis two weeks later.

Lyon was aware that the commander of the arsenal was in sympathy with the secessionists of Missouri and feared that should an attack come there would be little resistance if this officer had his way. As technically he outranked that officer, Lyon agitated the new Lincoln administration through the influential Blair to get himself placed in command of the arsenal. He promised that should he be placed in charge there would be little need to worry about such an attack. He warned, "There cannot be . . . a more important occasion, nor a

The Arsenal at St. Louis

better opportunity to strike an effective blow at this arrogant and domineering infatuation of secessionism, than here."[12]

Lyon was well aware of the evils of the slave system and of the desire of the South to maintain and extend it. An ardent supporter of Franklin Pierce in the election campaign of 1852, Lyon had been in Washington early in 1854 and had witnessed the debate on the Kansas-Nebraska Bill. [13] Its passage and acceptance by President Pierce had been a bitter disappointment to Lyon.[14] He soon had a chance to see its effects, for in March 1854 he was transferred to Fort Riley, Kansas, where he served intermittently for the next seven years. Almost simultaneously with Lyon's arrival in the new territory, the fight for "Bloody Kansas" began, and although not an active participant in the struggle, he enthusiastically supported the Free State party throughout this period.[15]

Hammond reports that Lyon was bitter in denouncing Pierce, [Stephen A.] Douglas, and others who supported the Kansas-Nebraska Act. At the time Hammond knew him, Lyon was a strong advocate of William Cullen Bryant's *New York Evening Post*, an abolitionist paper, which Hammond describes as "the gosped by which he [Lyon] swore." Lyon often spoke at Free State meetings, and "above all other things slavery met with his most thorough detestation."[16]

In Kansas, Lyon had ample opportunity to see Missouri slaveocracy at work, and during this time he formed a bitter hatred of that group. He was extremely indignant at the wrongs he felt were perpetrated upon the Free Staters by the "border ruffians" and strongly denounced the practices carried on by this group in the territorial election of 1855.[17] In December of that year he wrote: "I have seen so much of the overbearing domination of the pro-slavery people in Kansas towards the free state men, that I am persuaded the latter have either to fight in self-defense, or submit ignobly to the demands of their aggressors. This conduct, backed as it has been in some measure by the present administration, ought to be effectually rebuked by the indignation of the North."[18] Lyon was tired of making concessions to the South and was ready to fight if need be, but the army in Kansas was caught between the two factions so that whichever side won, the army would have its condemnation.[19] During the summer of 1856, things became so bad that Lyon seriously considered resigning his commission and would have done so had he been ordered to back up the enforcement of the proslavery Kansas legislature.[20]

In Missouri in 1861, Lyon was faced with a similar situation, except that the issue of secession was also involved. Claiborne F. Jackson had been elected governor of Missouri in 1860 on the Douglas Democratic ticket. Although this was considered to be one of the two conservative parties participating in the election, Jackson was a staunch Southern slaveholder and upheld the Douglas banner merely as a matter of expediency.[21] Lyon was doubtless familiar with the campaign of 1860 in Missouri, for he had always taken an active part in politics and during this particular year wrote a series of articles for the *Western Kansas Express* of Manhattan, which strongly presented the Republican cause. Included in these were bitter denunciations of Douglas who Lyon believed was flirting with the South.[22] Lyon wrote, "To render the whole power and patronage of the Government subservient to the interests of the slaveholders, and struggling with a resolution and desperation peculiar to his character, is, and ever has been, the true mission of Mr. Douglas."[23] He accused Douglas of entering the race merely to divert Northern votes from Lincoln and to throw the contest into the House of Representatives where (he thought) [John C.] Breckinridge would be chosen. He called on Douglas to withdraw and let Lincoln defeat the Southern Democrat. In an effort to prove his point, Lyon mentioned the alliance of the Douglas party with the proslavery Know-Nothing group in New York.[24] He needed only to look next door to see a similar situation, and it is highly probable that he did so.

Soon after the inauguration of Lincoln, Blair's efforts to secure for Lyon the command of the arsenal proved successful. Lyon was thwarted by General William S. Harney, however, who was the commander of the Department of the West, of which the arsenal was a part, and had his headquarters in St. Louis. Lyon had served with Harney previously in Mexico and at Fort Scott, Kansas, so that the two were no strangers. Harney interpreted the order giving

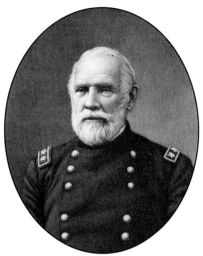

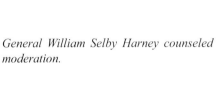

General William Selby Harney counseled moderation.

Lyon command as affecting only the men stationed within the arsenal walls, and therefore, Lyon's rival continued to have charge of the buildings, arms, ammunition, and other stores. In order to obtain any of these, it was necessary for Lyon to get a requisition from Harney. This greatly hindered and depressed him, and he wrote Blair seeking to get the situation corrected.[25] In speaking to prominent Unionists concerning the same situation, Lyon showed his impetuousness by promising that should circumstances demand, he would seize the arms in order to protect the arsenal.[26] This was typical of Lyon, for he seldom allowed technical or legal barriers to deter him from a course of action once he had decided upon it.

After the Confederate attack on Fort Sumter when President Lincoln issued his call for 75,000 volunteers, Missouri was given her quota to fill, but Governor Jackson refused to supply it.[27] Lyon and Blair, thereupon, offered immediately to enroll their Union guards to meet the state's quota. On April 21, Lyon received instructions to carry out this plan. General Harney was relieved of his post at the same time, and the command of the department devolved temporarily upon Lyon, April 23. With this new power, Lyon quickly recruited the regiments and armed them. He then transferred the remaining munitions in the arsenal to Illinois aboard the steamer *City of Alton* on April 26.[28]

This last action upset the plans of the pro-Southern Jackson regime to take the arsenal. Plans for this move were far advanced already, having been instigated by a memorandum sent to the governor by General D. M. Frost, commander of the state militia, on April 15.[28a] This memorandum had suggested, among other things, that the General Assembly of the state be called into special session, that agents be sent south to secure arms, and that Frost be instructed to establish a camp of militia near St. Louis "to . . . do all things necessary and proper to be done in order to maintain the peace, dignity, and sovereignty of the State."[29]

These recommendations the governor proceeded to carry out. He sent two militia officers to Jefferson Davis requesting him to furnish them with siege guns and mortars for use by General Frost.[30] A proclamation was issued calling the General Assembly into special session beginning May 2.[31] To avoid the outright suspicion which the establishment of a camp near St. Louis without cause would bring, Governor Jackson, on April 22, called upon the commanders of the several militia districts throughout the state to assemble their men in some convenient place within their district for a six-day encampment to promote greater efficiency. The same order authorized General Frost to establish such a camp anywhere within the city or county of St. Louis.[32]

When the arms were removed from the arsenal on April 26 and the cause for the encampment had been taken away, the governor was dismayed, but he decided that a camp should be established in St. Louis anyway. General Frost therefore established Camp Jackson in Lindell Grove on May 6.[33] Two days later, the arms from the Confederates arrived and were taken to the camp. These had been taken from the Federal arsenal at Baton Rouge, Louisiana.[34]

Soon after the establishment of Camp Jackson, Lyon determined that it must be captured, as he thought it represented a definite threat to the peace of the city.[35] Apparently he little realized the consequences such a move would have, and he certainly ignored the factors which tended to minimize the significance of the camp.

Although the state administration was secessionist in sympathy, the large majority of the people of the state were conservatives. This group wanted to keep Missouri in the Union if at all possible but favored neutrality for the state in the gigantic struggle which was just beginning. As will be seen later, they were divided among themselves, however, on the question of what to do should force be applied by the Federal forces to assure Missouri's loyalty.

The dominance of the conservatives on the state scene had been manifested quite decidedly in February when the General Assembly called for a state convention "to consider the then existing relations between the Government of the United States, the people and Governments of the different States, and the Government and people of the State of Missouri; and to adopt such measures for vindicating the sovereignty of the State and the protection of its institutions, as shall appear to them to be demanded."[36] The election for delegates to the convention resulted in a victory for conservatism, much to the surprise of Governor Jackson and his followers. Most of the delegates chosen were Conditional Unionists, and in all a majority of about 80,000 votes were registered for the Union.[37] The convention met in Jefferson City and St. Louis from February 28 to March 22 and decided that there was no adequate cause for Missouri to leave the Union at that time. It adjourned to meet again on the third Monday of December or sooner should it be called together by a special committee.[38] Thus an official state organization representing the will of the majority of the people had decided against secession.

The General Assembly, which had been reconvened by the governor, was accomplishing little at Jefferson City as its efforts to give Jackson extraordinary powers were being hampered by a determined group of Unionists.[39]

As mentioned above, the removal of the arms from the arsenal did away with the motive for Camp Jackson. There was little object in the secessionists attempting to capture the arsenal following this move. They had but seven hundred men against ten thousand men under Lyon. Had they made their attack, they could have expected little help from the Confederacy, for neither Arkansas nor Tennessee had yet seceded. In addition, there were Union forces in Illinois, Iowa, and Kansas ready to move into Missouri should they be needed.[40]

In spite of these facts, Lyon had decided that the camp was a menace to the Union, and nothing would swerve him from his determination to destroy

Camp Jackson Flag

the danger. Hammond had observed this same trait in him during their years together at Fort Riley, for he wrote, "When, after due reflection, he [Lyon] had determined on a course of action he was firm to the point of obstinacy!"[41]

Lyon called a meeting of the Union Committee of Safety on May 9 and announced his decision. Although two of the members opposed it on legal grounds, Lyon overrode their objections by saying that Harney was due to arrive in a few days to resume the command of the department. The objections need examination, however, as they were important and show further that Lyon was past listening to even reasonable arguments. The two gentlemen had pointed out that the camp was organized only for a six-day period and that the state authorities who controlled it still recognized the Federal government. They argued further that the United States flag flew over Camp Jackson and that there had been no disturbances as a result of the camp. While they admitted that there was stolen United States property there (the arms sent by the Confederacy), they believed that the proper way to get it was for the United States marshal to issue a writ of replevin and serve it, asking only for Lyon's assistance should General Frost refuse to respect this. They did win Lyon's agreement to allow the marshal to accompany the troops, but when the meeting ended, this was forgotten.[42]

General Frost had heard rumors of an impending attack upon Camp Jackson and on the morning of May 10 sent a letter to Lyon commenting on the reports and asking for a verification of them. He denied that the camp had been set up for other than lawful purposes and stated that he had made several offers in the past to the proper authorities of the help of his forces in preserving the peace within Missouri and in protecting United States property there.[43] Lyon refused to receive the communication.[44] His course was determined, and he would let nothing alter it.

Lyon surrounded Camp Jackson the same morning and demanded that Frost surrender. He accused the camp of being pro-Confederate in sympathy and of harboring United States materials of war obtained from the Confederacy. He revealed his ignorance of the situation at Jefferson City by giving as another reason for his demand the passage of "unparalleled legislation, having in direct view hostilities to the General Government and cooperation with its enemies."[45]

Frost had no alternative but to capitulate or face certain destruction. He quickly surrendered. His men were placed under arrest and marched out of the camp. While they waited in lines enclosed by Union troops, the crowd of men, women, and children who had gathered to watch the procedure began taunting the German soldiers and hurling sticks and stones. Authorities differ as to exactly what happened next. Some say that shots came from the crowd, followed by volleys from the troops. Others deny that the crowd did more than taunt and throw missiles. At any rate the troops did fire into the crowd, killing fifteen persons immediately and fatally wounding a number of others, including two women and three prisoners.[46] Two Union soldiers were also killed. Lyon later disclaimed any responsibility for this occurrence, but by the time his statement appeared in the papers, a panic was well underway.[47] The next day there were frequent clashes between Union troops and proslavery sympathizers.

The majority of Missouri historians agree that the Camp Jackson affair was a colossal blunder. Instead of suppressing secessionist sentiment, the move strengthened it. Before Camp Jackson, the state government had little chance of removing Missouri from the Union. After this incident, the possibility that the state's star would shine in the Confederate flag became much greater. There are two reasons for this. First, the action of Lyon drove many heretofore Conditional Unionists into the secessionist camp. These were men who wished to keep Missouri in the Union if it could be done peacefully but who balked at the use of coercion. Foremost of these were Sterling Price, former governor and the president of the state convention, and John B. Clark, a member of the Missouri congressional delegation. Both men hastened to Jefferson City and offered their services to the governor.[48] Secondly, the move frightened the General Assembly into action. As soon as they heard the news, they were thrown into turmoil, and within half an hour, the military bill giving the governor extraordinary power over the state militia, as well as other far-reaching measures, was passed.[49]

General Harney returned to St. Louis to find the secessionists there in terror for their lives. He restored order and requested additional reinforcements from the War Department. Harney then issued a proclamation denouncing the military bill and the treasonable nature of the encampment at Camp Jackson.[50]

With the return of Harney, Lyon was relegated to a subordinate position, and all his plans to further subdue the secessionists became subject to the general's approval. Lyon's reaction is evidenced in his letter to Adjutant General Lorenzo Thomas: "The authority of General Harney . . . embarrasses, in the most painful manner, the execution of the plans I had contemplated, and upon which the safety and welfare of the Government, as I conceive, so much depend."[51]

Believing his ideas to be absolutely right, Lyon and Blair sent personal representatives to Washington to plead with Lincoln for the removal of Harney and the reinstatement of Lyon to command. Although a conservative

Clash of German Home Guards and Pro-Southern Sympathizers at Fifth and Walnut, St. Louis, on May 11

delegation had gone to Washington to protest Lyon's moves, the former group was immediately successful in obtaining their desires.[52]

On May 20, Blair received an envelope by personal messenger from Washington which contained the order for Harney's removal and Lyon's promotion to brigadier general of volunteers. Accompanying these was a letter from President Lincoln asking Blair to hold the orders until such time as he felt that the further retention of Harney in his post would work to the serious detriment of the nation.[53]

In the meantime, Sterling Price was appointed major general of the Missouri State Guard, provided for under the military act, on May 18.[54] Within three days, Price and Harney reached an agreement which bitterly chafed Lyon, Blair, and their supporters. By the terms of this agreement, Harney pledged (in effect) that the Federal government would respect the neutrality of the state government. Both governments were to help keep the peace. In this, however, Price was to have active control, and Harney's troops were to be used as a reserve when needed. Price agreed not to organize the State Guard under the military bill and promised that all citizens would be given equal protection whatever might be their views on the national conflict.

Patriotic meetings for either side were to be outlawed and dispersed where necessary, as it was felt that these tended to create excitement.[55]

By May 30, Blair decided the time had come to put into effect the orders from Washington. He had received many letters from Unionists throughout the state telling of violations of the agreement by the state government.[56] Harney had written Price concerning these and had been reassured that there was nothing to them. With this he was satisfied, but not so Blair and Lyon.[57]

With the second removal of General Harney, Lyon again assumed temporary command of the Department of the West. Blair, in his letter to Lincoln explaining the reasons for his action, asked that authorization be given to enroll citizens in the interior of the state into the Federal army. Lyon wrote Secretary of War [Simon] Cameron asking for reinforcements from Illinois and Iowa.[58] General Price, upon learning of Harney's removal, openly repudiated the agreement and hastened the enrollment of his state troops.[59] All seemed ready for the outbreak of open hostilities within the state. Lyon had no intention of seeing his plans stalemated longer.

Realizing the seriousness of the situation, the conservatives arranged for a meeting between the opposing leaders. On June 11, Governor Jackson,

The Fateful Meeting in the Planters' House, St. Louis

General Price, and Colonel Thomas L. Snead (the governor's secretary) met with General Lyon, Colonel Blair, and Major [Horace] Conant (Blair's aide) at the Planters' House in St. Louis. Lyon and Price were the chief spokesmen for their respective sides, and although Price had a long acquaintance with Missouri politics, Lyon proved his match in understanding the situation as it existed. It was evident to the state officials that Lyon "had not . . . been a mere soldier in those days [his years on the Kansas frontier], but had been an earnest student of the very questions that he was now discussing."[60] When, after four or five hours of heated discussion it became apparent that no agreement could be reached, Lyon rose to his feet and closed the meeting with this remark:

> Rather than concede to the State of Missouri the right to demand that my Government shall not enlist troops within her limits, or bring troops into the State whenever it pleases, or move its troops at its own will into, out of, or through the State; rather than concede to the State of Missouri for one single instant the right to dictate to my Government in any matter however unimportant, I would see . . . every man, woman, and child in the State, dead and buried. This means war. In one hour one of my officers will call for you and conduct you out of my lines.[61]

The three state officials did not wait for this courtesy but immediately departed for Jefferson City from where Governor Jackson issued a proclamation to the people of the state reporting the interview and its failure and calling for fifty thousand volunteers to fill the ranks of the State Guard.[62]

Fearing that Lyon would follow immediately and realizing that they could not easily defend Jefferson City, Jackson and his forces withdrew up the Missouri River to the more easily defensible position of Boonville. They were correct in their surmise, for Lyon lost no time in moving down the river, and on June 15 he occupied Jefferson City without opposition.[63]

Thus the determination of one man, Nathaniel Lyon, drove into exile the legally constituted government of the State of Missouri. Lyon followed the Jackson forces to Boonville and defeated them there, driving them into southwest Missouri.[64]

Lyon occupied Springfield on July 13 and held that city until his death a month later at the Battle of Wilson's Creek. In that month he continually requested reinforcements from the headquarters of the department in St. Louis where General John C. Frémont was the newly appointed commander of the department.[65] Because of threats in southeast Missouri, however, Frémont was unable to send Lyon additional troops. Lyon received a dispatch from

Lyon's Death at Wilson's Creek

Frémont on August 9 advising him to fall back toward Rolla and await reinforcements there if he thought he was not strong enough to maintain his position at Springfield. To this Lyon replied that he would hold his position and could resist attack if not surrounded.[66] The next day he attacked the forces of General Price at Wilson's Creek and was soundly defeated, losing his life in the battle. John M. Schofield, who served as Lyon's adjutant throughout the Missouri campaign, later reported that he felt that the sacrifice at Wilson's Creek was wholly unnecessary and, under the circumstances, wholly unjustifiable. He believed that the retreat to Rolla was open as late as the night of the ninth; however, Lyon had a great sense of loyalty to the people of southwest Missouri and refused to abandon them. Schofield reported that Lyon was greatly depressed the evening before the battle and felt that he was being sacrificed to the ambition of another (Frémont).[67] In this mood, Lyon went to his death. In this last situation, he was badly outnumbered, but believing firmly in the cause for which he fought, he did not hesitate a moment to sacrifice himself and many of his men.

It is interesting to compare the situation in Missouri with that in Kentucky during the same period. In the latter state, strict neutrality was accorded the state by the Federal government at the request of its administration. As a result, Union sentiment became greatly strengthened. War came to Kentucky only when the Confederates invaded the state, thereby violating its neutrality.

By that time Union sentiment was sufficiently strong that Federal troops had little trouble entering the state.[68]

In Missouri, a staunch New England abolitionist had charge of the Federal forces, and the state suffered through four long years because of his blunders. Even after the Camp Jackson affair, Missouri might have been saved this ordeal had the Price-Harney agreement been allowed to operate. General Price tried to carry out this agreement, as evidenced by the breaking up of the large group of State Guard which had gathered in Jefferson City and their return home.[69] While a policy of neutrality might not have endured permanently in Missouri, the Union forces certainly had all the factors on their side in letting such a condition exist. They far outnumbered the state forces, and these latter were poorly organized and equipped. The Confederacy had little to gain by invading Missouri as it had moved into Kentucky. Had such a move been attempted, the Union could have put it down fairly easily, and in such action it would probably have had the support of the majority of the populace. Undoubtedly, the vast preponderance of opinion was conservative in nature and opposed to any move which would disturb conditions in the state. Only when Lyon showed his force did many of them join the Southern ranks, believing this to be the only course left to them by which they could save themselves and their property.

As most men are influenced by their upbringing and experiences, so was Lyon's character shaped by his past. This made him the right man but in the wrong place. He was a pillar of strength for the Union, but his support could have been much better applied to a sector where his fighting qualities rather than his powers of executive decision would have been used.

NOTES

1. James Peckham, *Gen. Nathaniel Lyon, and Missouri in 1861* (New York: American News, 1866), 59.

2. William A. Hammond, "Recollections of General Nathaniel Lyon," *Annals of Iowa* 4 (July 1900): 416.

3. Ashbel Woodward, *Life of General Nathaniel Lyon* (Hartford, CT: Case, Lockwood, 1862), 29.

4. Ibid., 18-26. Lyon's ancestral roots went back to Scottish emigrants who came to New England in the seventeenth century. Both of his grandfathers had fought in the Revolutionary War.

5. Ibid., 29-33.

6. Peckham, *Lyon and Missouri,* 58-59.

7. Ibid., 42-43.

8. Hammond, "Recollections," 434. Hammond says, "I am quite sure that if he (Lyon) had possessed the power he would have killed every northern upholder of what he called the 'slave power' upon whom he could have laid his hands. Indeed, I have often heard him exclaim that they had equitably forfeited their lives and that they were outlaws whom anyone ought to be empowered to destroy."

9. Woodward, *Life of Lyon*, 181.

10. Nathaniel Lyon, *Last Political Writings of Gen. Nathaniel Lyon* (New York: Rudd & Carleton, 1861), 209.

11. Woodward, *Life of Lyon*, 236.

12. Peckham, *Lyon and Missouri*, 66-68.

13. Woodward, *Life of Lyon*, 198.

14. Ibid., 203.

15. Ibid., 204.

16. Hammond, "Recollections," 423-425.

17. Woodward, *Life of Lyon*, 209-211.

18. Ibid., 213.

19. Ibid., 214-215.

20. Ibid., 219.

21. Walter H. Ryle, *Missouri: Union or Secession* (Nashville, TN: George Peabody College for Teachers, 1931), 126-167. This presents a thorough discussion of party thought and structure in Missouri during this period.

22. Lyon, *Last Political Writings*, 131-133.

23. Ibid., 151-152.

24. Ibid., 158-159.

25. Peckham, *Lyon and Missouri*, 68-71.

26. Ibid., 74-75.

27. *The War of the Rebellion: A Compilation of the Official Records of the Union and Confederate Armies* (Washington, DC: Government Printing Office, 1880-1901), ser. 3, vol. 1: 82-83 (hereinafter cited as *OR*).

28. *OR*, ser. 1, vol. 1: 669-675.

28a. Brigadier General D. M. Frost was born in Schenectady County, NY, in 1823. He was admitted to West Point Military Academy when sixteen years of age and graduated with high honors in 1844, being the first up to that time who had been "among the first five" in every branch he had studied. He took part in the Mexican War and acquitted himself with honor. In 1851 he married Miss [Eliza] Graham of St. Louis, granddaughter of John Mullanphy, and in 1853 resigned his commission and engaged in the lumber business and later in fur operations in St. Louis. In 1854 he was elected to the state senate for four years. In 1858 he was elected brigadier general commanding the First Military District of Missouri, embracing the city and county of St. Louis. See J. Thomas Scharf, *History of Saint Louis City and County* (Philadelphia: L. H. Everts, 1883), 1: 497-501.

29. Thomas L. Snead, *The Fight for Missouri* (New York: Scribner's Sons, 1888), 148-149.

30. *OR*, ser. 1, vol. 1: 688.

31. Buel Leopard and Floyd C. Shoemaker, eds., *Messages and Proclamations of the Governors of the State of Missouri* (Columbia: State Historical Society of Missouri, 1922), 3: 384.

32. Snead, *Fight for Missouri*, 151-152.

33. Ibid., 162-163.

34. Peckham, *Lyon and Missouri*, 136.

35. Ibid., 137.

36. *Laws of the State of Missouri . . . 21st General Assembly* (Jefferson City, 1861), 20-21.

37. William F. Switzler, *Switzler's Illustrated History of Missouri* (St. Louis: C. R. Barns, 1879), 323.

38. Snead, *Fight for Missouri*, 78-94.

39. John McElroy, *The Struggle for Missouri* (Washington, DC: National Tribune, 1909), 73.

40. Edward C. Smith, *The Borderland in the Civil War* (New York: Macmillan, 1927), 233.

41. Hammond, "Recollections," 415.

42. Peckham, *Lyon and Missouri*, 139-142.

43. *OR*, ser. 1, vol. 3: 5-6.

44. Peckham, *Lyon and Missouri*, 146.

45. Ibid., 149-151.

46. Ibid., 153.

47. *St. Louis Missouri Democrat* (weekly), 14 May 1861.

48. Snead, *Fight for Missouri*, 181.

49. McElroy, *Struggle for Missouri*, 88-89.

50. Proclamation of 14 May 1861, *OR*, ser. 1, vol. 3: 371-374. William Selby Harney had a distinguished military career which included the Indian Wars and, particularly, the Black Hawk War, where his courage was outstanding. In the Seminole War, he was brevetted for meritorious conduct in 1841, and in the Mexican War, his valor was so marked that he was brevetted brigadier general. During the Civil War when he was stationed at St. Louis, his sympathies were strongly pro-Union. In his proclamation he said, "Missouri must share the destiny of the Union. Her geographical position, her soil, productions, and, in short, all her material interests, point to this result. . . . I desire above all things most earnestly to invite my fellow-citizens dispassionately to consider their true interests as well as their true relation to the Government under which we live and to which we owe so much."

51. 12 May 1861, ibid., ser. 1, vol. 3: 9.

52. Peckham, *Lyon and Missouri*, 194-202.

53. Ibid., 209-210. Lincoln feared removing Harney a second time so soon after his reinstatement.

54. Snead, *Fight for Missouri*, 184.

55. *OR*, ser. 1, vol. 3: 374-375.

56. Peckham, *Lyon and Missouri,* 213-222. These letters have since been destroyed, but Peckham saw them and quotes several.

57. *OR*, ser. 1, vol. 3: 378-381.

58. Peckham, *Lyon and Missouri*, 222-225; Snead, *Fight for Missouri*, 194.

59. Snead, *Fight for Missouri,* 196-197.

60. Ibid., 197-199.

61. Ibid., 199-200. Both Snead and Conant, the two aides, left versions of this meeting. The quotation above has been used by the great majority of Missouri historians in their accounts of this conference. Conant's version, which appeared in the [*St. Louis*] *Missouri Democrat* of June 13, 1861, and was copied by Peckham, quotes Lyon as follows: "Governor Jackson, no man in the State of Missouri has been more ardently desirous of preserving peace than myself. Heretofore Missouri has only felt the fostering care of the Federal Government, which has raised her from the condition of a feeble French colony to that of an empire State. Now, however, from the failure on the part of the Chief Executive to comply with constitutional requirements, I fear she will be made to feel its power. Better, sir, far better, that the blood of every man, woman, and child of the State should flow than that she should successfully defy the Federal Government." Peckham, *Lyon and Missouri*, 248.

62. Snead, *Fight for Missouri*, 200-206.

63. Ibid., 206-211.

64. *OR*, ser. 1, vol. 3: 12-14.

65. Ibid., ser. 1, vol. 3: 394ff.

66. John M. Schofield, *Forty-six Years in the Army* (New York: Century, 1897), 40-41.

67. Ibid., 39-42.

68. Smith, *Borderland in the Civil War*, 263-312.

69. Snead, *Fight for Missouri*, 187-188.

The Battle of Lexington
as Seen by a Woman

SUSAN A. ARNOLD McCAUSLAND

It was war time in the land, and Missouri was feeling the stir of the situation throughout all her bounds. In the little town of Lexington on the river there was, in the early months of 1861, an eager impulse towards matters military, without however, any pronounced feeling of taking the side of either the North or South in the then undetermined policies of the two sections. Still, militancy in any direction was so pronounced that companies were formed, and our inexperienced eyes made acquainted with the stirring evolutions of the army drill. Later, and when further developments had set definite bounds to bent and affiliation, the men who formed these early half-play companies parted company, some to enlist under the stars and bars, others loyal to the stripes. The place of this first military practice was the wide and beautiful campus of the old Masonic College, and the drills were conducted by Capt. George Wilson, an ex-officer of the U.S. army, and Major Arnold, of the Virginia Military Institute.

Time ran on into May of that year when occurred the tragedy of Camp Jackson, in St. Louis, when some raw recruits under Gen. [Nathaniel] Lyon fired upon a crowd of citizens without known provocation, killing a young woman, a boy, and wounding some others. This act set the state in a flame of feeling, with the result that an immediate alignment was made for one side or the other about to enter upon the great modern tragedy of the War Between the States. Small Confederate flags began to be displayed from private residences, and the old flag was set afloat to the winds from all public buildings of the town. A month of this and Gov. Claiborne F. Jackson named Lexington a place of military rendezvous, and soon after the middle of that month came

F. Domenico, a Hungarian artist, painted this scene of the Battle of Lexington during the fighting. It later came into the possession of Susan McCausland, the author of this memoir, who donated it to The State Historical Society of Missouri.

Gen. Sterling Price at the head of the newly formed State Guards, and with him Governor Jackson. Then began the organization of companies and regiments, and the buckling on of such accoutrements of war as a hitherto peaceful people could muster from the country's store of bird guns, turkey and deer rifles, and such sidearms as belong to times of peace. "Old Sacramento," a twelve-pound brass cannon—a relic of the Mexican War, and which had been used here time out of mind as a reliable noisemaker for Fourth of July antics—was the heaviest piece of ordnance we had acquaintance with up to that time and furnished the largest show of preparation going forward, and the old gun remained staunch to the end of the four years of conflict, being always in Col. Hi Bledsoe's battery, and his confidence-holding sweetheart of utter faithfulness to the last. It has been told that he more than once, after an especially satisfactory deadliness of his gun, would throw his arms around the brass body and set his lips to it fondly. With the running out of the last week of June went also General Price and the governor, with what of men and military supplies had been here gathered up. This left us with no other signs of what had been but the many small homemade Confederate flags still made to show from the homes of those who affiliated with the South. These remained only until [Charles G.] Stifel, following close upon Gen. Price's going, came at the head of a regiment of foreigners, some of whom spoke English not at all, to take possession of the place as a fixed-for-the-war military post. When the transport bringing this regiment showed her smokestacks abreast of Gratz Bluff, all Confederate bunting quickly faded from sight, save and alone one small flag which, from the time of Virginia's secession, had been proudly flouting the world from a pole set on the lawn of the Dr. E. G. Arnold home on the corner of Broadway and Third streets. Broadway was the then thorough-fare from the levees up into the town, and when Stifel's debarked troop had come abreast of the Confederate colors, the line was moved up to surround the group of women who stood on the lawn in intent curiosity as to this next phase of military procedure. Ignorance of the meaning of war was at that time, and for us all, of the profoundest, and certainly the very young woman owning the flag never doubted her right to show it upon her own premises at her pleasure, besides holding an idea of the largeness and liberal protectiveness of all mas-culinity called "man" in a way befitting Eden, alone.

But here she found herself amazingly confronted by a body of folk hostile and threatening, with guns and bayonets, who made threats to her as she stood

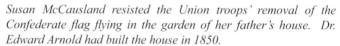

Susan McCausland resisted the Union troops' removal of the Confederate flag flying in the garden of her father's house. Dr. Edward Arnold had built the house in 1850.

upon her own ground and demanded that she surrender to them her flag—the flag of her native state. Such an unflawed confidence in civilized man's attitude towards womanhood it is just as well to record, since it is now gone from us forever, though, at that time, held as an unquestioned truth by all women of the old South.

The young woman refused him the flag, of course, and when one man moved to take it from the low staff, she ran to take it into her own hands. So she faced the regiment with the statement of her right, as a woman and citizen of a free country and state, to hold and defend her convictions and her property on her own freehold of earth. Amusing enough in the light of later events, but nevertheless the universal feeling of a large section of the country at that time; we of the old South being yet of the chivalric age of knighthood in so much that the rest of the world had left behind. But Stifel rode away with the offending little colors as well as with the young husband of the rash bride of a few months, who owned them. This even rasher young husband came rushing into the fray with his bird gun, with the intent to so lay low the enemy; the young wife then let fall the flag in order to grasp and lower the hand holding the gun, and so it was picked up, distinctly not captured, by a soldier, and carried away.

Stifel established headquarters at Masonic College, where he was soon joined by Lieut. Col. [Robert] White with his regiment. By the last of August, five companies of militia and two battalions of the First Illinois Cavalry, under Col. [Thomas] Marshall, had been added to the army of occupation. After the coming of Col. Marshall, he inaugurated the felling of the splendid grove of primeval oaks and elms on the college campus and the surrounding hills, and the making of the first earthworks was begun.

Early in September underground information was given us that Gen. Price, with a much-enlarged army, would soon be back to Lexington on an errand militant, and for the purpose further of getting into possession supplies of ammunition and arms, of which the Confederates, or more correctly, the State Guards, of the Southern wing, were in need. In preparation for this event, Col. [James A.] Mulligan came near the first of the month to reinforce the garrison with the Twenty-third Illinois Infantry, called throughout the war the Mulligan Irish Brigade. Col. Mulligan began at once the construction of intricate military entrenchments and to add to the earthworks formed by Col. Marshall. A cavalry charge would be possible only from the east side, the college, now a citadel, being set upon a height and protected by steep declivities on all other sides, so that here was digged a perfect checkerboard of pits, disguised sufficiently to entrap the unwary. A mine was also set in that direction for added security. While all this was being done, there came in Major [Robert T.] Van

Chicago lawyer James A. Mulligan, colonel of the Twenty-third Illinois, the "Irish Brigade," commanded the Union forces at Lexington. He was killed during the Battle of Winchester, Virginia, in July 1864.

Horn and Col. [Everett] Peabody with their commands, these soldiers being of the regular army. By this time information of the movements of the rapidly approaching army from the south was easy of access. Gen. Price's advance was already encamped upon the county fairgrounds, about a mile from town, and the thin line of Federal pickets was no stay to the adventurous who might wish to go out. While Gen. Price waited at the fairgrounds for the coming up of his ammunition wagons, Col. Mulligan continued to strengthen his defenses. During these days of waiting, continual skirmishing went on between the soldiers in town and small squads of those outside. The Southerners, becoming impatient of delay, daily came dashing into town in small groups to give an exchange of shots and out again. In one of these daring and useless exploits, I saw a friend go down, unhorsed, wounded by bayonets as he lay on the ground. This was Mr. Withrow. He was sent from here to St. Louis and died of his wounds in Gratiot street prison.

And now came the seventeenth of the month, when proclamation was made to the citizens that their undoubted safety lay in the direction of a temporary abandonment of their homes. So there went out from the town an army of women and children to take refuge in country houses in numbers sufficient to tax the hospitality of these to the utmost.

By the middle of the forenoon of Wednesday, the eighteenth, the stars and bars floating within the city limits, and the strains of "Dixie" came ringing clear through the gold of the perfect day. I needed to go but a single square from my father's residence—the Arnold home of the earlier flag episode—to look up the extent of Main Street, and this I did so soon as I caught the sound of "Dixie." What I saw there was an army without any pretense of uniform of any kind, but moving in orderly precision into some determined-upon position. This was Gen. [Mosby M.] Parsons' line, drawn along Main Street. Gen. [James S.] Rains' division took position on the east of the college, with Bledsoe's battery. Gen. [William Y.] Slack's column was extended along the west side, joining that of Gen. Parsons on the south. I think that [Henry] Guibor's battery was moved about from place to place from time to time, as it was stationed near the intersection of Third and Tenth streets this first day, but went to Gen. Parsons' division the next day, then back again west afterwards. On the morning of the second day of the investment, Gen. [Thomas A.] Harris and Gen. [James H.] McBride completed the cordon by placing their lines along the north, on the riverfront. This line was supported throughout by [E. V.] Kelley's and [James] Kneisley's batteries. Until the last of the three days of the siege, Bledsoe's battery was under the command of Emmet McDonald, Col. Bledsoe being hors de combat from illness, but on the last day, he was again with his guns. Gen. [Alexander E.] Steen's division, with Congreve Jackson's force of [Churchill] Clark's division, while held as reserves, were all the time in active service in one quarter or another of the field.

As I stood looking upon the line on Main Street take position, the first day of the entry, a friend, Charley Wallace, said on seeing me there, "What are you doing in town? You would better go to shelter at once, as we are about to fight, right away."

At this time Guibor's battery was stationed at the intersection of Third and Tenth streets, only three squares from the Arnold residence, and the admonition to go find shelter sent me to the crossing two squares above the battery's place, from which very advantageous position I witnessed what went on at that part of the field while the siege lasted.

Almost on the heels of Lieut. Wallace's "We are to fight now, right away" was opened the first thunder of the guns. The noise of the firing was heavier this first day than at any time until the hour just before the surrender and was heard at Carrollton, thirty miles away, also heard with such effect by Gen. [Samuel D.] Sturgis as he was marching to Mulligan's relief on the north of the river that he turned his column and marched away again. Very shortly after shot and shell began the hoarse noise of war in earnest, there came the need for surgeons and nurses, and while this battle has been called an almost bloodless one, this is true only in the light of what came later, when the loss of life made a new world record of what man could do to man in deadly strife. In the light of civilization, the battle of Lexington, Missouri, was sufficiently red. Many of those killed lie here sleeping the last long sleep; others were removed by kindred when the war was over.

The family residence of Col. Oliver Anderson stood in such proximity to the college grounds on the west that it was, from the time of the first occupancy of the college, taken into use as a hospital. The last outer entrenchments in that direction met Mrs. Anderson's flower garden, the house being so situated that the upper windows almost overlooked the interior of the works. Thus, its advantage meant so much to the Confederates that a running assault was determined upon, with the hope to make its capture without the firing of a gun. This use of arms could not be resorted to since the house was used as a hospital, so a sufficiently heavy column from the division of Gen. Harris was ordered to the assault, if this could be done without too heavy a loss of life, the assaulting column not to be allowed to respond to the fire from the building. The men took the chances, making the charge most gallantly, but with losses, of course. The building was held but a few hours only, and until a countercharge was prepared from the citadel. This assault was heralded by the sharp cracking of minie rifles, some of which sent the dreaded minie balls to the desired end, so that there were wounded Southerners in the building when retaken later by the Irish. When this charge of the Irish Brigade was made, I was standing at my post of observation, the middle of Third Street, a position overlooking the Anderson house, the long line of earthworks behind

State Guard forces captured the William Oliver Anderson house, which the Union had used as a hospital, during the battle. The house, built in 1853, is now a part of the Battle of Lexington State Historic Site.

it, and the besieging column on the west. I think it was between one and two o'clock when I took up, on this day, my post of observation. I had been there but a very short time when a double line of human forms appeared on top of the embankment, rushed over, followed by the serried ranks of others, all firing upon the house as they hurtled down upon it. And how they fell! some of them, on the way, and lay there amongst the flowers of the garden until all was over and the bodies could be moved. And how they yelled as they charged! It was a daring and brilliant sortie. We were told afterwards that these men were made very drunk before they could be sent out. Let this be believed, because of their after acts. The recapture of the building was so quickly accomplished that the dislodged Confederates were forced to leave behind some disabled comrades. There was nothing for it but to think that the gentle treatment accorded the sick they found in house would be returned to their own. Vain trust! But one escaped the crimson fury of that hour—Capt. Tip Manser. He, when the massacre began, drew the edge of the blanket covering one of the Federals over himself, and so passed for one of the enemy. All others suffered death in one way or another. About two hours more and the place was again in possession of the Confederates. When the again victorious besiegers poured into the house it was to find those they had so lately left there dead, murdered really. One man had both eyes ground quite out [of] his head, and the handsome, the gallant young Fayette Quarles, of Richmond, showed both hands with gaping holes through the palms, having been ground through by bayonets. Whether these injuries were inflicted before they were killed or not can never be known, but the then supposition was that this was the case. The night of this sad day was a lurid one. Hot shell sent from the entrenchments had started fires in three or more quarters, and as night fell, these flamed and spread, luridly reddening the sky and turning a new dread loose upon the town.

The cannonading on Thursday, the nineteenth, was comparatively light, but a ceaseless sharp cracking of rifles went on throughout the day. The possessors of those squirrel rifles hidden behind every available tree, stump, or elevated ground did deadly work whenever a human target inside appeared within range. Some of this was done from the vantage of tree limbs, which many men climbed and sat at ease to watch their opportunity. This practice must have been more galling to the besieged than had been the cannonading, for when all was over and an account gained of the happenings inside, we heard that, on this day, many hasty and shallow burials were made after nightfall. Certainly, in going about the place long afterwards, when deserted by both armies, I came upon a human foot pathetically protruding from a grave so shallow that it appeared to be only earth heaped shallowly upon a body placed on ground untouched by a spade.

At twilight of this day, some men of Gen. Harris's division inaugurated the beginning of the end by bringing from the warehouses of McGrew, Anderson and Sedwick the hemp bales with which movable breastworks were to be made on the tomorrow. All along Gen. Price had refused to order an assault on the defenses, though advised to this by his staff. "It is unnecessary to kill off the boys here," he said. "Patience will give us what we want." So he quietly awaited the event.

The men of the hemp bale strategy slept that night behind their movable defenses, and early next morning operations which brought about the surrender began. While Bledsoe's battery, he himself being in charge now, thundered away east in a way to rip open the walls of the old collegians' boarding-house and tear great holes in the walls of the one-time halls of learning, the men on the west went quietly on up the bluff behind the rolled hemp bales. It was not long, however, until a heavy fire was drawn upon these movable breastworks, but with little effect. On they came, crawling, as implacable as fate, and when the day was run on towards the morning's close, the end came. The Confederates were inside the defenses, the white flag of surrender was

Missouri State Guard troops using water-soaked hemp bales as moveable breastworks to attack the Union defenders brought about the surrender of Mulligan's force on September 20.

run up over the citadel, and a shout to reach the heavens was shouting from a thousand throats.

Upon the surrender, all the ranking officers conducting the defense were found to be suffering from wounds. Lieut. Col. White, handsome, debonair gentleman, had been shot through the lungs and died a few years afterwards. Col. Mulligan received only a slight wound in one arm and was not much disabled from the effects. Still, upon paroling him, Gen. Price put his private carriage at his disposal to drive to Warrensburg, where railroad transportation was to be had. But Mulligan refused a parole, as he had no wish to remain long inactive, and chose to be accounted prisoner awaiting exchange. It was much the same thing, however, as Gen. Price with his wife took him to Warrensburg in his carriage and, I think, turned him loose there on his word of honor. There was a general parole on the terms of no future service against the South, not a man being held as prisoner. In some instances, where the men captured were citizens of the town, they were laughingly handed over to their wives to be kept out of future mischief.

Only a very few years ago, when an extension of Central College was going forward (The old Masonic College is now Central College, a school for girls.), two skeletons were exhumed. These were of bodies shallowly interred and undoubtedly belonged to men killed in that long-gone day of the sharpshooters' deadly aim. It is probable that others still are left there, under the tread of schoolgirl feet, but like Omar's voice for Bahram, "That can not break their sleep."

"Springfield is a Vast Hospital": The Dead and Wounded at the Battle of Wilson's Creek

WILLIAM GARRETT PISTON

Although Wilson's Creek has been the topic of significant study, existing works pay minimal attention to the treatment of the wounded and the burial of the dead following the battle fought on August 10, 1861, some nine miles southwest of Springfield, Missouri.[1] This subject deserves closer examination for several reasons. While the neglect of medical treatment and burial services was quite common early in the Civil War, it exacerbated the suffering of both soldiers and civilians. The battle's consequences for the soldiers are easy to imagine; civilians were affected at several other levels. The fight obviously had a disastrous impact on those living on or adjacent to the battlefield. It also thoroughly disrupted life in Springfield and resulted in significant property damage. In addition, because Civil War regiments were raised at the community level, the battle affected the families in the soldiers' hometowns.

Wilson's Creek occurred only twenty days after the Battle of Bull Run in Virginia, making it the second major battle of the war. By early August, Brigadier General Nathaniel Lyon had occupied Springfield with the Union Army of the West, a force numbering some 5,400 men, yet he was so short of supplies that he felt compelled to retire to Rolla, the nearest railhead. The Western Army, 10,125 men strong, was camped dangerously close by, where the Wire, or Telegraph, Road crossed Wilson Creek.[2] This was a composite Southern force comprising Confederate troops serving under Brigadier General Ben McCulloch, including the Arkansas militia led by Brigadier General Nicholas Bartlett Pearce and the Missouri State Guard led by Major General Sterling Price. By agreement McCulloch exercised overall command of the alliance that posed a tremendous threat to Lyon. Rather than risk being cut

Even with the violent battle raging around them, soldiers bore their wounded comrades away from the combat area and took them to the overcrowded and unprepared dressing stations and field hospitals.

up during withdrawal, the Federal leader decided to launch a surprise attack, intending to stun the Southerners and inflict enough damage so as to allow the Union soldiers safe passage to Rolla. Lyon split his army into two columns. The first, under Colonel Franz Sigel, initially struck the rear of the enemy's camp with great effectiveness but was eventually driven from the field in a panic. Lyon led the second column and approached the Southerners from a nameless ridge that would soon be christened Bloody Hill. After five hours of combat, Lyon's column was forced to retire, although it did so in good order. Following Lyon's death during this action, command passed to Major Samuel Sturgis. The Federals regrouped in Springfield and left early on the morning of August 11, making it safely to Rolla.[3]

Compared to later Civil War battles, the number of men engaged at Wilson's Creek and the number of casualties suffered there appear modest. But when the casualty figures (the combination of killed, wounded, and missing) are placed in the perspective of earlier conflicts in American history and viewed as a percentage of the forces engaged, Wilson's Creek emerges as a major and costly battle. The best estimate for McCulloch's Western Army is 277 dead and 945 wounded (no soldiers were recorded as missing), producing a casualty rate of 12 percent. The total number of Southern dead and wounded, 1,222, exceeded the number suffered by Americans in any single battle of the Mexican War. As a percentage of the force engaged, the Southerners suffered a higher casualty rate than in all but three of the nine major battles of the Mexican War. Lyon's Army of the West had an estimated 285 killed, 873 wounded, and 186 missing, for a casualty rate of 25 percent. Both in total numbers and as a percentage of the force engaged, Lyon's losses were greater than those of any battle in the Mexican War. Indeed, over the course of the Civil War, only six Union regiments suffered a larger number of dead and mortally wounded in a single engagement than did the First Kansas Infantry, which sacrificed 284 men at Wilson's Creek.[4]

The primitive state of medical knowledge in the nineteenth century meant that men wounded during the Civil War faced a far greater chance of dying than do modern combatants. Yet a statistical analysis of the casualties at Wilson's Creek does little to convey the suffering of the men who struggled there. Events during the weeks after the battle demonstrate that the tragedy embraced an area far wider than the slopes of the battlefield and a much larger population than just those in uniform. Like all battles in the war, Wilson's Creek was, in part, a community experience. Its impact on civilians, both on the battlefield and in Springfield, proved devastating. The response of civilians to news of the battle underscores the continuing close relationship between military units and their home communities.

The Greene County Courthouse, unfinished at the time, served as the official military hospital after the battle.

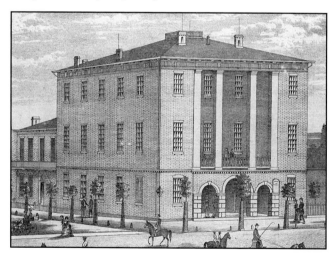

Early in the Civil War, few commanders prepared adequately for their men's medical needs. Shortly after his arrival in Springfield, Lyon ordered Dr. E. C. Franklin to establish a military hospital. Franklin chose the unfinished courthouse building under construction on the town square. Although sometimes styled "chief surgeon," he was in charge of the Springfield hospital only, having previously been attached to the Fifth Missouri Volunteer Infantry. Why Lyon selected Franklin, a novice military man, over three regular army doctors serving with the Federals remains unknown, but soldiers praised the cleanliness of the hospital and the dedication of the physicians. Most of Lyon's units had both surgeons and assistant surgeons attached to them, but there was no medical director for the Army of the West and no coordination among the fifteen doctors present, at least two of whom were described as incompetent by their peers. Medical supplies considered adequate by the standards of the day reached Springfield but were not equally distributed. In the volunteer regiments, the doctors relied upon instruments from their civilian practices, as the army had nothing to give them.[5]

Lyon's concern had been for illnesses, not battle casualties. When the Federal troops marched into the fray on August 10, each unit looked after its own wounded. As the force became heavily engaged on Bloody Hill, surgeons began treating the wounded immediately behind the lines. For example, Dr. W. H. White of the First Iowa Infantry had the patients brought to him laid out in a triangle and moved back and forth among the three divisions to treat them. Eventually, Captain John M. Schofield of Lyon's staff established a central field hospital in a ravine. This was probably the ravine that opened toward Gibson's Mill, although a few sources suggest it was another just north of Bloody Hill. No field hospital was established for the men who accompanied Sigel because they frequently changed positions. Since the army's retreat was preplanned and better facilities existed in Springfield, the Union doctors did not attempt major surgery on the field. According to one report, the surgeons performed no amputations. Dr. H. M. Sprague of the regulars confessed candidly, "The attention shown the wounded was good, but not specially praiseworthy."[6]

The Southern forces were surprised in their camps but kept possession of the ground. While this gave them an advantage in treating their own men, it left them burdened with the enemy's wounded following the Federal retreat. There were at least twenty-four surgeons assigned to the Missouri State Guard units on the field. Records, however, were incomplete, and the actual number of doctors present was probably higher. All five "divisions"—as the subunits of the guard were called—had chief surgeons, at least three of whom were appointed prior to the battle, but coordination was lacking. A soldier in

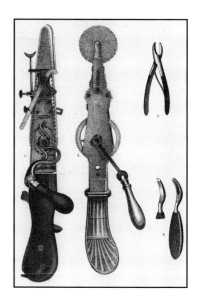

These surgical instruments were used to remove shot that was imbedded in bone.

Clark's Division complained that the State Guard had "no organized hospital corps, no stretchers on which to bear off the wounded." Unfortunately, little is known about the medical personnel in Pearce's Arkansas state troops or the Confederate units under Ben McCulloch's direct command. Nothing suggests that an effort was made above the regimental level to prepare for the inevitable consequences of battle.[7]

The plight of the Union wounded was arguably worse than that of their foes. Fearing that the rumble of wheeled vehicles might betray his surprise march, Lyon initially ordered all ambulances to be left in Springfield. After Sturgis pleaded with him, he reluctantly allowed two ambulances to accompany the main column, but none went with Sigel. The ambulances apparently did not attempt to make round trips to Springfield during the battle but remained at the battle site until Sturgis ordered the retreat. Even burdened far beyond capacity, they could not have brought more than two or three dozen of the hundreds of Federal wounded from the field. Once Sturgis gave the order to retire, Union soldiers confiscated wheeled vehicles of every description from nearby farms and pressed them into service; however, their numbers were few. Almost all of the severely wounded Federal soldiers were left on the battlefield while those with lesser injuries, the so-called "walking wounded," scrambled for safety with no help from officialdom. Such conditions suggest almost criminal neglect to modern analysts, but they were hardly unusual in the initial phases of the Civil War.[8]

The commanders' failure to prepare for the medical consequences of battle robbed their forces of combat strength. Like other Civil War soldiers, the volunteers who fought at Wilson's Creek were enlisted in companies raised at the community level. Generally, a person of local prominence organized seventy to one hundred men from his hometown or county into a company, which usually elected him captain. These units almost always carried a flag made by local women and pledged in public departure ceremonies to uphold the honor of the community sponsoring them. Ten companies formed a regiment, which in turn elected its higher-ranking officers.[9]

Community spirit helped sustain the common soldiers in combat because the men in the ranks stood literally side-by-side with neighbors from home. But when men fell wounded, their comrades often dropped out of the battle to care for them because there was no one else to do it. In a letter to his hometown paper in Atchison, Joseph Martin of the First Kansas Infantry related without apology how he left the fight to attend to his friend George Keith. "I found him, took charge of him and carried him to one of the hospital wagons, dressed his wounds and placed him in a wagon to be carried to town," Martin wrote. "Many of the wagons were heaping full, every man was trying to get friends into them, but I succeeded. . . . He depended upon me to take care of him, which I did."[10]   Martin clearly did not worry about being accused of cowardice, of using his friend's medical needs as an excuse to seek cover. He was reporting to his homefolk that they need not worry; in the First Kansas the men looked after each other. Similarly, when Hugh J. Campbell of the First Iowa captured some abandoned horses, he gave them only to wounded fellow Iowans. Shot in the foot himself, Campbell nevertheless managed to steal at gunpoint a horse ridden by a Northern officer's servant, giving it to his wounded friend Newton Brown. Campbell gleefully related this larceny at the expense of "a darkey" to readers of the *Muscatine (IA) Weekly Journal.* Conduct unthinkable under ordinary circumstances—horse theft—became not only acceptable in the context of unit solidarity but also a source of humor to share with the homefolk.[11]

If the lack of medical services and the strength of community bonds gave men socially acceptable reasons to quit the fight, how many promptly returned? Where was the dividing line between helping a friend and shirking one's duty? Some soldiers doubtless found excuses never to return to the fight, but the absence of even those who returned promptly diminished unit strength during the very time they were needed most. This occurred on the Southern side as well. John D. Bell of the Missouri State Guard recalled that when a man was wounded, "it took from two to four of his friends to bear him to some shady nook, where he was left with a canteen of water." While Bell contended that "in almost every case" these Good Samaritans returned speed-ily to the fight, his postwar recollections are probably too forgiving.[12] Over 900 Southern army soldiers were wounded, so it is reasonable to speculate that at least another 900 to 1,000 men withdrew from the fight for a significant period of time to care for comrades. This withdrawal effectively reduced McCulloch's combat strength more than 17 percent. Since the Federals lost 873 wounded, and it is likely that just as many more absented themselves tem-porarily or permanently to assist them, Federal strength was probably reduced by 32 percent. Battles have turned on less. The lack of medical preparedness, added to the fact that the soldiers fighting at Wilson's Creek were volunteers raised locally who could not ignore each other's plight, considerably reduced the effectiveness of both the Northern and Southern armies.[13]

The Southerners established several impromptu field hospitals along the banks of Wilson Creek, perhaps because the wounded crawled there seeking water and shade. Trees and underbrush grew thick beside the stream, and soldiers instinctively carried their wounded friends to cover. Since the battle took place amid their camps, the Southerners used their various wagons to transport the wounded to safety even during combat. This was done spontane-ously, for there was no organized effort to collect the wounded until after the battle ended. The positions of the battle lines meant that no place was truly safe. Artillery and small arms fire passed constantly above the Southern hos-pitals, and they were occasionally targeted by accident. Confederate surgeon William A. Cantrell set up a hospital "near the centre of the battlefield" shortly after firing commenced. Amazingly, he escaped injury, but a physician in the Missouri State Guard and several wounded soldiers from both sides were killed at a creekbank dressing station.[14]

Cooperation in regard to medical care was one of the few humane notes amid the general carnage as surgeons attended men without regard to po-litical affiliations. "I have never before witnessed such a heart-rendering scene," wrote Colonel John Hughes of the State Guard. "State, Federal, and Confederate troops in one red ruin, blent on the field—enemies in life, in death friends, relieving each others' sufferings."[15] Indeed, before the last firing died away, an unidentified Federal doctor risked his life to contact McCulloch and open negotiations concerning the joint treatment of the wounded.[16] Even so, the surgeons were overwhelmed by the task facing them. Despite the doc-tors' best efforts over long hours, the wounded suffered terribly. The Federals started moving their wounded to Springfield during the afternoon and evening of August 10, and the Southerners followed suit the next day. On August 12, however, a Missouri State Guard surgeon wrote in his diary: "Many of the wounded are lying where they fell in the blazing sun, unable to get water and

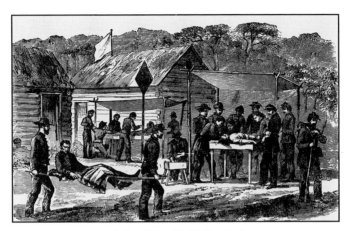

A Civil War Field Hospital

any kind of aid. Blow flies swarm over the living and the dead alike. I saw men not yet dead [with] their eyes, nose & mouth full of maggots."[17]

Presumably, men still lay without cover because every house, cabin, and barn in the vicinity of the battlefield already overflowed with wounded. The battle was obviously an unmitigated disaster for all civilians living nearby, but detailed information has survived only in relation to the Sharp and Ray families.

On a plateau along the southwestern edge of the battlefield, Joseph Sharp's farm was the site of Sigel's rout and some of the fiercest combat of the day. When the fighting erupted, Joseph, his wife, Mary, son, Robert, and daughters, Margaret and Mary, took shelter in the cellar. Artillery projectiles crashed through the house, devastating the interior. The barn and other outbuildings sustained extensive damage as well. The crops that had not been eaten by the encamped Southerners were probably trampled during the fight. Fence rails were knocked down, and dead horses from Sigel's luckless batteries lay scattered about.[18]

Three stories exist concerning the reaction of the Sharps. Writing long after the war, Joseph Mudd of the Missouri State Guard recalled that from a distance he had seen Mary Sharp vigorously encouraging the Southerners as they drove Sigel from the field. Also writing from memory, William Watson of the Third Louisiana Infantry described how he had broken into the Sharps' locked house and found the family cowering in the cellar behind a barrel of apples. They did not object when his comrades promptly appropriated the apples, but Mary protested in a shrill voice that the morning's cannoneering had rendered Joseph deaf. "I felt like saying that, considering her gift of speech, a worse thing might have happened to the old man," Watson wrote. Mary climbed cautiously from her refuge, "but on seeing the wreck, and looking out and seeing the dead men and horses lying in the front of the house, she broke into a greater fury than ever," he wrote. "Who was going to pay for all this?" she exclaimed. "Who was going to take away them dead folks and dead horses? Was she to have them lying stinking around her house?" Mary continued in this manner until Watson quite happily left to rejoin his regiment. Finally, in a letter written just a few days after the battle, Colonel Elkanah Greer wrote to a friend in Texas: "The battle raged hottest around the house of an old gentleman named Sharp, near the centre of the battlefield. After the roar of cannon and the rattle of small arms had ceased for a short time, an old lady came out of the house with a bundle of clothes on her arm, passing over and around the dead Dutch that lay in the yard, and near the fences, to hang out clothes. Placing her spectacles high up on her nose, her right arm akimbo, she exclaimed in a singular and doleful tone, 'Well dese folks have kicked up a monstrous fuss here to-day.'"[19]

These accounts demonstrate the difficulty historians face in evaluating evidence. Can the accounts of Mudd and Watson be reconciled? Does Greer's letter refer to Mary Sharp or (note the dialect speech) one of the Sharps' slaves? Regardless of their differences, the stories told about the Sharps serve as a reminder that civilians were intimately affected by the battle. Approximately one hundred people lived in the neighborhood of Wilson's Creek, and they lost property worth thousands of dollars without receiving a penny in compensation from either the Union or Confederate governments. If their homes were not shattered by artillery or musket fire, they sustained damage when beds and every square inch of floor space were covered with the wounded. In some cases, injured soldiers remained for weeks. Finally, dollar amounts cannot measure the psychological trauma that these families doubtless suffered.

The Ray family endured as much misery as did the Sharps. Located northeast of the Sharp homestead, the Ray farm was also the scene of particularly heavy fighting. John Ray boldly watched the carnage unfold throughout the day, seated on his front porch while the rest of the family took cover in the cellar. Although artillery fire hit a chicken coop and slightly damaged some other outbuildings, the family dwelling was not struck. Early that morning Southerners had appropriated the house for their wounded, and a large yellow hospital flag spared the site from all but accidental fire. Even if the buildings were essentially unscathed, the family's ordeal was severe. For some five hours, Roxanna Ray and eight of her children, the Rays' slaves, Rhoda and her five children, and Julius Short, who resided with the Rays, sat in a dark, cramped cellar. When they emerged, wounded men covered the floors and occupied every bed in the house. Unlike Mary Sharp, Roxanna did not waste time venting her feelings about the unfairness of what had happened. She, Rhoda, and perhaps some of the older children immediately began to assist in caring for the wounded, primarily by hauling water from the nearby spring-house. Some of the wounded, too badly injured to be moved to Springfield, remained in the Rays' home for six weeks. John Ray may also have participated in caring for the wounded. That evening he acted as a guide for a group of prisoners being escorted to Springfield. Since all of his horses had been stolen, he walked. The family was greatly anxious for his safety, but John may have been more worried about his losses of grain and livestock. Although a Unionist, he was never compensated.[20]

It is not possible to estimate how many women in the neighborhood volunteered their services as nurses, but many did so. On August 13 a Missouri State Guard surgeon wrote in his diary: "The fair sex, God bless them, are doing all they can in the way of cooking, serving, and nursing for [the] sick and wounded."[21] He may have been referring to women from Springfield as well as locals, for the town was completely caught up in the tragic aftermath of the battle.

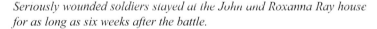

Seriously wounded soldiers stayed at the John and Roxanna Ray house for as long as six weeks after the battle.

Many of Springfield's citizens fled prior to August 10, heading for Rolla with one of several columns of Federal soldiers who were either sick or nearing their date of discharge. According to Franc Wilkie, a civilian newspaper correspondent, all who remained awoke before dawn on the fateful day, listening for the sounds that would mark the opening of the battle. "About ten minutes past five," he wrote, "the heavy boom of artillery rolled through the town like the muttering of a thunder storm upon the horizon, and sent a thrill through every heart, like a shock of electricity."[22] Although Wilkie soon departed to view the battle firsthand, the townfolk endured hours of anxiety before learning anything about the conflict's outcome. Shortly after 3:00 p.m., the first of the wounded began streaming in on foot and horseback, bringing news of Lyon's death. Ambulances, wagons, carriages, and other wheeled conveyances followed, all overflowing with men needing attention. When the hospital in the courthouse was filled, the Union authorities took over the Bailey House Hotel. After the hotel filled up, the wounded were sent to local churches and schools. Once these became crowded beyond capacity, military officials requisitioned private houses. According to one account, the wounded occupied between thirty and forty private homes. This probably represented a large portion of the houses in Springfield; another eyewitness stated that "nearly all the private dwellings" were taken over. The total dollar value of damage to the town as a result of medical treatment was unquestionably large. Property owners received only a small amount of compensation, and that came after the war.[23]

Most of Springfield's citizens were pro-Union. Once it became clear that the battle had been lost and the Federal forces would retreat, many civilians began preparing to evacuate. Some merchants, who had been charging exorbitant prices to the Union troops enduring half rations, now gave away food or dumped it into the streets rather than leave it for the enemy to confiscate.[24] Wilkie wrote: "Springfield was the scene of great confusion—citizens anticipating an instant attack were packing up their effects and flying in crowds to all parts of the state for safety."[25] When the Southern forces arrived in town, they noted that relatively few citizens, particularly women, remained. Their absence made civilian property easy pickings for looters, despite the guards McCulloch posted to maintain order. In some cases, Springfieldians in the Missouri State Guard may have been retaliating for damage inflicted on their own homes by the fleeing Unionists. Harris Flanagin, whose company of the Second Arkansas Mounted Rifles was detailed for guard duty, estimated that not twenty women remained in the whole town. "We treat the union men much better than the Missourians do," he noted.[26]

As Sterling Price's men celebrated their victory, well-wishers and prospective recruits for the Missouri State Guard flocked to Springfield in large numbers. "The flag of the Confederacy was raised amidst the wildest enthusiasm by all the people," wrote one Southerner. "Everyone seemed wild with joy except a few sad faced Dutch who had been left behind by their army."[27] Elation soon gave way to more somber emotions amid the lingering evidence of victory's cost. "Springfield is a vast hospital," wrote Dr. Cantrell, surgeon of the First Arkansas Mounted Rifles, to friends back in Little Rock. "There is not sufficient medical aid here—a hundred doctors could be employed constantly," he lamented, estimating that four months would pass before enough soldiers recovered to alleviate the situation.[28] John B. Clark, a wounded Kansan forced to stay behind, made an equally discouraging evaluation. "Springfield is the most offensive place you was ever in; the stench from the dead and dying is so offensive as to be almost intolerable in some quarters," he informed his relatives.[29] Indeed, a Union doctor who remained with his patients recalled that days passed before the surgeons "succeeded in bringing partial order out of utter chaos."[30] Ben McCulloch and Bart Pearce took pains to visit not only their own hospitalized men but the Union wounded as well, a fact reported favorably in Northern newspapers.[31] But they, like Sterling Price, were too busy with strategy to give medical affairs more than scant attention.

Major General Sterling Price

Fortunately, the physicians did not have to work alone for long. Thanks to telegraphic communications and newspapers that copied stories from other journals, news of the battle spread quickly, and help began to arrive. The telegraph lines that ran along the Wire Road to link Fayetteville, Arkansas, and Jefferson City, Missouri, apparently had been cut both north and south of Springfield, as the earliest news came out of Rolla, where the Army of the West halted its retreat. From there, word of the battle reached St. Louis. Information first published in that city's newspapers was soon relayed west to Kansas City and throughout Kansas, north to Davenport and across Iowa, and southeast to Memphis, Tennessee. From there, it traveled to Little Rock, Arkansas, to Baton Rouge and New Orleans, Louisiana, and finally to parts of eastern Texas, covering all the states that had sent troops to the battle. Southerners initially heard only Northern accounts of the fight. Their own accounts did not spread until a week or more after the battle, when hard-riding messengers reached the telegraph offices in Little Rock.

While reports of the battle tended to be highly partisan, those printed in hometown newspapers, North and South, shared important commonalities. In earlier wars, civilians had waited months to learn the fates of loved ones, but the families of those who fought at Wilson's Creek obtained information quickly, often within a few days. Newspapers printed long lists of the names of the killed and wounded. Many of these lists were annotated, including the locations of wounds and estimates of chances of survival. As more information became available, the newspapers updated, expanded, and corrected the lists. They were remarkably accurate overall, which meant that either relief or grief came immediately.

In addition, hometown newspapers often printed letters attesting that individual wounded soldiers had fulfilled the implicit social contract that had been formed between the community and its company when the men volunteered. In *Embattled Courage*, historian Gerald Linderman noted that Victorian Americans tended to define courage in terms of fearlessness and expected all wounded soldiers, even those mortally hurt, to maintain proper spirit and decorum. The soldiers who clashed in Missouri were clearly concerned about courage. In the days following the fight at Wilson's Creek, the survivors reassured their homefolk that those who had fallen in battle had suffered manfully, thereby upholding the reputations of their companies and, by extension, the good names of their hometowns.

The first two weekly editions of the *Little Rock Arkansas True Democrat* containing detailed information about the battle illustrate a community's interest in matters of courage and honor. Accounts of the battle contained specific information about the behavior of the wounded. A soldier in the Fourth

Brigadier General Ben McCulloch made a point of visiting both the Confederate and Union wounded in the hospitals.

Arkansas Infantry wrote of his friend: "Poor Joe, as he fell, waved his hat to his men, and cried, 'onward, boys, onward.'" A member of the First Arkansas Mounted Rifles related: "When young Harper fell, they went to him, but he desired them not to stop, but to go on and whip them; and when he learned that we had taken their artillery, he pulled off his hat, gave three cheers, and said he was satisfied. Brown, of the V[an] B[uren] F[rontier] Guards, after he had received a mortal wound, cheered his brave boys to advance."[32] Dr. Cantrell continued the story: "Harper had become a favorite with the regiment and they thronged around his dying bed to see him and part with him. I could not go near him without feeling almost overcome by the spectacle of his sufferings and his magnanimous disregard for them. Poor fellow! he never murmured or complained once, but died like a soldier and a hero."[33] Pulaski Light Battery commander William Woodruff also praised a fallen comrade: "Poor Omer Weaver fell like a hero, with his face to the foe, and died some two hours later, as befits a man. During the fight he refused to get under any shelter at all. No man ever died a more glorious death."[34] Similar testimony appeared in newspapers throughout Louisiana, Texas, Missouri, Kansas, and Iowa.

Newspaper editors reminded readers of the contributions made by the fallen men to their communities in obituaries, formal eulogies, or as parts of larger articles. They frequently mentioned how long a person had lived in the community, his place of employment, civil accomplishments, and surviving relatives. For example, the *Mount Pleasant (IA) Home Journal* reported the death of former law student Frank Mann, who had resided in the community only briefly prior to joining the First Iowa Infantry. The editor noted that "in that short time he had made many warm friends. . . . He was a young man of strict morals, rare attainments and of unusual promise." Likewise, the *Atchison (KS) Freedom's Champion* lauded Camille Angiel, who fell while leading the town's company in the First Kansas Infantry. He was, the editor proclaimed, "known to our citizens as a modest, unassuming young man, faithful in the interests of his employer, courteous and genial in social life, industrious and active in his business and duties, and an intelligent and scholarly gentleman." The *Emporia (KS) News* remarked that Hiram Burt, the only fatality from the town's Union Guards, was the stonemason who had built the local Methodist Episcopal church. In an article entitled "Martyrs of Freedom," the *Lawrence (KS) Weekly Republican* eulogized three men of the city's Oread Guards. "Messers. Pratt and Litchfield were among the very first settlers of the town, and through all the trials and troubles of Kansas were esteemed among the truest friends of Freedom. . . . Mr. Jones leaves a wife now with her father in Olathe, and Mr. Litchfield leaves a wife and child in this place."[35] Many parallel examples exist in other newspapers, North and South.

Communities recognized the need for continued support of their hometown volunteers. As soon as news of the fight at Wilson's Creek reached Lawrence, two private citizens, James C. Horton and Edward Thompson, started for Springfield to assist in caring for the wounded. "Acts of mercy like this, having no motive but the purest philanthropy, show how deeply such men as Pratt, Jones . . . and others are entwined in the affections of our people," commented the *Weekly Republican*.[36] A citizen of Des Arc, Arkansas, whose name is not known, undertook a similar mission of mercy, as did Mrs. George Reed of Emporia, Kansas, who joined her wounded husband in Springfield shortly after the battle.[37] Most Missouri citizens had shorter distances to travel. One soldier recalled, "Ladies whose husbands, fathers, and brothers were in the service, some of them wounded, began to arrive and gave social life and enjoyment to the society of Springfield."[38]

Although many of the wounded probably remained in Springfield until December, the less seriously injured men were discharged from the hospitals as early as the first week in September. After receiving their paroles, wounded Federals traveled to Rolla. Those who had enlisted for ninety days were discharged, and most of the others received furloughs to complete their recovery. For weeks after the battle, Northern newspapers noted the homecomings of wounded soldiers, lauding their sacrifices and suffering on behalf of the hometown. While the editors highly praised enlisted men, recuperating officers naturally received disproportionate attention. For example, Colonels Robert B. Mitchell and George W. Deitzler, commanders of the First and Second Kansas Infantry, respectively, were cheered wherever they went in the state.[39]

With fewer railroads to utilize, most homeward-bound, recuperating Southerners faced a difficult journey. To facilitate the evacuation of men down the Wire Road, McCulloch authorized the impressment of civilian wagons in the Springfield area. Although paid for their use, citizens were naturally reluctant to surrender their private property to the military. Harris Flanagin recorded the daylong efforts of Mary Phelps, wife of U.S. Congressman John Phelps, to prevent her family's vehicles from being used. According to Flanagin, she "would scold and rage until she got tired and then she would cry," but her protests fell on deaf ears.[40]

The families of those who lost their lives were concerned with how and where their loved ones were buried. Unfortunately, the military authorities had made even fewer preparations for the interment of the dead than they had for the treatment of the wounded. On the morning of August 11, Western Army officers detailed soldiers for the grim process. Because of the weather and the number of dead, most were laid to rest in mass graves; a few were even placed in a sink hole atop Bloody Hill. The Southerners buried their own dead (assuming they could be identified) and left Northern corpses for a party of Union soldiers who had stayed behind. "The process of burying the dead was toilsome and got on slowly," William Watson recalled. "By the early part of the forenoon the sun got intensely hot, and some of the bodies began to show signs of decomposition, and the flies became intolerable, and the men could stand it no longer." A fellow Louisianian also described how the workers quickly sickened "and were unable to finish the task."[41]

By the best estimate, 535 bodies lay on the field. Each corpse had to be located, identified if possible, and then dragged or carried to a grave site. Digging the grave pits was time-consuming, fatiguing labor in the August sun, yet these difficulties and the unpleasantness of the job hardly excuse the poor performance of the burial parties. If one estimates that it took an average of three man-hours of labor to put each fallen soldier beneath the sod, one hundred men could have completed the task in sixteen hours—two days of labor. No one knows how many men were assigned to the burial details, but clearly not enough as the process took much longer than two days. Shortages of implements may have contributed to the problem. Interments continued through August 12, but when the Union workers did not show up on August 13 (they had apparently departed for Rolla), the Southerners were angered at the prospect of handling the remainder of the enemy's dead as well as their own. By that time the Western Army was shifting to new camps in and around Springfield; the rest of the Northern corpses simply rotted where they lay. Most of those abandoned were casualties from Sigel's routed column. A Missouri State Guardsman recalled: "I was a member of a detail of fifty men that was sent over that part of the field to gather up the arms strewn along their wild flight. The stench was awful then, and what it must have been two days later would baffle imagination." When the Third Louisiana marched past the Sharp farm on August 14, a soldier reported: "The bodies of those that fell in the road near the battery had been thrown to the side of the road and were festering in worms and the advanced state of putrification; it was horrible and loathsome beyond description." Given these conditions, the Sharp family probably evacuated. A full week after the battle, a large number of bodies remained unburied. According to one account, a captured Union officer, understandably outraged by these circumstances, finally offered civilians five hundred dollars of his own money to do the job.[42]

Not all of those who died on August 10 were buried amid the oak-covered hills. The bodies of fallen soldiers who had been residents of Greene County and its environs may have been claimed almost immediately. Others were taken home as well, depending upon geographic distance and their ranks. The Pulaski Light Battery provides an illustration. Both Lieutenant Omer Weaver and Private Hugh Byler fell while serving the guns, but they received quite different treatment in death. Captain William Woodruff went to great lengths to obtain a zinc-lined coffin for Weaver's body and then ship it home for a hero's funeral, one of the largest ever witnessed in Little Rock. Byler, however, was interred on the field.[43]

Because Nathaniel Lyon was the first Union general to fall in combat, it is hardly surprising that his corpse was treated differently from the others. The tragicomic story of its interment demonstrates both the confusion of the military and the degree of animosity between North and South. At the same time, it underscores the necrolatry inherent in Victorian mourning customs. Sturgis had ordered Lyon's body placed in a wagon, but the vehicle was later drafted to remove the wounded. In the haste of the retreat, the body was left behind. Since Lyon did not carry a sword and wore a plain captain's coat without any insignia of rank, there was little reason for his corpse to be noticed amid so many others. When the Southerners accidentally discovered it, they brought it to Federal surgeon S. H. Melcher, who had stayed on the field to treat the wounded. Melcher took the body to the Rays' home where, with proper military decorum, it occupied a bed while wounded enlisted men from both armies writhed in agony on the hard, blood-soaked floorboards. The privileges of rank went unquestioned, even in death. Nor did Melcher

Brigadier General Nathaniel Lyon

apparently feel any guilt in abandoning his suffering patients when, during the night, he carried the lifeless hero back to Springfield under a military escort supplied by the Missouri State Guard. The body was placed in Lyon's former headquarters, where Dr. Franklin, who had also remained behind, failed in his attempts to embalm it because he did not remove the internal organs. Since no airtight coffins were available, Franklin ordered a black walnut one from a Springfield cabinetmaker. A number of local women sat with the body throughout the night, a typical mourning custom of the times.[44]

Preoccupied with organizing the Federal retreat to Rolla, Sturgis and Sigel and the column had tramped several miles before they realized their commander's corpse had again been left behind. Sturgis sent an armed guard back to Springfield to fetch it, but on arrival they found that other arrangements had been made. By this time, Lyon's body was rapidly decomposing. Dr. Franklin somewhat concealed the smell by sprinkling it with bay rum and alcohol and then decided to store it in the icehouse at Congressman Phelps's nearby farm. A detachment of the State Guard once again escorted the coffin, which lay in an ordinary butcher's wagon. During the next two days, however, soldiers camped near the icehouse threatened to desecrate the remains; to keep it safe, Mary Phelps had the coffin buried in a cornfield on August 13.[45]

When Lyon's kinfolk in Connecticut learned of his death, his cousin, Danford Knowlton, and brother-in-law, John B. Hassler, made haste for Springfield. General John C. Frémont, the Federal commander in Missouri, sent Captain George P. Edgar of his staff to assist them in passing through the Southern lines. Knowlton and Hassler had Lyon's body disinterred from the Phelps farm on August 23, packed it in ice, and placed it in an iron coffin brought from St. Louis. Departing Springfield on August 24, the party reached St. Louis on August 26. At his headquarters, Frémont placed Lyon's coffin under a guard of honor.[46]

The next day witnessed the first of a series of ceremonies as the North began to mourn one of the first martyrs to its cause. Large crowds came to view the casket, which was transferred with full military honors to a steamboat late in the afternoon. The Adams Express Company had contracted to ship the body. Once across the river, the remains were placed on a train and conveyed to Cincinnati.[47] The casket was on display in the city throughout August 29, attracting many mourners. Entrained once more, the party passed through Philadelphia and New York, where flags flew at half-mast. They arrived in New Haven on the last day of the month. The coffin was on public view at City Hall for the next three days. Late in the afternoon of September 3, it went by rail to Hartford, where it rested briefly in the capitol under military guard. Connecticut's fiery general lay in state, the highest honor the community could render his memory. From Hartford the casket traveled by rail to the town of Willimantic, where a four-horse hearse provided by the state government carried it to the Congregational Church in Eastford. The September 5 funeral was well attended; the procession to the graveyard was reportedly a mile and a half in length.[48]

As time passed, heroes arose whose names outshone Lyon's, and in the decades following the war, all of the dead were eventually removed from the battlefield for reinterment in either private, national, or Confederate cemeteries. Ironically, the combat at Wilson's Creek was not the greatest threat to the lives and the property of the civilians living along the stream's winding course. Like many others, the Sharps' home survived the battle only to be burned during the vicious guerrilla warfare that characterized so much of the conflict in Missouri. Of all the civilian dwellings in the area, only the Ray house still stands. The National Park Service appropriately uses the former hospital site to teach visitors to the Wilson's Creek National Battlefield about the experiences of civilians as well as the wounded during one of the Civil War's most significant battles.

NOTES

1. The only two modern studies of the battle provide only casualty figures. See Edwin C. Bearss, *The Battle of Wilson's Creek* (Bozeman, MT: Artcraft Printers, 1975), 136; William R. Brooksher, *Bloody Hill: The Civil War Battle of Wilson's Creek* (Washington, DC: Brassey's, 1995), 234-236. The standard biographies of the commanders at the battle provide even less information. See Thomas W. Cutrer, *Ben McCulloch and the Frontier Military Tradition* (Chapel Hill: University of North Carolina Press, 1993), 240, 246; Albert Castel, *General Sterling Price and the Civil War in the West* (Baton Rouge: Louisiana State University Press, 1968), 46; Christopher Phillips, *Damned Yankee: The Life of General Nathaniel Lyon* (Columbia: University of Missouri Press, 1990), 257.

2. Wilson Creek is the correct name of the stream. Northerners usually referred to the battle as Wilson's Creek. Southerners used that term as well but also called it the Battle of Springfield or the Battle of Oak Hills.

3. Richard W. Hatcher III and William Garrett Piston, "The Battle of Wilson's Creek," *Blue & Gray* 14 (Fall 1996): 9-18, 48-62.

4. Comparisons are based on the figures given in Bearss, *Battle of Wilson's Creek*, 161-164; David Eggenberger, *A Dictionary of Battles* (New York: Thomas Y. Crowell, 1967), 63-64, 83, 88-89, 104, 280, 284, 321, 359; E. B. Long with Barbara Long, *The Civil War Day by Day: An Almanac, 1861-1865* (New York: Doubleday, 1971), 717. Buena Vista (15.1 percent), Churubusco (14 percent), and Molino del Rey (22.8 percent) were the only Mexican War battles that exceeded the Southern casualty rate at Wilson's Creek.

5. B. to Editor, 22 July 1861, in "From Springfield," *Kansas City Western Journal of Commerce*, 6 August 1861; Joseph K. Barnes, *The Medical and Surgical History of the War of the Rebellion (1861-1865)* (Washington, DC: Government Printing Office, 1875), 2: 16-17; Phillips, *Damned Yankee*, 258.

6. Barnes, *Medical and Surgical History*, 2: 15-18.

7. John D. Bell, "Price's Missouri Campaign, 1861," *Confederate Veteran* 22 (June 1914): 416; Richard C. Peterson et al., *Sterling Price's Lieutenants: A Guide to the Officers and Organization of the Missouri State Guard* (Shawnee Mission, KS: Two Trails, 1995), 35, 108, 114, 137, 138, 143, 173, 175, 196, 203, 211, 215, 222, 232, 245, 248, 253, 257, 260, 267.

8. Barnes, *Medical and Surgical History*, 2: 16; Bearss, *Battle of Wilson's Creek*, 162.

9. For the most recent scholarship stressing the strength of community bonds and other social forces, see Reid Mitchell, *Civil War Soldiers* (New York: Viking, 1988); Reid Mitchell, *The Vacant Chair* (New York: Oxford University Press, 1993); Gerald F. Linderman, *Embattled Courage: The Experience of Combat in the American Civil War* (New York: The Free Press, 1987).

10. Joseph W. Martin to Geo. J. Martin, 20 August 1861, in "The Battle of Springfield," *Atchison (KS) Freedom's Champion*, 31 August 1861.

11. Hugh J. Campbell to Editor, 18 August 1861, *Muscatine (IA) Weekly Journal*, 30 August 1861.

12. Bell, "Price's Missouri Campaign," 416.

13. Bearss, *Battle of Wilson's Creek*, 164.

14. Robert A. Austin, "Battle of Wilson's Creek," *Missouri Historical Review* 27 (October 1932): 48; William A. Cantrell to Editor, 17 August 1861, "Extracts from a Letter Written at Springfield, Mo., by Dr. W. A. Cantrell," *Little Rock Arkansas True Democrat*, 29 August 1861; William Watson, *Life in the Confederate Army* (London: Chapman and Hall, 1887), 225; "Reliable Letter from Springfield," *Marshall Texas Republican*, 24 August 1861.

15. Punctuation and capitalization have been standardized by the author. Hughes was unforgiving. He continued, "President Lincoln ought to suffer death for this awful ruin, brought upon a once happy country." "Further from the Battle of Oak Hill," *Little Rock Arkansas True Democrat*, 5 September 1861.

16. Watson, *Life in the Confederate Army*, 221-222.

17. Punctuation added by the author. Orval Henderson Jr., ed., "A Confederate Diary Maintained by a Surgeon of the Missouri State Guard, 1 August 1861-9 January 1862," 9-10, Missouri State Archives, Jefferson City.

18. Watson, *Life in the Confederate Army*, 222.

19. Joseph A. Mudd, *With Porter in North Missouri: A Chapter in the History of the War Between the States* (Washington, DC: National Publishing Co., 1909), 124; Watson, *Life in the Confederate Army*, 222-223; Elkanah Greer to R. W. Loughery, n.d., in *Marshall Texas Republican*, 28 September 1861.

20. "Mrs. Ollie Burton Recalls Wilson Creek Battle," *Springfield Press*, 5 April 1961.

21. Henderson, "A Confederate Diary," 11.

22. "The Battle near Springfield," *Burlington (IA) Daily Hawk-Eye*, 21 August 1861.

23. Barnes, *Medical and Surgical History*, 2: 15-16; "Army Correspondence," *Dubuque (IA) Herald*, 18 August 1861; Harris Flanagin to M. E. Flanagin, 24 August 1861, Harris Flanagin Papers, Arkansas History Commission, Little Rock.

24. Eugene Fitch Ware, *The Lyon Campaign* (Iowa City, IA: Press of the Camp Pope Bookshop, 1991), 341.

25. "Army Correspondence," *Dubuque (IA) Herald*, 18 August 1861.

26. Harris Flanagin to M. E. Flanagin, 24 August 1861; "Latest from Missouri," *Emporia (KS) News*, 31 August 1861; "Further Interesting News About the Doings at the Battle of Oak Hills," *Shreveport (LA) Weekly News*, 2 September 1861.

27. Henderson, "A Confederate Diary," 10; Richard H. Musser, "The War in Missouri: From Springfield to Neosho," *Southern Bivouac* 4 (April 1886): 684.

28. Cantrell, "Extracts from a Letter."

29. "Latest from Missouri," *Emporia (KS) News*.

30. Barnes, *Medical and Surgical History*, 2: 16.

31. "From Springfield, Mo.," *Olathe (KS) Mirror*, 24 October 1861.

32. All quotations from "Latest from Missouri," *Little Rock Arkansas True Democrat*, 22 August 1861.

33. Cantrell, "Extracts from a Letter."

34. "Latest from Missouri," *Little Rock Arkansas True Democrat*.

35. "The Noble Dead," *Mount Pleasant (IA) Home Journal*, 24 August 1861; "Killed," *Atchison (KS) Freedom's Champion*, 24 August 1861; "Latest from our Army in Missouri," *Emporia (KS) News*, 24 August 1861; "The Martyrs of Freedom," *Lawrence (KS) Weekly Republican*, 29 August 1861.

36. "For the Battlefield," *Lawrence (KS) Weekly Republican*, 22 August 1861.

37. "The Late Battle Near Springfield," *Des Arc (AR) Weekly Citizen*, 4 September 1861; "Letter from Lieut. Hills," *Emporia (KS) News*, 31 August 1861.

38. Musser, "The War in Missouri," 684.

39. "From Springfield," *Emporia (KS) News*, 21 September 1861; "The Reception of Colonel Mitchell," *Leavenworth (KS) Weekly Conservative*, 19 September 1861; "Arrival of Colonel Deitzler," ibid., 26 September 1861.

40. Harris Flanagin to M. E. Flanagin, 6 September 1861, Flanagin Papers.

41. Watson, *Life in the Confederate Army*, 229; "Full and Authentic Particulars of the Doings at the Camp, Before & After the Battle of Oak Hills," *Shreveport (LA) Weekly News*, 2 September 1861.

42. Bearss, *Battle of Wilson's Creek*, 161-164; J. H. Rockwell, "A Rambling Reminiscence of Experiences During the Great War Between the States," n.p., Missouri State Archives; "From Springfield, Mo.," *Olathe (KS) Mirror*; "Full and Authentic Particulars," *Shreveport (LA) Weekly News*; William E. Woodruff to Dear Pa, 15 August 1861, "Extract of a Letter from Capt. William E. Woodruff, jr.," *Little Rock Arkansas True Democrat*, 5 September 1861; Cantrell, "Extracts from a Letter."

43. W. E. Woodruff, *With the Light Guns in '61-'65: Reminiscences of Eleven Arkansas, Missouri and Texas Light Batteries, in the Civil War* (Little Rock, AR: Central Printing, 1903), 42; Woodruff, "Extract of a Letter."

44. According to two accounts, Southerners cut up Lyon's coat for souvenirs, but the report of Dr. S. H. Melcher, the Federal surgeon who took charge of the body, refutes the story. Likewise, two accounts say that the body was bayoneted. One states that it occurred in the heat of the battle, just moments after Lyon's death;

according to the other, it took place long after the fighting ended. Melcher reported no bayonet wounds on the body. Apparently another corpse was mistaken for Lyon's and despoiled. Return I. Holcombe and W. S. Adams, *An Account of the Battle of Wilson's Creek, or Oak Hills* (Springfield, MO: Dow and Adams, 1883), 98-102; Thomas W. Knox, *Camp-Fire and Cotton-Field: Southern Adventure in Time of War* (New York: Blelock, 1865), 79; "Further Interesting Particulars About the Doings at the Battle of Oak Hills," *Shreveport (LA) Weekly News*, 2 September 1861; Alf to Dear Mother, 12 August 1861, in "The Battle of Oak Hills, near Springfield, Mo.," *Shreveport (LA) South-Western*, 4 September 1861; Martin J. Hubble, comp., *Personal Reminiscences and Fragments of the Early History of Springfield, Greene County, Missouri* (Springfield, MO: Museum of the Ozarks, 1979), 93.

45. Phillips, *Damned Yankee*, 258-259; Hubble, *Personal Reminiscences*, 90-96; Holcombe and Adams, *An Account of the Battle of Wilson's Creek*, 98-104.

46. Phillips, *Damned Yankee*, 259-260; "Gen. Lyon's Body," *Ste. Genevieve Plaindealer*, 30 August 1861.

47. J. C. Frémont to John M. Schofield, 27 August 1861, John M. Schofield Papers, Library of Congress, Washington, DC; "Remains of Gen. Lyon," *Burlington (IA) Daily Hawk-Eye*, 29 August 1861; Phillips, *Damned Yankee*, 260.

48. Receipt from State of Connecticut to Trustees, Hartford, Providence and Fishkill Railroad, 6 September 1861, Nathaniel Lyon Letters, Connecticut State Library, Hartford; Phillips, *Damned Yankee*, 260-261.

Hamilton R. Gamble, Missouri's War Governor

MARGUERITE POTTER

At an early hour on the morning of January 12, 1861, St. Louis was buzzing with excitement. Main Street was a brilliant spectacle; flags of every size and description, busts of [George] Washington, [Henry] Clay, and [Daniel] Webster, and huge banners bearing the words "John J. Crittenden's Compromise" decked it from one end to the other. At twelve o'clock, a salute of thirty-three guns was fired from the levee and another at two in the afternoon. At noon, all business houses closed, and crowds thronged the streets. Fourth Street from Market to Chestnut was a living sea of people. Never before had St. Louis beheld such a meeting; never before had the West displayed such an interest in the fate of the country. By two o'clock, the vast throng was surging around the speaker's stand. Enthusiastic applause greeted the tall, slender, distinguished gentleman who rose to address them. He had the carriage of a general, the sensitive face of a scholar. When he began to speak in slow, deep, resonant tones, the crowd was hushed. Then and there Missourians heard Hamilton R. Gamble, for forty years respected, admired, and trusted throughout the state, take his stand for compromise and against secession.[1]

Thus, at a critical time in Missouri history, there returned to her political stage the leader whose statesmanship was to prove a dominant force in shaping the destiny of the state and perhaps, to a lesser degree, of the nation. He came back to St. Louis at a critical moment when people there, as elsewhere in Missouri, were halting between union and secession, and when amid the confused thinking of the time, the persuasive voice of one constructive thinker could formulate and sway public opinion. Tied to the South as

Although a Virginia native with ties to the South, Hamilton R. Gamble urged Missourians to remain loyal to the Union.

he was by blood and sympathy, Gamble overcame his prejudices and placed his loyalty where reason and common sense told him it should be placed, with the Union. The position of the border states in the conflict was never more perspicuously pointed out than by Gamble, who declared on the floor of the Missouri convention that if Missourians listened to their hearts they would go with the South, but if they were guided by their heads they would stay with the North. From the outset, therefore, it was evident to thinking Missourians that Gamble was unaffected by war hysteria and presented a clear, logical, defensible policy for individuals and the state to pursue. Around him public opinion crystallized. The hour and the man had met!

In Missouri, leadership was a more potent force in keeping the state loyal than in any of the other border states. Men like Gamble worked for the maintenance of state loyalty, unaided by the show of force which materially strengthened leaders in Kentucky, Maryland, and Delaware. One should not overlook the fact that in Missouri there was lacking the compulsion to loyalty that existed elsewhere along the border. Doubtless, Kentucky was impressed and even awed by the tremendous strength of the Union. Lines of Union troops were constantly whipping down across her bluegrass region as grim reminders of the almost unlimited manpower and the great economic resources which were used to force obedience from the recalcitrant states. The same was true in Maryland and little Delaware; from border to border rang the unceasing tramp of marching feet. Delaware, Maryland, and Kentucky beheld the forts, arsenals, batteries, and supply stations of the North. Across

Missouri, though, there were no streams of Union soldiers pouring into the South. Missourians were not constantly impressed with the fact that war was the price of secession, nor were they so forcefully reminded of the superior resources of the North. [Nathaniel] Lyon's forces and his maneuvers were incentives to secession rather than loyalty. The Mississippi River, which tied Missouri to the South economically, served almost as a barrier between the East and the West and tended to give Missouri a sense of detachment from the North which the other border states lacked. It will be seen, therefore, that the leaders who fought to keep Missouri loyal had a more difficult task than those who hoped to accomplish the same thing in Delaware, Maryland, and Kentucky.

Always in hours of great crisis, there arise leaders who, by virtue of their character, their sanity of judgment, their ability to fire their followers with their enthusiasm and endow them with their vision, enunciate principles and pursue policies that forever alter the course of human destiny. Such a man was Hamilton Rowan Gamble, and to him, more than to any other man, belongs the credit for keeping Missouri in the Union.

When the clouds of secession darkened the South and began to overspread the border, Gamble was living quietly in his Pennsylvania home, removed forever, as he thought, from the political stage of the state in which he had made his fortune and his reputation. Alarmed by the import of what was going on in the Union, and realizing that Missourians would soon be compelled to make what at best would be a grievous choice between the North and the South, Gamble determined to return and do what he could to swing public opinion by showing "one grey head in favor of the Union."[2] He was a Nehemiah returned to build a wall for his people, a wall against war and disunion. No man was better qualified to do it than he, for his long residence in the state and his wide reputation as a lawyer and jurist had won him an unusual degree of respect and admiration from his fellow men. Although not a native Missourian, he had practically grown up with the state.[3] He came into the Territory of Missouri as a young lawyer in 1818 and served as prosecuting attorney in a large frontier district north of the river and later, for a brief period, as secretary of state.[4] The land disputes growing out of the transfer of the Missouri territory from the Spanish and French into American hands gave Gamble his opportunity. He became the foremost authority on land law in Missouri and one of the best lawyers in the West on constitutional rights. The law firm of Bates and Gamble, a partnership with his brother-in-law Edward Bates, counted among its clients a large number of the important men in St. Louis. Gamble had been so absorbed in his profession that his career in public office prior to 1861 had been brief indeed. Elected to the General Assembly while he was absent from the state, he served one term. Later, as a judge of the Supreme Court of Missouri, he won a high reputation, and some of his opinions, notably his dissenting opinion in the Dred Scott case, won him wide recognition. Ill health led him to resign his judgeship in 1854. Shortly thereafter, in order to provide adequate educational facilities for his children, he established his home in Pennsylvania.

The salient traits of character which enabled Gamble to command such a following among Missourians grew directly out of his experience on the Missouri frontier. As a young prosecuting attorney, his library was limited to the five or six books which he could cram into his saddlebags, and he was forced to prepare his cases as he jogged along on horseback over the fifty or sixty miles of backwoods trails that separated the courts of his circuit. To an unusual degree, therefore, he was forced to depend upon his own common sense, and consequently, his judgment was mature beyond his years. He had a retentive memory, and he made it serve him in lieu of a library. So thoroughly did he assimilate all that he read that other lawyers marveled at what seemed to be an inexhaustible storehouse from which he could always draw the needed facts. Those characteristics of self-reliance and self-sufficiency remained with him throughout his life. Calm, dignified, self-possessed, he always appeared perfectly at ease. The confidence which he had in himself caused others to place their confidence in him. He was slow and deliberate in his speech, yet so logical, clear, and forceful that he never left a jury in doubt about the strong points of his own testimony and the weak points of his opponent's. In no sense of the word was he a spectacular orator, for he disliked and avoided all kinds of show. His modesty and utter lack of pretension led many to undervalue his real ability, but they changed that opinion once they met him at the bar. Gamble was motivated by high principles from which he would not deviate for personal gain and which he displayed not only in his profession, but in all the relationships of his life. During his whole career as prosecuting attorney, he never failed to gain a verdict when he pressed for it at the conclusion of the case, but often he would say to the jury that on the basis of the evidence he considered the defendant entitled to a verdict of not guilty.[5] He left a splendid example of integrity in the law.

Because of Gamble's long association with the state, because of the confidence placed in him, Missourians paid heedful respect to his opinions and welcomed him as the champion of peace and the Union.

In view of the tragic circumstances which necessitated Missouri's taking a stand either for or against secession, the legislature determined to place the issue before the people. On January 16, 1861, it authorized the election of a state convention which should have authority to consider the relationship

Edward Bates, Gamble's brother-in-law and former law partner, served as Lincoln's attorney general. He helped convince Gamble to return to Missouri and run for the state convention.

existing between Missouri and the national government. However, the convention was to have no power to alter that relationship except by vote of the people.[6]

In the short, turbulent campaign that followed, three distinct groups emerged, the secessionists led by Governor [Claiborne] Jackson, the Unconditional Unionists headed by [Frank] Blair, and the Conditional Unionists under the leadership of Gamble. The latter group was so designated because its adherents favored the Union in principle but would not pledge themselves to support it under all circumstances. They were the largest group in the state, and they counted among their members the wealthy influential people of the state who feared war because they had much to lose by it. Gamble contended that Missouri would have greater influence in restraining the North from aggressive acts which might precipitate a war if she were not committed in advance to support the North under all circumstances. Likewise, he felt that declarations in opposition to the principle of secession would at the same time serve to deter the South. With his policy of refusing to hand a blank check to either side, the Conditional Unionists were in complete agreement.

Under Gamble's leadership, the stand of the Conditional Unionists became increasingly pro-Union during the course of the campaign. At the time they selected their candidates for the state convention, they drew up a declaration of policy which differed in one important respect from the stand they had taken at the mass meeting on January 12. They reaffirmed their advocacy of the Crittenden compromise and reiterated their belief that the possession of slaves was a "constitutional right," but it is significant to note that they omitted the resolution containing their threat to secede unless that right were recognized and guaranteed.[7] The party declared further that Missouri would not submit to any attempt by the general government to coerce the seceding states by force, a stand from which Gamble tried to dissuade them. In a carefully written letter in which he accepted their nomination as a delegate to the forthcoming state convention, he pointed out clearly the dangers involved in taking an attitude which would hamstring the general government and expressed his unwillingness to stand for election on such a platform.[8]

On the same day that Jefferson Davis was inaugurated, Missourians went to the polls to vote on the most momentous question ever placed before them. Probably, it is not too much to assume that their vote determined in a great measure the failure of the Confederacy under Davis. The vote was an overwhelming victory for the Conditional Unionists. Gamble proved himself the strongest man on the ticket, for he was elected by a vote one-third larger than that cast for any other successful candidate.[9] Of the ninety-nine men elected, eighty-two had been born in slave states, thirteen in the North, and three in foreign countries.[10] Although decidedly southern in tone, there was not one out-and-out secessionist in the group, a fact which surprised Governor Jackson and the legislature.[11] It was well not only for Missouri, but also for the Union, that it was such a man as Gamble whose "legal authority, great circumspection, and personal popularity most happily guided the policy of the Convention."[12]

Immediately following organization, the convention named Hamilton Gamble chairman of the committee on federal relations. It was the duty of this committee to consider the question of secession and recommend a course of action to the convention. Of the group, Gamble was the leader. The other twelve were men of more than average ability; however, they were all at least ten years younger than Gamble, and although every member was either a practicing lawyer or a judge, none had attained his prominence in the profession or received the wide recognition accorded him throughout the state. In the committee room, they deferred to Gamble's judgment. The report was largely his work. Defending it in the debate which ensued on the floor of the convention, he declared, "I am responsible for every word and sentence in the report, for I wrote it."[13]

The report which the committee submitted to the convention was embodied in seven resolutions. The first was by far the most important for it contained the pronouncement that all were waiting anxiously to hear: that there was then "no adequate cause to impel Missouri to dissolve her connections with the Federal Union, but on the contrary she will labor for such an adjustment of existing troubles as will gain the peace, as well as the rights and equality of all the states."[14] Thus, as Gamble had desired from the first, Missouri was pledged to the Union. He never for a minute admitted the possibility of secession. "No matter what other slave states may do," he remarked on many occasions, "there is no danger of Missouri."[15] Unionists were jubilant, and even secessionists found some cause for rejoicing. Missouri was pledged to the Union. But not under all conditions! At the present there was no "adequate cause," but what of the future? With events moving so swiftly, might not a fortuitous turn of circumstances provide that "adequate cause?" Every man read the report in the light of his own hopes. To the Northerner, it was a pledge of continued loyalty. To the Southerner, looking ahead to possible attempts of coercion on the part of the North, it was an invitation to bide his time. To the great mass of Missourians, it was a highly satisfactory document, for above all else they desired peace and union, and the report showed the possibility for restoring both. Although the Southerner might hope, the report was basically a Union victory; every day that Missouri remained loyal, Union sentiment grew stronger.

Gamble did more than write the report; he introduced it, defended it, and secured its final adoption. From the time debate began upon it until its final passage, Gamble was almost constantly on the floor. In his opening defense,

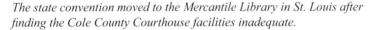

The state convention moved to the Mercantile Library in St. Louis after finding the Cole County Courthouse facilities inadequate.

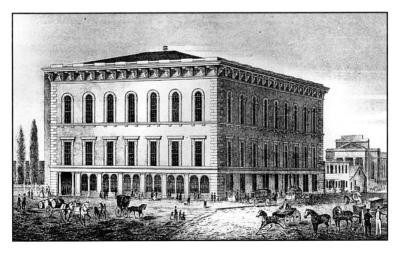

he pointed out the folly of involving Missouri in a revolution over slavery; even if the South should win, Missouri could scarcely hope to continue as a slave state because of her exposed position. He ended with an appeal for peace. "Missouri was brought forth in a storm and cradled in a compromise. She can resist the one and recommend the other."[16] He was the target for all opposition, and almost singlehandedly, he met and turned back every assailant. Gamble was no orator, but those who met him in that debate soon learned why the greatest orators of the state dreaded to appear against him. Logic was the rapier with which he parried blows and made his thrusts. One after another, those who tried to weaken the report went down in defeat. Gamble would not allow Missouri's hands to be tied by pledging in advance to aid either side. He contended that to commit her to any particular course of action was to lessen her influence in effecting a peaceful settlement. If she were to play the role of peacemaker, she was to be conciliatory and fair to both sides, and as he pointed out, she could not do that by announcing to the world that she was "prepared to be insulted." Thus, with the adoption of Gamble's report, a month before actual hostilities began, Missouri, with her great manpower, rich lead deposits, and strategic command of the two great rivers, took her stand against secession.

One other important step remained to be taken before the first session of the Missouri state convention closed. At Gamble's suggestion, provision was made whereby the convention could be reassembled if the need arose.[17] Within a few months the state was to see the capital city deserted, the governor pursued by an army, the legislature in full flight, and a condition of anarchy prevailing from border to border. Under such circumstances, one wonders what would have happened had the convention adjourned *sine die*.

There was no one in the state and probably no one in the United States who believed more firmly than Gamble that the war could be averted. He believed to the very last that sane statesmanship could have prevented what Lyon, Blair, and others called the "inevitable" conflict. It was this belief which caused him to back every movement for peace. Immediately following the adjournment of the Missouri state convention, he went as a delegate to the border state convention at Frankfort, Kentucky.[18] It must have been apparent from the first, even to him, that the efforts of that group were doomed to failure, for only two states bothered to send representatives.[19] "We ask both sides," Gamble had urged in a speech before the Missouri convention, "to shed no blood. Wait, wait until all peaceful means are exhausted."[20] After all "peaceful means" had failed, he was practically the last man to leave the final meeting for preventing a civil war. With a heavy heart, he returned to his family in Pennsylvania. No doubt, he knew that soon he would have to be back in Missouri, in a Missouri torn by the civil conflict which he dreaded and which he had tried so hard to avert. There, in the midst of war, he was to take up again the work of making peace.

The call came sooner than he had expected. Union men, dismayed at the rash action of Lyon, telegraphed Gamble to accompany one of their number to Washington to confer with the president.[21] Innocent people had been killed; loyal militiamen, including Gamble's own son, had been captured and made prisoners of war. Under Gamble's leadership, Missouri's natural tendency toward secession had been restrained on the grounds that the national government had not taken from the people of Missouri any of their rights, and it had been further checked by Lincoln's declaration that "this government will not assail you." Yet, under the leadership of a young hotspur, the national government had assailed a state which professed to be loyal! Gamble, who could never feel that fighting a people was the best way of winning them, saw that Lyon and Blair might easily push Missouri into the arms of the Confederacy and in their rashness undo all that he had accomplished by careful, painstaking diplomacy. In company with [James E.] Yeatman and Edward Bates, he had an interview with the president. They did not ask that Lyon be removed, but they did insist that [William S.] Harney be left in command and that regular troops be substituted for the irregular "Dutch Guards."[22] Their suggestions were not followed, and Lyon was free to make war upon the state. Had Gamble's counsel prevailed, the course pursued would have been less dramatic than that followed by Lyon, but it certainly would have produced more desirable results. From that point on, Lyon and Blair impugned Gamble's motives. Those who serve their country with the sword often mistrust and misjudge the efforts of those who would do the same by diplomacy.

The chaos that resulted from Lyon's maneuvers necessitated the calling together of the convention. The government had broken down; from county seat to state capital, anarchy reigned. Two courses presented themselves to the harassed convention members. Either they were to submit to the establishment of a military government, which was distasteful to all save a few extremists, or they were to take matters into their own hands and establish a provisional government.

Gamble was still in Pennsylvania when the session opened, but upon the earnest entreaties of leading Missourians, he returned immediately to St. Louis. "I am persuaded," wrote Edward Bates from Washington, "that your presence in the convention may exert a most benign influence in favor of peace."[23] Samuel T. Glover commented, "What a windfall it was that Judge Gamble came to the Convention. It would have been utterly impossible to have got along without him."[24]

Frank Blair, a U.S. representative from St. Louis, was a leader of the Unconditional Unionists.

Almost instantly upon arrival, Gamble was thrust forward as the champion of those who favored the establishment of a provisional government. His opponent was Uriel Wright, a fiery orator who contended that the convention had no power to replace the Jackson government. Doubtless, Gamble defended the weaker side, but he advocated the course dictated by grim necessity, and public calamity provided him with powerful arguments. Silenced, but not convinced, Wright went down in defeat. On Tuesday, July 30, 1861, the state convention by a vote of fifty-six to twenty-five declared the executive offices of the state vacant.[25]

With a unanimity born of instinctive trust, men of both parties turned to Gamble as the logical leader of the new government. He had always shunned public office, and it was only after the most urgent petitions had been made that he submitted to nomination. The vote given for him was an indication of the esteem in which he was held by other members of the convention. Even Uriel Wright, who asked to be excused from voting because he felt the convention had no power to replace the executive, declared, "There is no man in the limits of the State upon whom I would more readily confer the important trust which must devolve upon a chief executive. By all the habitudes of his mind, by the maturity of his intellect, by the solidity of his judgment, by the unstained purity of his moral character, I know of no man . . . who challenges more unqualified approbation than Hamilton Rowan Gamble."[26] Throughout the state, gratification and satisfaction were expressed. The

Missouri Republican and the *New York Times* expressed their satisfaction in the action of the legislature.[27]

Gamble entered his office with an alert mind trained in the law, a deep understanding of human nature, an innate love of right, and a predisposition to afford justice to all. He was not an experienced executive, but he commanded the confidence and trust of the people. He was not a politician; he was a man whose actions were dictated by principles of right rather than party polity. Little concerned about personal glory, he allowed men under him to take all the credit for any public service; it was enough for him that the desired end was brought about. As a fellow member of the bar declared some time later, seeing with what fortitude Gamble met the multiple difficulties of office, "His strength was of the Doric order, and granite in its material."[28]

The new governor turned his hand first to the challenging yet disheartening task of pacifying a turbulent people. The whole state was in confusion. No authoritative voice had been raised to quell the strife until Gamble issued his inaugural address to the people. It was a document characterized, as were all his state papers, by calm dignity, and it did much to quiet Missouri.[29] The most outstanding quality Gamble possessed as a lawyer was his ability to go directly to the core of any problem and analyze it objectively. His address shows that from the first he had a thorough grasp of the fundamental problems with which he was to grapple. He turned his attention to the most troublesome of these—slavery, the impending social war, and the amnesty for past offenses.

Loyal and secessionist slaveholders were comforted by his words on the slave question. Since slavery was legal in the state, he had no choice but to pledge himself to enforce the laws concerning it. He removed, as much as he was able, the element of uncertainty which had contributed so largely to the prevalent agitation. His remarks were not made with the idea that he could thus settle the question, but rather with the hope that if he could diminish its importance in the public mind, he would have taken a step in the direction of peace.[30]

Of equal magnitude and interwoven with the slavery question was the problem of keeping peace among the people. Class had been set against class, neighbor against neighbor, and even families were divided. This condition, soon to produce guerrilla bands that made the war in Missouri so terrible, might be mitigated, Gamble pointed out, if each citizen would refrain from intemperate discussion.[31] But the governor soon learned that reasonable appeals were unheeded. Time, not reason, is the antidote for popular hysteria and hate.

Upon the assurance that the federal government would cause his promise to be respected, Gamble extended amnesty on August 3, 1861, to all who, having taken up arms under the Jackson government, would voluntarily return to their allegiance.[32] Many citizens with no intention of disloyalty had responded to Jackson's call, and unless some plan had been provided by the new government, they would have been forced to remain in the false position in which they found themselves. Numerous letters poured into his office from men who wished to avail themselves of his offer. In each case, Gamble investigated carefully in order to give protection only where it was justified and in order not to overstep his powers. The presence of other legal authorities in the state complicated matters, and the governor was careful to establish his own purview before he acted. He scrupulously avoided assuming any power over cases of martial law declared by [John] Frémont in St. Louis and throughout the state. In such cases, he had no authority to act, and he never tried to assume powers not legally his. Likewise, Gamble was cautious not to grant amnesty to anyone who had committed offenses after he had an opportunity of claiming security under the August proclamation. To give personal attention to these cases was a heavy task but one that paid large dividends.[33]

Gamble's position was weakened somewhat by the fact that his government was a provisional rather than a duly elected one. However, he did not consider his administration as an experiment, nor did he for a moment admit the possibility of failure. In his proclamation to the people, he dismissed the subject thus: "I could give you no stronger expression of my deliberate judgment that their [state convention] action was both constitutional and necessary, than is afforded by my acceptance of the office."[34] To Missouri at large, that simple statement, from the man recognized as the greatest constitutional lawyer in the state, sufficed to settle the question. The *Missouri Republican* declared that "the only lawful governor of Missouri is Governor Gamble," and that, of course, was the sentiment of many of the outstanding leaders of the state.[35] Yet, like the ghost of Banquo, there came stalking upon the scene the shadow of the old Jackson government. Gamble ignored it, but its continuance was a source of irritation and an actual threat in event of military failure on the part of the new government. Even the death of Jackson himself did not serve to dissolve this shadow government.[36] Strong military forces within the state made its return impossible, but Gamble's opponents hoped that a fortuitous turn of circumstances might make its restoration possible.

The legality of his government caused Gamble less concern than the problem of the restoration and maintenance of peace within the state. If he could solve the latter problem, the former would take care of itself. Before Missouri could be of any aid to the Union at all, internal discord and fighting had to be obliterated. He realized that Missouri with her iron, lead, and hemp resources and with her strategic position on the two great waterways could be a great asset to the Union if internal strife were removed. Gamble did not try to raise a state militia immediately, partly because of his fear that secessionists would enroll for the sake of obtaining arms and partly because of the financial condition of the state. Missouri was bankrupt, interest on the debt was in arrears, and state credit was dead.[37] Moreover, the source of income had been shut off. Local government had broken down, tax books were missing, tax collectors had gone south, property had fallen in value, and sheriffs were resigning their offices to avoid having to collect the taxes already due from the last year. As late as June 1862, after comparative quiet had been restored throughout the state, the report of the state auditor showed that only forty-one of the counties had given receipts for the tax books of the previous year. Even in those counties, one-third of the amount due remained to be collected.[38]

By the last of August 1861, Gamble felt that lines between secessionists and Union men were sufficiently well drawn, and he had enough faith in the true sentiment of the people of the state, to proceed to raise a state force. Therefore, on August 24, he issued a proclamation calling for 42,000 volunteers. This was to be a force enrolled for six months "unless peace be sooner restored."[39] Gamble's patience was sorely tried by the subsequent delay and difficulty in obtaining the number of troops he desired. Men and officers in the United States regiments, in order to swell their own numbers, represented to the prospective militiamen that there was slight chance of their receiving their pay and the proper clothing and subsistence. The known condition of the state treasury lent color to the arguments of the federal soldiers.[40] Appeals by

Mustering In

Governor Gamble to the brigadier general were of no avail.[41] As a result, not 42,000, but only slightly more than 6,000, entered the state service in response to the governor's call.[42] The bad feeling thus engendered between the two groups of soldiers continued, and although Gamble did what he could to improve matters, Frémont's hostility to the state troops counteracted his work.

The military situation in Missouri was further complicated by the presence of the Home Guards. That force, formed during the early days of secession, proved a source of trouble and irritation from the first. They were an organization "half-soldier, half-citizen" over which the governor had no control whatever. He suggested to the president that they should either be disbanded or else united and disciplined with the regular army.[43] Instead, however, under Frémont this force was actually enlarged.

In an effort to procure sufficient funds to maintain a force capable of restoring peace in the state, Gamble proposed a plan to the president whereby the federal government would pay, clothe, and subsist the troops raised in Missouri. Shortly after his inauguration, Gamble sent John S. Phelps to confer with Lincoln on the possibility of working out some plan by which this could be done. Phelps was not successful, and Gamble went to Washington to make a personal plea. Although the president would not agree to Gamble's plan, he did agree to grant the governor arms and money to carry out his proclamation. Two hundred and fifty thousand dollars was to be placed to Gamble's credit in the subtreasury.[44] Upon his return to St. Louis ten days later, Gamble was able to assure the people of the state that the provisional government had the moral backing of the administration and that aid was forthcoming. A month elapsed and the promised funds did not arrive. In despair, Gamble wrote to Bates and asked him to investigate. With Gamble's letter in his hand, Bates went immediately to the secretary of the treasury. [Salmon] Chase seemed surprised, because he had ordered the money sent sometime earlier and supposed it was already at Gamble's disposal. He asked Bates to assure the governor that it would be sent immediately, as indeed it was.[45] There was the same disheartening delay in obtaining arms. Gamble had delegated [William M.] McPherson to get them for him. After having secured in Washington an order for guns and infantry equipment for 4,000 men, McPherson went immediately to New York to get them. At the New York arsenal, however, he found that only 2,710 guns were available, and they were old patterns of the Springfield musket loaded with ball and buckshot. Even those were obtained with the greatest difficulty, and only then by special order of the president.[46] Gamble was disappointed; even the full 4,000 would have been insufficient. Bates assured him, "The government is not so much to blame as you may suppose. The demand is very great for Tennessee and Kentucky as well as

Missouri."[47] His words were small comfort to a man who, charged with the task of restoring peace, had to stand helplessly by and see the state ravaged and had to turn a deaf ear to appeals from Union men for arms with which they could at least have mitigated the conditions. Another trip to Washington was necessary before Gamble was able to convince the president that the only hope was for the national government to do as he had first suggested, arm and subsist a state militia.

The difficulties which the governor had to face were needlessly augmented by General Frémont, the very man who could have done the most to help make his task lighter. Gamble had expressed gratification over Frémont's appointment, and apparently he made an honest and persistent effort to cooperate with the general. Psychologically, the two men were incompatible. Frémont, vainglorious, dictatorial, and intolerant, assumed that Gamble was also avaricious for power and prestige. Personal praise was of little importance to the governor, and he was perfectly willing that Frémont should have it all. Gamble was interested primarily in the restoration of peace and order in the state. Had Frémont taken Gamble into his confidence and been willing to talk with him about the problems in Missouri, surely he would have discovered Gamble's fine spirit of cooperation and unselfishness. Whatever else one may say of Gamble, it can never be truthfully charged that as governor he tried to arrogate praise and power to himself. Frémont gave orders to him as arbitrarily as though he had been a subordinate, refused to grant him interviews, and proceeded from the first on the theory that Gamble was a usurper, trying to assume powers not rightfully his in the hope of appearing more important and powerful than the general himself.

The first friction had developed over the matter of appointments in the militia. Immediately after Gamble assumed office, Frémont telegraphed a demand that Gamble make no appointments without consulting him.[48] In that case, and in Frémont's subsequent requests, Gamble attempted to cooperate whenever possible. He appointed the adjutant and quartermaster general suggested by Frémont, but he had to refuse to comply with his wishes in regard to appointing brigadiers because he had no power to do so. Under Missouri law, the field officers of the brigades elected the brigadiers. Gamble liked that arrangement no better than Frémont did, but he was powerless to change it. He explained this carefully to Frémont in a letter.[49] He was surprised twelve days later when Frémont requested that Gamble commission Frank Blair with the rank of brigadier general.[50] Either Frémont had paid no attention whatever to Gamble's letter—and that is the more plausible reason, since he was hazy on the other facts contained in the letter—or he made the request knowing in advance that Gamble could not legally grant it and thus tossed the hot poker

As commander of the Department of the West, John C. Frémont was a constant source of friction to Gamble.

to the governor. If the "hope and pride" of the Blair clan were to be refused a commission, it was better that the refusal came from the governor than from the general; at least, it was better for the general.

The second cause of friction arose when Frémont demanded that the police commissioners of St. Louis be replaced by men of his own selection.[51] He presumptuously ignored Gamble's right to make his own appointments and the fact that legally the commissioners could be removed only upon proof of misconduct. When a vacancy occurred, Gamble did appoint one of the men from Frémont's list; however, he did not make wholesale removals on mere suspicions. He asked Frémont to examine the records of the board and assured him that if there were evidences of misconduct, removals would be made immediately. This the general would not do. Gamble had the books sent to Jefferson City, examined them himself, and when he found evidence strong enough to warrant removals, he made them.[52] Gamble's unwillingness to make the removals without investigation exasperated the impetuous general; his flat refusal to overstep his authority infuriated Frémont, who had no such scruples.

Probably many in 1861 who felt that Frémont was deliberately trying to cripple the provisional government were unfair to him. Yet, he must bear a heavy responsibility for making a decision that abandoned a very large part of the state to the Southerners, a part rich in lead deposits. Lyon, who was in command of the small Union force in southwest Missouri, begged Frémont and Gamble for reinforcements. Although personally Gamble had no great faith in Lyon's judgment, he supported him in his campaign in every way possible, and he did everything in his power to make it successful. Both in person and in writing, he begged Frémont to reinforce Lyon, but to no avail.[53] The governor's requests were unheeded, and Lyon's special messengers cooled their heels on the steps of the Brandt mansion.[54] Reinforcements were not sent in time to be of any use. The Battle of Wilson's Creek was a Southern victory. Lyon met his death, and half of the state of Missouri was abandoned to the Confederates. That great defeat, coming as it did closely upon the establishment of the provisional government, lessened Union prestige and made the governor's position even more precarious.

On his way to Washington, DC, to see the president, Gamble stopped in St. Louis to confer with Frémont. The general was deep in the preparation of the famous emancipation proclamation and refused to grant him an interview. The proclamation came as a complete surprise to Gamble; his first information about it was gained from the newspapers.[55] It ran counter to Gamble's views at nearly every point. He felt it would split the Union forces, as indeed it did; he felt that it would be more politic to try to hold the slaveowners of Union sympathy to the Union rather than to alienate them. He did not consider Missouri as a conquered province, which was the attitude taken by Frémont; he opposed increasing strife by stirring up the slavery question; he resented the implication that civil government had broken down and that military government should take its place. What discussion he and Lincoln had on the subject is not known, but on his return, Gamble brought with him a letter from the president which ordered Frémont to grant him an interview.

As the demand of the president could not be ignored, Frémont arranged to see the governor shortly after his return from Washington. Upon being admitted to Frémont's presence, Gamble handed him the letter Lincoln had sent and waited in silence while he read it through. "Governor," said Frémont, when he had finished, "it is proper that we should be frank. I sent you a list of names of persons whom I wished appointed to offices in the militia in order that I might assign them to positions, and no such appointments were made." In view of his carefully written explanation, this doubtless amazed Gamble, but he very patiently explained the contents of that letter to Frémont, pointing out how his hands were tied in the matter and how he had done everything he could do legally in complying with the request. At the mention of the letter, Frémont acted as if he were trying to recall something that had faded from his memory, and although he admitted having received it, he did not remember its contents. Gamble tried to clear up the entire affair of the police commissioners and other minor matters in order that no misunderstanding might remain. During nearly the whole interview, Frémont sat silent and distracted. Finally, he remarked that his mind was not clear upon the subjects discussed and that he would think them over and communicate later with the governor. After making arrangements for getting a 10,000 stand of arms within the next sixty days, the governor took his leave.[56] Commenting to his nephew, he stated, "I expect no arms from him."[57] He judged correctly, for he got none.

The next day Major [Richard M.] Corwin[e] brought the governor a note from Frémont requesting that he call again before he left St. Louis in order that they might go further into the matters they had discussed the day before.[58] He promised to notify him about a time for the appointment. Gamble agreed.[59] He waited all the next day, but no word came until that night when he received another note from Corwin[e].[60] An interview was arranged for 11 o'clock the next day, and precisely at that time, Gamble presented himself at Frémont's headquarters. At the desks in the outer office were several men busily engaged in writing. One of them stopped long enough to state that he had been asked by Frémont to entertain the governor. Some time later, a secretary came into the room, evidently from Frémont's private office, handed some papers to one of the men, and went out. Another long wait ensued. Finally, after having waited nearly an hour, Gamble rose to depart; whereupon, one of the men asked if he would call again before leaving the city. Gamble replied that he would if he found time.[61] He left St. Louis without either seeing or hearing from Frémont again.

All of this was reported to Lincoln through Gamble's nephew and personal agent at Washington, Charles Gibson. Gamble, Gibson, and Bates urged Lincoln to remove Frémont, but their efforts met with no success. When Gamble made his next trip to Washington, he carried with him and presented to Montgomery Blair the charges which Frank Blair, then under arrest at Frémont's order, had entrusted to him.[62] This embroilment with the Blair clan proved to be the last straw, and Frémont was replaced. Unfortunately, the removal of the general did not carry with it the removal of the discord his acts had engendered. His proclamation was the starting point for the division of Union men in the state, and that division accounts for much of the unhappy history of the next few years in Missouri.[63]

By the end of October 1861, the first crisis of the provisional government was safely past. It had been a trying three months for the new governor. He had not succeeded in convincing Lincoln that the national government should extend financial aid to the state; he had not been able to procure an adequate supply of arms; he had found his call for 42,000 men almost ignored because of open opposition from the United States forces; he had been successively ordered, upbraided, and ignored by a general who tried to assume civil authority himself; he had seen every military encounter end in Confederate victory; and in vain he had importuned good men to accept the meagerly paid state offices. Later in 1861, however, the outlook was brighter. A new financial arrangement had been made with Washington, and Frémont had been removed. As it became increasingly evident that the provisional government would be able to maintain itself, men who had previously refused, accepted office, and new recruits came into the militia. It was not an easy path that lay ahead, but at last Gamble could feel that his government rested on a solid foundation.

Shortly after his return from the first official trip to Washington, Gamble summoned the convention to meet in special session on the tenth of October 1861.[64] His reasons for doing so were obvious. Actual war existed in half of the state. Following the Confederate victory at Wilson's Creek, [Sterling] Price had moved northward as far as Lexington. It was not so much Price's maneuvers as the psychological reaction of the people to those maneuvers that wrought the havoc. Union prestige was badly impaired, the people felt unprotected, and there were wild rumors of invasion by great Southern armies.[65] In addition to the intermittent threat of invasion, there were guerrilla bands which ravaged the country, making war on their personal enemies and living by plunder.

At the time it had established the provisional government, the convention had made arrangements for submitting its action to a vote of the people on the first Monday in November 1861. At that time, also, new state officers were to

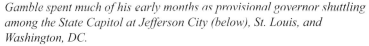

Gamble spent much of his early months as provisional governor shuttling among the State Capitol at Jefferson City (below), St. Louis, and Washington, DC.

be elected.[66] By the time the convention met in October, it was apparent that if any election were held the following month the secessionists would certainly win, for they had control of southern and western Missouri. In some places, the broken-down condition of the local government made the holding of any election impossible. Under the circumstances, Gamble recommended that the election be postponed until a more suitable time. As that entailed his continuance in office longer than the convention had intended and longer than he had anticipated in accepting, he urged that the convention select a successor to serve in the interim.[67] "We need no better officers," declared the *Missouri Republican*, and the convention agreed.[68] The election was postponed until the first Monday in August 1862.[69] However, certain changes were necessary if the state were to be prepared to hold an election even on that date. Consequently, a test oath was required, the first ever imposed in the state. The offices of all civil officials in the state who did not subscribe to the oath within sixty days were to be declared vacant.[70] By this measure, loyal local government was reestablished and the hand of the provisional government immeasurably strengthened.

To improve the military situation in the state, the convention, at the request of the governor, enacted a new military law to replace the inadequate, cumbrous one then in effect and authorized the issuing of Union defense bonds to the amount of $1,000,000 to help finance the state troops.[71] Gamble was delegated to go to Washington to borrow money from the federal government on the bonds.[72] The enactment of these bills, of course, relieved the governor from immediate embarrassment, but the measures were inadequate for the full support of a considerable force for any great length of time. If the troops were to be kept in the field long enough to become efficient, more permanent provisions had to be made.

In his interview with the president, Gamble pointed out that if the Missouri troops could be put on a sound financial basis, a considerable force could be raised, and Union soldiers then in the state could be released for service elsewhere. Many who feared to leave their homes to the mercy of guerrillas would enlist if assured that they would not be called out of the state. Likewise, many who did not care to join the Union army to invade and subjugate the South would be willing, nevertheless, to take up arms against an invasion of Missouri. At Lincoln's request, Gamble drew up a draft which, with minor changes, became the basis for the extension of federal aid to the state.[73] At [General George] McClellan's suggestion, it was agreed that the governor should name as the major general of the state forces the major general of the War Department, who had been appointed by the president. To this the governor assented without hesitation.[74] Gamble suggested in his draft that the money be paid out through regular United States paymasters rather than through state officers, but another system was adopted.[75] The funds were deposited to Governor Gamble's credit and paid out on his personal check.[76] Although vast sums passed through his hands, no charge of fraud was ever made against him even by his bitterest enemies.

Now that he had secured adequate backing for a state force, Gamble wished to disband the old Missouri state militia, which had been called out for six months, and to incorporate its members into the new force. He realized the endless and unnecessary confusion that would result if it were kept in existence at the same time that the new troops were being raised. Then, too, the old militia had been very expensive because it had been organized under the old military law which allowed an undue proportion of officers. As regular pay and sufficient subsistence were guaranteed in the new organization, he felt confident the Missouri state militiamen would reenlist. However, as they were already entitled to pay which they had not received, only a small number did reenlist.[77]

According to the agreement between Gamble and the president, Major General [Henry] Halleck became the major general of the new state militia, but immediate command of the state was turned over to J. M. Schofield, who was the brigadier general of the volunteers. This choice was a most fortunate one, for he was one of the few able military men in Missouri during the war. His relations with the governor were most cordial at all times. Schofield states in his autobiography:

> It is due the memory of Governor Gamble to say that although partisan enemies often accused him of interfering with the operations of the militia in the interest of his supposed political views, there never was, while I was in command of the militia, the slightest foundation for such accusation. He never attempted to interfere in any manner with the legitimate exercise of the authority of the commanding general, but was, on the contrary, governed by the commander's views and opinions in the appointment and dismissal of officers and in other matters in which his own independent authority was unquestioned. [78]

Halleck's efficient military control and the unusually rigorous weather gave Missouri comparative peace during the winter of 1861 and 1862. Early in the spring, before Price considered the weather moderate enough for the movement of troops, [General Samuel] Curtis, who had taken the field under Halleck, started his march toward Springfield. Price began his retreat, a retreat that ended with his defeat at Pea Ridge.

That decisive Union victory assured Missourians that they need have no further fear of invaders and secessionists. Also, there was no further hope of reestablishing the old Jackson government. From then on, Missouri was firmly in the Union. Thus, the state had passed successfully through two great crises. The Gamble government, the only hope of the Union forces, had endured the test and had successfully warded off invasion and thereby preserved the sovereignty of the state.

In the spring of 1862, petitions poured into Gamble's office asking him to become a candidate in the coming election for state officers. Two men, James H. Birch and George W. Miller, announced their candidacy in January and March, but neither was as widely or favorably known as Gamble.[79] It was not until the fifteenth of May that Gamble consented to have his name placed on the ticket.[80]

There was little doubt about the main issue. As early as March, the *Missouri Republican* stated that the August election would be fought over emancipation.[81] It is interesting to note that the abolitionists did not begin preparation for their campaign until Gamble's candidacy was announced. Apparently, only then were they convinced that the election was actually going to be held and also that they had an opponent strong enough to challenge all their forces. Accordingly, they issued a call for a radical convention to be held at Jefferson City in June.[82]

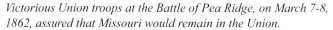

Victorious Union troops at the Battle of Pea Ridge, on March 7-8, 1862, assured that Missouri would remain in the Union.

Five days before the radicals met, the state convention "stole their thunder" by postponing the election for state officers until 1864. The convention had first voted to proceed with the election as scheduled in 1862 but postponed it to the later date when, to their amazement, the members learned that Gamble looked upon their action as a censure of his administration.[83] Certainly, it was not their intention, and one is at a loss to understand his attitude. It was a grave error in judgment on his part and, without doubt, his greatest blunder. Surely, it would have been wiser for him to insist that the election take place and that the emancipation question be settled as soon as possible. However, he acted in accordance with the principle which he had advocated in the Dred Scott decision. He stated then that a vital issue which affected so many people should not be made a political issue, particularly in times of distress. He refused to see that whether leaders liked it or not, emancipation had already become a political issue, and one of such magnitude as to demand immediate settlement. The year 1862 was the psychological time for a test of strength; Gamble was stronger then in popular favor than at any time subsequently. The *Missouri Republican*, ordinarily a very accurate barometer of public opinion in the state, predicted that three-fourths of the Union men in Missouri were then opposed to any scheme of emancipation and that the abolitionists would be unable to poll more than 20,000 votes against Gamble.[84] Certainly, Gamble would not have received all the votes of the Union men in 1862, but the indications are that he would have won easily. The radicals had no leader to compare with him. George W. Miller, the other Union candidate, withdrew in Gamble's favor. Birch, who was suspected of courting secessionist favor, was in jail charged with treason before the date on which the election was to have been held. The fact that in the November election the emancipationists won the state is no proof that they would have done so in an August election with Gamble at the head of the opposition ticket, for their success in electing legislators in November was largely the result of the president's emancipation proclamation of September.[85] Had the governor thrown aside his "lawyer caution" and gambled for all and won, as he doubtless would have done, then how much more vigorous, how much more constructive his leadership would have been in the emancipation fight to follow. The endorsement of the people would have been the strongest of all weapons and would have disarmed his enemies and rendered them powerless. Duly elected, Gamble could possibly have inaugurated his moderate emancipation policy and kept the executive branch of the government in conservative hands until 1866. If strong leadership during that time had effected peace and established a workable plan of emancipation, the radical element would probably never have captured the state, and Missouri would have been spared the needless reconstruction at their hands. It was that "tide in the affairs of men" which should have been, but was not "taken at the full."

Three other measures of importance resulted from the fourth session of the convention. A test oath was imposed upon voters, which excluded the disloyal voters from the polls.[86] This measure accounts, at least in part, for the fact that Missouri polled only 82,000 votes in 1862 as compared with the 170,000 votes in 1861. Although the election of executive officers was postponed until 1864, provision was made for electing members for a new legislature in November 1862, and for abrogating entirely the ordinance providing that the people should vote on the action of the convention in establishing the provisional government.[87] Again, it was at Gamble's own insistence that this action was taken. There was certainly some truth in his contention that it was foolish to ask the people to decide between a provisional government and no government at all. Yet, the vote of approval by the people upon his government was the reinforcement he most needed and would have removed his government from the extralegal category. Missourians have always been a conservative group in whom respect for legality is strongly ingrained, and though they have obeyed extralegal governments, they have always been inclined to view allegiance to them as less obligatory. Many of the difficulties Gamble met during his last months in office revert to the fact that, although the provisional government existed for three years, it was never approved by a vote of the people.

Early in April of 1862, General Price, who had gone south, issued an appeal to Southern sympathizers in Missouri to follow him. From that time on, much of the fighting in the state was between Union forces and the bands of men trying to work their way south to join him. Also there were the guerrillas and the incursions of Kansans which, beginning shortly after the Battle of Wilson's Creek, continued with vigor and violence all along the border during the rest of the war. Property was destroyed, stock driven off, and towns were sacked and burned by the invaders. The loyal and disloyal factions in the state were so intermingled as to facilitate the bandit raids, and there were no adequate forces to deal with such an irregular mode of warfare. Gamble believed that if a militia were equipped and stationed as a guard throughout the state, the bushwhacker invasions could be checked.[88]

These conditions led him to authorize General Schofield to issue Order No. 19, which required every able-bodied man in the state to enroll in the militia.[89] The force was raised, controlled, and paid by the state. Of the 50,000 men so enlisted, about 30,000 were armed.[90] Since Gamble and Schofield ordered all those who had aided or supported the South to be enrolled also, they were severely criticized. This action was taken, not with the intention of using those men, but rather for the purpose of keeping them under surveillance. They were to be registered but not incorporated into the militia. There was no intention either on the part of Gamble or Schofield to arm them and make them a part of the fighting force. However, a few officers whose zeal exceeded their discrimination did exactly that.[91] When Gamble and Schofield discovered the mistakes, the men were released from service. Schofield issued Order No. 24 declaring that all Southern sympathizers would be permitted to remain at home as long as they attended quietly to legitimate business.[92]

Gamble's intention had been to have these men available for service when trouble arose. That plan proved to be impracticable, and eventually, only the best trained men were used. They were selected according to fitness and loyalty and put under Schofield's command. At the suggestion of Lincoln, the entire work of keeping order north of the Missouri River was delegated to this enrolled militia, and Union soldiers in the state were released to reinforce [Ulysses] Grant at Vicksburg.[93]

Thus, there existed in Missouri in 1863 three distinct military groups: the old Missouri state militia, raised under an agreement between Lincoln and Gamble, used only in the state but subsisted entirely by the national government; the national troops; and the new enrolled militia, subsisted by the national government and paid by the state.

One of the most troublesome questions of the Gamble administration was the status of the old Missouri state militia raised under the special agreement. The matter was brought sharply to focus when Gamble, acting as he believed

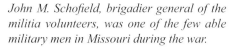

John M. Schofield, brigadier general of the militia volunteers, was one of the few able military men in Missouri during the war.

with full authority, dismissed a colonel who had been proved incompetent by an examing board.[94] Halleck declared that in dismissing a colonel "in the service of the United States," Gamble was exceeding his power.[95] The governor agreed that if the man were in the "service of the United States," he had no authority over him. Unusual importance was attached to this question by officials at Washington who contended that it involved the right of the president to command the militia of other states.[96] Gamble could not agree that a public admission by the War Department of his right to make appointments and removals in the Missouri force would carry with it the tacit admission that other governors had a similar power over the volunteer forces in their states. The Missouri militia was a special force, existing in one state only and raised under a special agreement between the national and state governments. A careful analysis of the agreement itself convinced Gamble that the troops were in actuality state troops. If they had been considered national troops from the first, then the document, as he pointed out, was "solemnly expressed nonsense."[97] Lincoln took the stand that strictly speaking, the force was neither state or national and that each question should be settled separately as it arose.[98] This was not a satisfactory arrangement for Gamble, for it left him with no criterion by which to judge what he could and could not do.

The uncertainty regarding his power only increased his difficulties. The president seemed to feel that the governor wished to force him to declare that the status of the troops was such that he could arrogate powers to himself, but there is little evidence that such was the case. Although the president granted Gamble the right to make appointments in the militia, he denied him the right to remove his own appointees even after grave dereliction of duty had been proved. Every petty offense had to be settled at Washington. Even in the matter of disbanding the troops, approval as to the time, place, and method had to be secured before action could be taken. The president's authority in the matter very effectively tied Gamble's hands and made his position weaker.

Almost as persistent and troublesome as the question of the troop status was the one regarding assessments on Southern sympathizers. The policy of assessments had been started by Frémont and continued by his successors. From the first, Governor Gamble had disapproved of it because Union men might easily fall under some slight suspicion and be assessed. As Gamble had reason to know, in such disturbed times everyone's sympathy was subject to question, and there existed no possible means of proving or classifying shades of opinion. Since that was true, it was almost impossible to make fair assessments. Injustice was inherent in the system. Halleck did what he could to prevent fraud by improving the method of assessing and collecting the funds. But under his successor, Curtis, the policy was prosecuted with more vigor and less discretion.[99] Both Lincoln and Gamble tried to persuade Curtis to abandon the policy of collection, but Curtis was obdurate and defended it on the ground of necessity.[100] The money thus collected was used for the support of the enrolled militia and their families. However, Gamble and Lincoln made arrangements for raising the money by some other method, thus clearing the way for the abandonment of the system.[101] By executive order in January 1863, Lincoln suspended all action for assessments in the state, and the system fell into disuse.[102]

The assessment question was one more issue to widen the breach in the Union ranks. By the time of the election in 1862, Missouri was definitely split into two factions: the "clay-banks," led by Gamble and Blair, and the "charcoals," led by B. Gratz Brown. As the name would imply, the "charcoals" were the blackest of the black Republicans, that is, the party that favored immediate and unconditional emancipation. The "claybanks" had opposed the radical policy of emancipation advanced by Frémont, and with his removal, they continued their opposition against the radicals who supported his ideas. Although there was a small element whose hybrid character caused them to be called "chocolates," their number was so small that they are seldom given political existence at all. The test oath had excluded all except the two main groups of Union men from the polls.

The bitterly fought contest in the fall of 1862 ended with victory for the emancipationists, who gained control of the state legislature.[103] It was expected of course that this group would take immediate action on the emancipation question. The governor urged them to do so in order to abate the agitation which the campaign had engendered. Ignoring the mandate of the people and the request of the governor, they spent their time wrangling over the selection of senators and ended the session with one of the two senators still to be elected.

The bad feeling which had arisen between Union men during the campaign was made worse when General Curtis was placed in charge of the federal troops. Of all the bad generals with which Missouri was cursed during the war, Curtis was undoubtedly one of the worst. Gamble disliked and distrusted him and felt that he was conniving with the radicals to promote the establishment of a military government in Missouri. Curtis permitted and even encouraged his officers to meddle with the internal and social affairs of the state; he allowed his officers to slander the governor and the militia; he ignored rather than cooperated with the governor; and he was found guilty of notorious speculation and of meddling with state politics. Over the protest of Gamble and other Missouri leaders, he secured a new military arrangement whereby part of Missouri was joined with a Kansas district under the

control of General [James] Blunt. As the governor suspected, the old border hostilities flamed again, and once more western Missouri was ravaged
by war.[104] Petitions, pleas, evidence, testimonials, and personal interces-
sions on the part of Governor Gamble, John B. Henderson, Edward Bates,
and Charles Gibson were necessary before Lincoln would consent to Curtis's
removal.[105] Henderson, before leaving for Missouri, called at the White House
and presented the facts quite plainly to the president. "He gave me his word
to act and he will do so," he wrote to Gamble, and then added realistically,
"I hope."[106] Finally, the change was made; Curtis was replaced by Schofield.
Although the radical press clamored with vehemence against the change, responsible citizens agreed with Bates, who said, "It was the only course that
could have saved Missouri from social war and utter anarchy."[107]

The removal of Curtis had an unfortunate repercussion. Lincoln's letter
of instruction to the new commander, though intended to be private, some-
how appeared in the St. Louis papers. Its general tone was derogatory to the
governor. Lincoln wrote that General Curtis was, "perhaps not from choice
. . . the head of one faction, and Gamble that of the other . . . . as I could not
remove Governor Gamble I had to remove General Curtis."[108] Surely, even if
Lincoln had no confidence in Gamble whatever, to voice it thus was a needless
discourtesy that abased him before his own people. The delight of the radical
faction was unbounded in seeing the governor thus publicly humiliated by the
president.

*Union General Samuel Curtis's
victory at the Battle of Pea Ridge was
a turning point of the war in Missouri.
Five months later he became
commander of the Department of the
Missouri.*

Gamble smarted under the injustice of the whole matter. He had known for some time that a whispering campaign was being carried on against him in Washington. In fact, Bates had spoken plainly and boldly to the president and the secretary of war and had charged them of listening to imputations against Gamble, holding him as a "suspected person," and making him powerless to aid the general government by degrading and belittling him before his own people.[109] It was a surprise to Gamble that the president should resent his having opposed Curtis, for he had done so on the grounds of the corruption and misconduct which had been alleged and proved against the general. For the president to imply that of the two he would prefer to keep Curtis in office was, as the governor said, a "most wanton and unmerited insult."[110] It was true that Gamble was the leader of the conservative element but equally untrue that, as the president implied, he had built up or purposely headed a faction. Certainly, a faction had grown up in opposition to him and his policies, but unless he were willing weakly to submit to and endorse all of their measures, there was no escape from being termed an opposition leader. Perhaps Schofield came nearest to a sane analysis of the situation when he commented that the nature of the quarrel was not fully understood in Washington. The president, he thought, labored under a misapprehension as to who his friends really were. "If the so-called 'claybank' faction are not altogether friendly to the president and the administration," he wrote, "I have not been able to discover it."[111]

One need only to examine Gamble's reaction to the Delaware resolutions to discover how unmerited Lincoln's suspicions and accusations really were. Those resolutions drawn up and adopted by the Delaware legislature condemned the emancipation proclamation and censured President Lincoln for arbitrary acts which violated the Bill of Rights. They contained the suggestion that the border states unite in calling a national convention to end the war. Gamble's answer was a stinging rebuke not only to the Delaware legislature but also to his Missouri critics. "It is cause of the deepest regret," he wrote, "in the present condition of our nation, when the government is struggling to maintain its own being, that the authorities of any state should add to its embarrassment by the adoption of resolutions which are calculated to withdraw the attention of the people from the present rebellion."[112] In regard to the protests against Lincoln's violation of individual rights, he insisted that the matter be viewed in its proper perspective. "The stupendous violation of the Constitution engrosses my attention," he declared. "If we prevent the success of that we can attend to other violations afterwards."[113] His answer demonstrates clearly how sincere he was in his support of the Union and the president. If he had favored slavery at heart, as was charged, he had an opportunity to agree with the border state legislature which disapproved of the efforts being made toward emancipation; if he had opposed the administration of Lincoln, as even the president himself seemed to believe, he had a splendid opportunity to voice that opposition by agreeing with the state of Delaware that the president's acts were unconstitutional. Actually, there were many unconstitutional usurpations of personal rights under Lincoln to which even men who lacked Gamble's training in constitutional law were not blind. The governor proved himself a diplomat in handling that point. He could not defend Lincoln's acts as constitutional, but he would not condemn him. Not one word did he utter in favor of the resolutions. When he might have given tacit approval, he chose to speak out. He wished his stand to be clear, and he sent to the legislature a vigorously denunciatory message. His course of action speaks for the sincerity of his purpose.

The vile and fierce condemnations of the radical press he had consistently ignored, but he felt the rebuff from the president was the last straw. In a letter as stinging as that of the president, but not as well known, since Gamble did not give it to the press, he stated: "Mr. President, I have disapproved of acts of your administration but I have carefully abstained from denouncing you or those concerned with you in conducting the government and this because there is nothing of a 'factional spirit' in me and because I thought I might damage the cause of my country by weakening public confidence in you."[114]

No explanation is needed of the fact that close upon the heels of this episode, Gamble handed his resignation to the Missouri state convention.[115] The leaders of the convention, however, convinced that there was no one in the state who could so capably fill the unenviable position of governor, persuaded him to withdraw his resignation. At the time he addressed the convention and announced that he would yield to their wishes and retain his office, he allowed himself to indulge in vindictiveness—the only time in his whole career when he did so, either in writing or in his public addresses. It was not his nature to stoop to such, but the recent humiliation had cut deep. He stated to the convention: "I . . . will again involve myself in the cares . . . of office; not to be, as the sagacious President of the United States regards me, the head of a faction, but . . . above all party influences, and careless of everything but the interests of the state."[116]

An interesting parallel may be drawn between the attitudes taken by Lincoln and Gamble on the slavery issue at the outbreak of the war. Lincoln declared in his inaugural: "I have no purpose, directly or indirectly, to interfere with the institution of slavery in the states where it exists." Gamble stated in his address to the people that as slavery was legal in the state, he would protect it and enforce the laws regarding it. Both men felt that such a provocative question should not be pushed to the front at a time when conditions were already chaotic; both agreed that Union slaveholders would be alienated needlessly by agitation of the slave issue; and both were convinced that the troublesome problem should and probably would be settled on a basis of compensated emancipation.

During the course of the war, Gamble's ideas on slavery changed considerably. Although not a slaveowner himself, he had no natural antipathy against it, and it might be said that he underestimated the moral aspect of the question. In 1861 he had declared that nothing would make him an antislavery man, and indeed nothing ever did.[117] However, that statement does not warrant the assumption that he was an anti-emancipationist. Even before the Civil War, he had contended that Missouri's interests would be promoted better under a system of free labor than under a slave system, and he had expected that slavery would in time die out in the state.[118] His opposition to emancipation in 1861 was based on his belief that the question could be settled more justly when people were calm and were thinking more rationally; his advocacy of emancipation in 1863 was based on his conviction that conditions were such that it was both expedient and necessary to settle the question at that time and to remove it from politics.

When the Missouri convention met in June 1862, the national government had declared in favor of gradual, compensated emancipation. However, nothing tangible had been done in the way of providing funds for the states proceeding in accordance with that principle.[119] The convention voted down [Samuel M.] Breckinridge's gradual emancipation proposal but, at Gamble's

Gamble came to favor gradual emancipation of Missouri's slaves.

suggestion, sent a favorable reply to the federal government commending the action Congress had taken. Gamble did not urge the convention to go into the emancipation problem, for a new state legislature was to be elected in November. Since the legislators would come with a fresh mandate from the people, and since the question more properly lay in the province of the legislature's power, it was his suggestion that that body was the proper one to deal with it.[120]

As has been stated, the 1862 election put the legislature into the hands of the emancipationists, and Missouri looked to see the immediate adoption of some scheme for liberating the slaves. The governor's message which dealt almost exclusively with that problem was forceful and clear. Since the Missouri Constitution provided that the legislature might free slaves only by consent of the owners or by giving full compensation, Gamble suggested that the New Jersey and Pennsylvania plans be studied. Both of those states had freed the children of slaves. Missouri, he thought, could do likewise and thus avoid a great outlay of money. In addition to the fact that such a plan of gradual emancipation would allow time for both Negro and white to make necessary adjustments, he pointed out other advantages:

> This plan, while it leaves the present generation of slaves with their condition unchanged, prevents any sudden diminution of labor, attracts emigration by the assurance it gives that slavery is to be extinguished, conforms to the examples of other states in which the same change has been successfully made, is in accordance with the views of those exercising the powers of the Federal Government, and thus secures the aid of that Government, satisfies the requirements of our own Constitution and does justice to the owners of this description of property, while it provides that those who are to enjoy freedom under it shall be prepared for that condition before they exercise its privileges. This plan I recommend to your consideration.[121]

The legislature ignored both the counsel of the governor and its own mandate from the people, neglected the emancipation issue, and spent the entire time in petty disagreement. It was a splendid opportunity for the legislature; it was a failure commensurate with that opportunity that attended its work. The people had clearly voiced a demand for emancipation. As the legislature had refused to provide for it, Gamble decided to call another session of the convention. Violent and prolonged was the storm of protest raised by the radicals. They declared that he was asking the convention to do what he had said earlier they ought not to do.[122] True, he had stated to the convention in 1862 that the legislature was the proper group to deal with the matter. It should be noted, however, that he did not deny that the convention possessed the legal power to act. Throughout his term in office, he held that a convention called by the people had all the power of the people themselves and that their actions had the force of law.[123] If the legislature would act, he favored letting them do so. In view of the legislature's refusal to take action, he believed the convention could and should dispose of the matter. Gamble delayed summoning it for a while in order to see what action would be taken by the federal government regarding compensation. Two Missourians, [John B.] Henderson and [John W.] Noell, were pushing bills to appropriate money to finance emancipation measures. Due largely to the shortsightedness of Missouri's own congressmen, however, the measures were not adopted.[124] Their defeat accounts for Gamble's action, for he knew that the legislature of Missouri would be faced with exactly the same dilemma at its next meeting; it had no power to free slaves without compensation, and the state was not financially able to free them with compensation. A new convention could not be called to deal with the matter, for the legislature had refused to authorize such a step. Therefore, if Missouri were to take any action on emancipation, it would have to be taken by the old convention. The radical press charged that, by placing the matter before that body, Gamble hoped to secure an emancipation measure which would be so weak that it would defeat the emancipation principle.[125] The charge was utterly unfounded, for in the convention he worked consistently for a more liberal plan than that which was finally adopted, and his support was more often given to [Charles D.] Drake, the radical, than to [James H.] Birch, the conservative. Equally untrue was the charge that he called the old convention into session to keep from calling a new convention. It was he, not a radical, who suggested that a new convention be called rather than that a technical six-part ordinance be submitted to a vote, an action which he knew was sure to defeat any emancipation plan regardless of its merits.[126]

It was indeed unfortunate that the vigorous leadership which Gamble displayed in the first session of the convention was lacking in the last one. He was a member of the committee on emancipation, but his attendance was irregular because of the press of official duties which kept him commuting between St. Louis and Jefferson City, his rapidly failing health, and his anxiety for his wife who was fast losing her eyesight. The report of the committee did not embody his ideas on the subject and, as he predicted, really suited no one.

His suggestions regarding emancipation were placed before the convention in the form of an amendment to the committee report. He proposed that slavery should cease in 1866 but that from that time until 1874, the slave should be under the care of his master whose duty it would be to see that he

Charles Daniel Drake, a St. Louis lawyer and bitter opponent of slavery, led the radicals in demanding immediate emancipation.

was prepared for his freedom. Those slaves who were over forty years of age were to be free but were to remain with their masters for the rest of their lives.[127] As he saw it, the master, after having enjoyed the benefits of their labor during their working years, should assume the responsibility of caring for them in their old age. He saw what many chose to ignore, that striking off the chains of servitude was very much like changing the label on a can—one did not thereby change its contents. No lawmaking body could by enactment remove the shackles of ignorance, superstition, or dependence bred by a life of servility. "We must have no such Utopian notion as that. Act upon the subject as you know it to be," he urged. It was no kindness to the Negro, he felt, to free him, to throw him suddenly upon his own resources, and make no attempt to help him adjust himself to new circumstances which at best he would find difficult. "Your own children are not treated so," said he, "and the Negro still more needs the advantage of direction and guidance."[128] His plan, he felt, would help Missouri to make the transition from one labor system to another as easily as possible.

Gamble took a decided and logical stand on the question of submitting the action of the convention to the people. "To submit the question, whether an ordinance of five or six sections shall become a Constitutional law of the state (I do not care how wise or politic its provisions may be) would be sure defeat."[129] It would be voted down, he contended, by people who opposed one part or another. He proposed that three schemes of emancipation be submitted, and that the people first vote "yes" or "no" on the question of freeing the slaves, and then on the three methods of emancipation, with the understanding that the method which received the largest vote should be enforced. Leaders representing every possible opinion should be invited to lay their views before the committee, and the three plans should be carefully drawn so as to embody those differences. In the light of subsequent emancipation history in Missouri, one can realize how wise his suggestions really were. What personal and party animosities Missouri could have been spared had they been adopted! Unfortunately, his official duties forced him to leave Drake and [L. C.] Marvin to sponsor his plans. Under his leadership, his plan could have been adopted, but under the leadership of Marvin and Drake, nothing was accomplished.

The emancipation plan finally adopted was a weak compromise measure which pleased no one. No slaves were to be freed until 1870. Those over forty years of age were to remain slaves for life, and those under twelve were not to be freed until they were twenty-three. In the meantime, slave trade was to be restricted in no way, and after 1870 it was still to be allowed between residents of the state.[130] The lack of compensation to the owners was the only feature of the ordinance which received Gamble's commendation.[131] His attitude toward the convention's work may best be summed up in his own words: "This ordinance . . . is not in all its different provisions such as I myself approved . . . . yet as the subject is one which has always produced a diversity of opinion in regard to details among those who are the most earnest friends of emancipation, the ordinance was accepted . . . as the best measure that could be agreed upon. It cannot be expected of me that I shall enter into a vindication of the ordinance in all its details as I voted against some of its provisions."[132]

In spite of its weakness, Gamble believed that the adoption of this measure would close the matter, for those interested in slave property would not seek to disturb it, and no one else would have any interest in doing so. He commented that further agitation of the question, "while it may promote the organization of political parties, and keep up a contest for office, will contribute neither to the peace or the prosperity of the state." That statement explained why he was willing to let the question rest and why the radicals were not.

Gamble ignored the wordy invective of the radical press, but he could not afford to ignore the course of action which the radical party tried to urge upon the state. In the hope of influencing the legislature to change the emancipation law, that party called a convention to meet at Jefferson City in September of 1863.[133] In carefully framed resolutions, the delegates demanded the resignation of Gamble, the replacement of Schofield by some "suitable man," such as General [Benjamin F.] Butler, and the establishment by the radicals of a committee of public safety. They proposed that the committee confer with Union men "to organize and arm them for the protection of their homes, and in event of no relief being obtained from our present trouble to call upon the people of this state to act in their sovereign capacity, and take such measures of redress as shall be found necessary for their welfare."[134] Gamble became genuinely alarmed at this thinly veiled threat of revolution. He was persuaded that the radicals, having failed in their efforts to control the provisional government, were determined to overthrow it.

The threat to replace the provisional government by force had been a persistent one. As early as 1861, there had been talk of placing Frémont in control, and in 1862 some radicals had openly advocated a plan to establish a military government.[135] When it became apparent in 1862 that the convention would deter the state election, the *St. Louis Anzeiger* openly proposed that if such a procedure were even suggested, the provost marshal or a military governor should put an end to the convention.[136] In August of that year, Charles Gibson wrote from St. Louis to warn the governor that serious efforts were being made to have the president replace him. The plan was that both Gamble and Schofield should be seized and imprisoned. Word of it came to Schofield through Blair, who, while refusing to reveal the names of the conspirators, did attest to the fact that there was such a plot.[137] Gamble had known for some time of the delegations sent to Washington for the purpose of undermining Lincoln's faith in the provisional governor. When young Hamilton Gamble visited Washington in March of 1863, he was alarmed to discover how widespread and serious such plots really were. He wrote to his father, "I had no idea of the number of persons who have been plotting against you till I came here. Your loyalty has not only been doubted but actually denied by committees and by petitions for your removal."[138]

In view of the action taken by the radicals in their convention, Gamble determined to meet threat with threat. In a letter to Lincoln, he suggested that a presidential order be sent to the general in charge of Missouri to uphold the provisional government.[139] Its publication would discourage revolutionary schemes by recognizing them as such.

After waiting twelve days without receiving a reply from the president, Gamble determined to accomplish what he could through a statement of his own. The proclamation which he issued was not a plea to the people to perpetuate the provisional government without demanding the necessary changes, but an earnest entreaty to them to discountenance all revolutionary means of effecting a change.[140] "It was a document," state [John] Nicolay and [John] Hay, "so clear in its statements and so quiet and firm in its tone as to appeal to the good sense and moderation of all except those intent upon mischief."[141]

A week after he had issued the proclamation, Gamble received what he considered an unsatisfactory reply from the president. "I have delayed so long to answer . . . because it did not appear to me that the domestic violence you apprehend was very imminent," Lincoln wrote.[142] Certainly, Gamble was no alarmist. Neither was Schofield, who had reinforced the governor's demands to the president and who had insisted that the matter actually was serious. Yet, in spite of the fact that both men were on the field and knew the actual conditions, the president ignored the significance of their reports. He questioned the governor's statement that the radicals were threatening an overthrow of the government. "Does the party so proclaim," he asked, "or is it only that some members of the party so proclaim?" Declaring, "No party can be held responsible for what individual members of it may do or say," the president dismissed the matter.[143] Gamble realized exactly the difference between threats made by a party and those made by individual members of a party. He had not run to the president with the persistent rumors of individuals who plotted against his government. It was not until the radical party in convention, speaking through its elected delegates, declared its intention to overthrow the provisional government that he asked for the protection of the federal government, protection which he had every right to expect but which he did not receive. He was left to take what comfort he could from Lincoln's order to Schofield to do his duty in regard to any "organized military force" which should appear in Missouri in opposition to the "General Government."[144] Lincoln's disposition to distrust Gamble, to give the benefit of the doubt to the men who opposed him, and to deny him the moral backing of the general government made the governor's position unnecessarily trying and unenviable.

In the face of such treatment, Gamble steadily refrained from criticizing the president; he did everything possible to uphold Lincoln and to reinforce and strengthen the Union. He reminded the president on one occasion that he had never denounced him or his administration because he felt it might damage the Union cause for him to do so. The president's rebuke cut deep, but it did not alter Gamble's course of action. He bore it in the same spirit as he did the insults hurled at him through the radical press. He said of them, "In patient silence I have borne the assaults in the past . . . and if it is my duty to the state to continue to expose myself to the detractions of bad men, I must encounter their attacks in the path duty points out. They shall never move me from that path."[145]

The strenuous months in office had left their mark on Gamble's health. He was never a man of vigorous constitution, and in his fifties he had resigned his position on the supreme court because of ill health. In his middle sixties,

President Abraham Lincoln tended to distrust Gamble even though he had always remained loyal to the Union and the president.

under the double strain of bitter personal abuse and oppressive official responsibilities, he failed rapidly. A fall on the icy steps of the executive mansion in December confined him to his bed, but even his own family did not realize until the very last that he was seriously ill. News of his death on January 31, 1864, came almost as a surprise to the state.[146] However, when his condition was realized at the last, word of his serious illness spread rapidly in the city of St. Louis, and crowds gathered and waited anxiously for news of his condition. A few hours before his death, he rallied slightly and recognized a friend, Carlos Greeley. After a few minutes, he said in his usual, slow, deliberate fashion, "I shall try to do what is right and proper to do, and shall prevent anything from being done which is wrong to do."[147] His last words reveal his high principles and justify all his actions.

From every side, tributes were given. In Washington, Edward Bates, aged and very much alone after the death of Missouri's other great conservative, in a vein of sadness recorded in his diary: "To me, this loss is a sore grievance—far greater than I had supposed—we had been friends forty years. . . . The services he had done the state, in patiently and successfully resisting the revolutionary violence of headlong Jacobins, are now seen and appreciated; and the purity of his personal character now shines all the brighter, because of the clouds of wicked calumny with which his and the state's enemies have so long labored to obscure him."[148] Even his most bitter foe, the *Daily Missouri Democrat*, reserving its vitrol for other and newer victims, declared, "His private character and personal reputation are unblemished."[149]

"A good man is dead."[150] With those words the *Missouri Republican* had announced to Missourians the death of their governor. But more than a good man had died. Unseen, unrecognized even by the most thoughtful, an era had passed too; for when Hamilton Gamble went to his grave, the conservative cause went with him. To the casual onlooker, conservatism still existed, but like a stone wall from which unseen the mortar has crumbled away, it was strong in appearance only. There was no one to take his place. It is futile to conjecture what would have happened had he lived, had he rallied the conservatives fresh from the advantages they had just gained in electing their candidates to the supreme court. The fact remains that upon his death the radicals swept into power. Could he have saved Missouri from the needless reconstruction at their hands? Could he have led the state to support the archly conservative emancipation plan? If not, could he have secured the passage and support of a plan of his own, one which was more nearly in accord with his own thinking and which might have prevented the emergence of strong race hatreds? It is impossible to say. In three years, Gamble had swung Missouri away from its natural inclination to stand with the other slave states; in six years, the radicals swung it back and made it in peace what it had not been in war, an integral part of the "solid south."

Gamble had returned to Missouri at a time when the Union cause needed him. He was an advocate of peace when hotheads cried for war, of reason when the unthinking were swayed by emotion, of sanity when zealots followed the mob mind, of justice when the intolerant favored persecution, of restraint when the rebellious chose excess, and of enduring principles when the opportunist advocated violence. He worked tirelessly to get Missouri in the Union, and when she was definitely in it, he insisted that she be treated on a par with the other states, not as a conquered province. Misunderstood, abused, slandered in his own day, he let the rectitude of his conduct counteract any injustice done to him, confident that the dispassionate judgment of time would bring him what measure of acclaim he deserved. Missourians, who have kept alive the memory of [Nathaniel] Lyon or of [Joseph] Porter, have not measured justly how far the quiet constructive work of this statesman transcends the colorful yet destructive work of those generals. To keep Missouri loyal, prevent anarchy, rebuild the civil government, ward off military control, repel invasion, reconstruct state finances, and pacify the people were only a few of the herculean tasks to which Gamble set his hand. In no one did he fail entirely.

NOTES

1. *St. Louis Missouri Republican*, 15 January 1861.

2. Ibid.

3. He was born in Winchester, Virginia, on November 29, 1798.

4. Commission signed by Governor Frederick Bates, 19 November 1824, Hamilton Rowan Gamble Papers, Missouri Historical Society, St. Louis.

5. *St. Louis Missouri Republican*, 4 February 1864.

6. Eugene M. Violette, *A History of Missouri* (Boston: D. C. Heath, 1918), 328.

7. *St. Louis Missouri Republican*, 15 January, 11 February 1861.

8. Ibid., 11 February 1861.

9. *In Memoriam: Hamilton Rowan Gamble, Governor of Missouri* (St. Louis: George Knapp, 1864), 75.

10. Violette, *History of Missouri*, 329.

11. James Peckham, *Gen. Nathaniel Lyon, and Missouri in 1861* (New York: American News Co., 1866), 29.

12. Robert J. Rombauer, *The Union Cause in St. Louis in 1861* (St. Louis: Nixon-Jones, 1909), 169.

13. *Proceedings of the Missouri State Convention, . . . March, 1861* (St. Louis: George Knapp, 1861), 178.

14. Ibid., 107-108.

15. *In Memoriam*, 6.

16. *Proceedings of the Missouri State Convention, . . . March, 1861*, 47.

17. Ibid., 258.

18. *St. Louis Missouri Republican*, 30 May 1861.

19. *Proceedings of the Missouri State Convention, . . . July, 1861* (St. Louis: George Knapp, 1861), 28.

20. *Proceedings of the Missouri State Convention, . . . March, 1861*, 68.

21. Peckham, *Gen. Nathaniel Lyon*, 191-193; Yeatman to Gamble, telegram, 23 June 1861, Gamble Papers.

22. Yeatman to Gamble.

23. Edward Bates to Gamble, 16 July 1861, Gamble Papers.

24. Samuel T. Glover to James O. Broadhead, 26 July 1861, James Overton Broadhead Papers, Missouri Historical Society.

25. *Proceedings of the Missouri State Convention, . . . July, 1861*, 131.

26. *St. Louis Missouri Republican*, 1 August 1861.

27. *New York Times*, 7 August 1861.

28. *St. Louis Missouri Republican*, 4 February 1864.

29. Ibid., 5 August 1861.

30. *Proceedings of the Missouri State Convention, . . . June, 1863* (St. Louis: George Knapp, 1863), 281.

31. *St. Louis Missouri Republican*, 5 August 1861.

32. Simon Cameron to Gamble, telegram, 3 August 1861, Gamble Papers.

33. Gamble to Major Henry Turner, 27 August 1861, ibid.

34. *St. Louis Missouri Republican*, 5 August 1861.

35. Ibid., 1 August 1861.

36. Ibid., 29 August 1861. See also James G. Randall, *The Civil War and Reconstruction* (Boston: D. C. Heath, 1937), 329.

37. *Proceedings of the Missouri State Convention, . . . June, 1862* (St. Louis: G. Knapp, 1862), 4-5.

38. Ibid.

39. Copy of General Orders, No. 1, Gamble Papers.

40. *St. Louis Missouri Republican*, 26 August 1861.

41. Gamble to Curtis, 17 October 1861, Gamble Papers. The original of the letter from Gamble to Curtis on October 5, 1861, is not in the collection, but the reply of Curtis is included.

42. *Proceedings of the Missouri State Convention, . . . June, 1863*, 10.

43. Gamble to Lincoln, 26 August 1861, Gamble Papers.

44. *St. Louis Missouri Republican*, 11, 30 September 1861.

45. Edward Bates to Gamble, 3 October 1861, Gamble Papers.

46. McPherson to Gamble, 3 October 1861, ibid.

47. Bates to Gamble, 27 September 1861, ibid.

48. Kelton to Gamble, wire, 2 August 1861, ibid.

49. Gamble to Frémont, 6 August 1861, ibid.

50. Frémont to Gamble, 18 August 1861, ibid.

51. Ibid.

52. Gamble to Charles Gibson, 20 September 1861, ibid.

53. *Journal of the Missouri State Convention, . . . June, 1863*, 10.

54. Richardson to Gamble, 10 August 1861, Gamble Papers.

55. Gamble to Gibson, 20 September 1861, ibid.

56. Ibid., giving a very complete account of the interview.

57. Gamble to Gibson, telegram, 14 September 1861, ibid.

58. Corwin[e] to Gamble, 12 September 1861, ibid.

59. Gamble to Gibson, 20 September 1861, ibid.

60. Corwin[e] to Gamble, 13 September 1861, ibid.

61. Gamble to Gibson, 20 September 1861, ibid.

62. Gibson to Gamble, 27 September 1861, ibid.

63. Galusha Anderson, *The Story of a Border City During the Civil War* (Boston: Little, Brown, 1908), 218-219.

64. *St. Louis Missouri Republican*, 23 September 1861.

65. Ibid., 11 October 1861.

66. Ibid., 9 October 1861.

67. *Journal of the Missouri State Convention, . . . October, 1861*, 5.

68. *St. Louis Missouri Republican*, 23 September 1861.

69. *Journal of the Missouri State Convention, . . . October, 1861*, 5.

70. Ibid., 10.

71. Ibid., 24-25.

72. Ibid., 26.

73. Lincoln to Gamble, 4 November 1861, Gamble Papers.

74. Gamble to Halleck, 10 October 1862, ibid.

75. Draft of the agreement between Lincoln and Gamble, ibid.

76. The canceled checks are among Governor Gamble's papers, ibid.

77. *Proceedings of the Missouri State Convention, . . . June, 1862*, 5.

78. John M. Schofield, *Forty-Six Years in the Army* (New York: Century, 1897), 55.

79. *St. Louis Missouri Republican*, 26 January, 15 March 1862.

80. Ibid., 16 May 1862.

81. Ibid., 29 March 1862.

82. Ibid., 21 May 1862.

83. McClurg to Gamble and Willard P. Hall, 12 June 1862, Gamble Papers.

84. *St. Louis Missouri Republican*, 10 June 1862.

85. John G. Nicolay and John Hay, *Abraham Lincoln: A History*, 6: 894.

86. *Journal of the Missouri State Convention, . . . June, 1862*, app., 13.

87. Ibid., app., 12.

88. *Senate Journal*, 22nd General Assembly, 1st sess., 30 December 1862, 15-17.

89. *St. Louis Missouri Republican*, 23 July 1862.

90. *Senate Journal*, 22nd General Assembly, Adjourned sess., 11 November 1863, 6-8.

91. *Journal of the Missouri State Convention, . . . June, 1863*, 7.

92. Ibid.; *St. Louis Missouri Republican*, 17 August 1862.

93. Lincoln to Gamble, telegram, 18, 27 December 1861, Gamble Papers.

94. Gamble to Halleck, 10 October 1861, ibid.

95. Halleck to Gamble, 27 September 1862, ibid.

96. Gibson to Gamble, 30 September 1861, ibid.

97. Gamble to Halleck, 10 October 1862, ibid.

98. Nicolay and Hay, *Abraham Lincoln*, 6: 385-386.

99. Anderson, *Border City*, 280.

100. Nicolay and Hay, *Abraham Lincoln*, 6: 388.

101. *Senate Journal*, 22nd General Assembly, 1st sess., 30 December 1862, 15.

102. Nicolay and Hay, *Abraham Lincoln*, 6: 390.

103. *St. Louis Missouri Republican*, 27 November 1862.

104. *Proceedings of the Missouri State Convention, . . . June, 1863*, 231; Howard K. Beale, ed., "The Diary of Edward Bates, 1859-1866," in *Annual Report of the American Historical Association, 1930*, 4: 292.

105. Schofield to Gamble, 2 February 1863; Gamble to Lincoln, 2 May 1863, both in Gamble Papers; Beale, "Diary of Edward Bates," 4: 292.

106. Henderson to Gamble, 30 March 1863, Gamble Papers.

107. Beale, "Diary of Edward Bates," 4: 294.

108. Schofield, *Forty-Six Years*, 68-69, quoting the letter from Lincoln of May 27, 1863.

109. Barton Bates to Gamble, 21 January 1863, Gamble Papers.

110. Gamble to Lincoln, 13 July 1863, ibid.

111. Schofield, *Forty-Six Years*, 87.

112. *Senate Journal*, 22nd General Assembly, 1st sess., app., 250.

113. Ibid., 253.

114. Gamble to Lincoln, 13 July 1863, Gamble Papers.

115. *Journal of the Missouri State Convention, . . . June, 1863*, 11.

116. *Proceedings of the Missouri State Convention, . . . June, 1863*, 368.

117. *Proceedings of the Missouri State Convention, . . . March, 1861*, 242.

118. *Senate Journal*, 22nd General Assembly, 1st sess., 30 December 1862, 21-22.

119. Randall, *Civil War and Reconstruction*, 484.

120. *Journal of the Missouri State Convention, . . . June, 1862*, 37.

121. *Senate Journal*, 22nd General Assembly, 1st sess., 30 December 1862, 24.

122. *Proceedings of the Missouri State Convention, . . . June, 1863*, 34.

123. *Proceedings of the Missouri State Convention, . . . July, 1861*, 75.

124. Nicolay and Hay, *Abraham Lincoln*, 6: 393.

125. *Proceedings of the Missouri State Convention, . . . June, 1863*, 35.

126. Ibid., 344.

127. Ibid., 283.

128. Ibid.

129. Ibid., 331.

130. Ibid., 367.

131. Ibid., 368.

132. *Senate Journal*, 22nd General Assembly, Adjourned sess., 11 November 1863, 10.

133. *St. Louis Missouri Republican*, 17 August 1863.

134. Nicolay and Hay, *Abraham Lincoln*, 8: 213.

135. Schofield, *Forty-Six Years*, 86.

136. *St. Louis Missouri Republican*, 9 June 1862.

137. Schofield, *Forty-Six Years*, 86; Gibson to Gamble, 14 August 1862, Gamble Papers.

138. Hamilton Gamble to his father, 6 March 1863, ibid.

139. Gamble to Lincoln, 1 October 1863, ibid.

140. *St. Louis Missouri Republican*, 13 October 1863.

141. Nicolay and Hay, *Abraham Lincoln*, 8: 227.

142. Lincoln to Gamble, 19 October 1863, Gamble Papers.

143. Ibid.

144. Nicolay and Hay, *Abraham Lincoln*, 8: 225.

145. *Proceedings of the Missouri State Convention, . . . June, 1863*, 368.

146. *St. Louis Missouri Republican*, 31 January 1864.

147. Ibid., 4 February 1864.

148. Beale, "Diary of Edward Bates," 4: 328-329.

149. *St. Louis Daily Missouri Democrat*, 1 February 1864.

150. *St. Louis Missouri Republican*, 31 January 1864.

Missouri's Secessionist Government, 1861-1865

ARTHUR ROY KIRKPATRICK

One of the least known, yet most interesting, chapters in the history of Missouri is the story of the state government which was elected in August 1860. It became a fugitive government-in-exile following the Battle of Boonville and was outlawed by the State Convention in July 1861. A number of accounts have been written of its peregrinations, but these have varied greatly in many details, even as to the most basic facts.

Following the Battle of Boonville on June 17, 1861, Governor Claiborne F. Jackson and his troops of the State Guard began a retreat to southwest Missouri where they hoped to make contact with Confederate forces under General Ben McCulloch. General Sterling Price left Lexington for McCulloch's camp about the same time.

On July 5, Jackson defeated a Federal force under Colonel Franz Sigel near Carthage and the following day made contact with Price and McCulloch. The state forces went into camp at Cowskin Prairie in McDonald County, where General Price spent the next six weeks reorganizing and equipping his troops to take the field against General Nathaniel Lyon.[1]

Meanwhile, on July 12, Governor Jackson left Cowskin Prairie for Richmond, Virginia, where he hoped to secure financial and military aid from the Confederate government. He was accompanied by former United States Senator David R. Atchison, his aide. On the 19th he was in Little Rock, Arkansas, where he was given an official welcome by Governor Henry Rector, and on the 22nd he reached Memphis, Tennessee.[2] There he consulted with Confederate General Leonidas Polk. General Polk agreed to send General Gideon Pillow into Missouri by way of New Madrid if the governor would

108

Governor Claiborne Jackson was loyal to the Southern cause and declared Missouri to be an independent state.

accompany his forces. General Pillow's "Army of Liberation" occupied New Madrid on July 28, but by then Governor Jackson was in Richmond, having decided that his presence there was essential to Missouri's future welfare and position in the Confederacy.[3]

While in Richmond, the governor became personally acquainted with President Jefferson Davis and received assurances of continued military aid. He was also promised substantial financial support as soon as money for the purpose was made available by the Confederate Congress. The president had conceived a dislike and distrust for Jackson following the agreement between General Price and General William S. Harney on May 14, 1861,[4] but the governor now managed to convince Davis of his honesty and loyalty to the Southern cause.[5]

In the meantime, other Confederate state officials in Missouri were having troubles. The whereabouts of Secretary of State B. F. Massey at this time are unknown, but State Treasurer Alfred W. Morrison had been captured at Hermann on June 18 and returned to Jefferson City as a prisoner. Since no money was found in his possession, he was released after turning his books and papers over to Colonel Henry Boernstein, the Federal commander there.[6] Although Attorney General J. Proctor Knott remained in Jefferson City, he refused to take the oath of allegiance to the United States and was held a prisoner.[7] Lieutenant Governor Thomas C. Reynolds had been in Richmond since about the middle of June but was back in Nashville, Tennessee, by July 8.[8]

On August 5, Governor Jackson was back on Missouri soil after a trip by rail from Richmond to Memphis. That day he issued from New Madrid a proclamation declaring Missouri an independent and sovereign state by virtue of the sweeping powers granted him by the General Assembly in the "Rebellion Act" of May 10, 1861. This declaration was of doubtful validity, and the Confederate government recognized the independence of the state only after the passage of an ordinance of secession by the General Assembly at Neosho in October. Lieutenant Governor Reynolds had already issued a similar provisional declaration of independence from General Pillow's camp on July 31.[9]

Jackson and Reynolds were both in southeast Missouri at this time, but apparently they never met. They either failed to learn of each other's presence, or else Reynolds deliberately avoided the governor, for he gave General M. Jeff Thompson orders directly contrary to those already issued by Jackson and signed himself "Acting Governor of Missouri."[10]

Early in August the Confederate Congress appropriated one million dollars for the use of Missouri troops cooperating with those of the Confederacy.[11] The governor learned of this on August 8,[12] and after making arrangements with General Polk in Memphis for requisitioning supplies for the Missouri State Guard under the terms of the appropriation, he left for General Price's camp at Springfield on the 13th.[13]

General Price, with the help of McCulloch, had defeated Lyon at Oak Hill (Wilson's Creek) on August 10 and five days later marched north toward the Missouri River. The governor caught up with him on the line of march, and they arrived at Lexington on September 12.

Following victory in the Battle of Lexington on September 18-20, Jackson issued a proclamation calling the General Assembly to meet in special session at Neosho on October 21. He also commissioned E. Carrington Cabell and Thomas L. Snead to negotiate an offensive-defensive treaty of alliance with the Confederacy and sent them to Richmond.[14]

On August 20 the Confederate Congress had authorized the negotiation of a treaty with Missouri. It had also provided for the admission of Missouri as a Confederate state as soon as the provisional constitution was ratified by the "legally constituted authorities of said state." Jackson's government was specifically recognized as the "legally elected and regularly constituted government of the people and State of Missouri."[15]

The special session of the General Assembly convened on Monday, October 21, at Neosho. One week later it passed an ordinance of secession

Missouri's First "Confederate Capitol," Masonic Hall, Neosho, Missouri. The "Confederate" legislature of Missouri met here, October 21-29, 1861, to pass an act of secession from the Union, pursuant to Governor Jackson's proclamation.

with but one dissenting vote and an act ratifying the provisional Confederate constitution. On the 29th the members adjourned to meet on October 31 at the courthouse in Cassville, Missouri. At this latter place a large number of bills were adopted, including one appropriating ten million dollars "now in the treasury or which may hereafter be paid into the treasury" to repel invasion and to maintain the sovereignty of the state. Authorization was made for issuing ten million dollars in state defense bonds, and delegates to the Confederate Congress were chosen.[16] The assembly adjourned on November 7 after adopting a resolution to meet again at New Madrid on the first Monday in March 1862.

Whether the Neosho-Cassville session of the legislature had a quorum present and was therefore legally able to act for the state has long been a matter of controversy, with the weight of opinion resting with the negative. Contemporary reports differ on the matter, and the truth, perhaps, will never be known unless some other source of information comes to light. The important fact is that the session and its acts were considered legal by the Confederate government and that Missouri was admitted to the Confederacy on the strength of its legality on November 28, 1861.[17]

Missouri's Second "Confederate Capitol," Barry County Courthouse, Cassville, Missouri. The "Confederate" legislature of Missouri also met here, October 31-November 7, 1861, to enact further legislation. In this building Governor Jackson is said to have signed the act of secession.

Governor Jackson returned to New Madrid shortly after the adjournment of the legislature, where he remained with General Thompson's troops until about the middle of December, helping to recruit and organize additional companies of the State Guard.

With things in southeast Missouri pretty well to his satisfaction, he left for Memphis on December 13, and after a conference with General Albert S. Johnston, he made a pleasant but uneventful trip by steamer to New Orleans. There he arranged for printing the bonds authorized by the legislature at Cassville.[18] At the same time he secured a large number of old guns, rifles and muskets, which he had retooled for use by troops. He even reported that six young ladies of the city were raising money to send a sword to General Price.[19]

General Thompson went to New Orleans to meet the governor. After a short period of conferences and sightseeing, they left for Missouri on January 11 with the supplies, the guns, the ten million dollars in bonds, and, it is presumed, General Price's sword. Upon his return, General Thompson used some of the bonds to pay his troops for the first time in several months.[20]

In order that more funds might be available for use by the Missouri government, the Confederate Congress on January 27, 1862, directed the secretary of the treasury to advance to the state the sum of one million dollars to be used in paying its troops and purchasing necessary supplies. Missouri was to deposit an equal amount in state bonds with the Confederate treasury until a final settlement was made between the two governments.[21] Another million dollars was made available on similar terms on February 15.[22]

Just before Christmas 1861, President Davis sent word to the governor of his anxiety to have the Missouri troops quickly reorganized and tendered to the Confederacy so that general officers could be appointed for them. By this means, he said, their efficiency would be increased, and "they will be relieved from the anomalous position they now occupy as militia of the Confederate States without being a part of their organized Army."[23]

Governor Jackson and General Price applied themselves to this problem, and by January 17, 1862, the latter was able to report to the secretary of war, Judah P. Benjamin, that he had already procured two regiments of infantry, one of cavalry, and two light batteries of artillery for regular Confederate service. This work continued until the defeat at Pea Ridge, Arkansas, on March 7, 1862, after which General Price and his Missouri division in the Confederate army were sent east of the Mississippi, and the governor remained with the remnants of the State Guard, now under the command of General M. M. Parsons. They also fought in the Battle of Corinth, but returned to Arkansas in July.

The one notable event during the period preceding the Battle of Pea Ridge was the meeting of the General Assembly at New Madrid on Monday, March 3, 1862, pursuant to the resolution adopted at Cassville. On that day a few of the legislators appeared, but Governor Jackson and others who were scheduled to come by steamer from Memphis did not show up. General Thompson had those present formally convene, and then he adjourned the session to meet at Caruthersville on March 6. The general wrote Governor Jackson that Federal troops were close enough to New Madrid to make the scheduled meeting hazardous and told him of the proposed session at Caruthersville.[24]

This letter was sent down the river by a committee of legislators who were to stop the governor and his party from coming on to New Madrid. Governor Jackson, however, was with Price at Pea Ridge, and no further session of the 21st General Assembly was ever held.

The movements of Governor Jackson following the Battle of Corinth until shortly before his death are more difficult to trace than the story up to this point. Some time during 1862 he purchased a home in Texas and moved his family there, perhaps in Red River County where his wife died on July 5, 1864.[25]

It has commonly been assumed that Governor Jackson himself set up a temporary state capital at Marshall, Texas, but the evidence is against this belief. When Thomas C. Reynolds became governor upon the death of Jackson, he reported that the records and officers of the state government were scattered throughout Texas and Arkansas. He found the largest share of the records at Camden, Arkansas, which suggests that such capital as Jackson had maintained must have been there, or nearby at Little Rock, where he is known to have spent his last days.[26]

Jackson is known to have been in Marshall in July 1862 when he met in conference with the governors of Arkansas, Louisiana, and Texas to consider uniting the resources and energies of their respective states.[27] However, no mention of any other visit to Marshall by either Jackson or Reynolds prior to the summer of 1863 is made in any issue of the Marshall papers now known to be in existence, nor in any other contemporary source which has been examined.

Governor Jackson apparently spent the next six weeks with his family, but early in September, he left for Little Rock to help draw up plans for a campaign into Missouri to be launched in the fall or winter.

The governor was reported to have suffered from cancer for a number of years, and about November 1 his condition became worse. He lived long enough to make his will and to see his family who were summoned from Texas, but died on the evening of December 7, 1862, in a boardinghouse just

Lieutenant Governor Thomas C. Reynolds led Missouri's refugee government after Jackson died. [Walker-Missouri Resources Division, SHSMO 018929]

north of the Arkansas River across from the capital city. He was buried in Mount Holly Cemetery in Little Rock and after the war was reinterred in the Sappington family cemetery near Arrow Rock.[28]

Upon the death of Governor Jackson, Thomas C. Reynolds, who had been in Columbia, South Carolina, since December 1861, became the head of Missouri's refugee government. He hurried to Richmond early in January 1863, where he conferred with President Davis and other Confederate leaders.

In March the new governor left for the West. He stopped off in Mississippi to interview the Missouri troops and then went to Shreveport to confer with General E. Kirby Smith, commanding general of the Trans-Mississippi Department. After spending a few days with General Smith, he started for Little Rock where he planned to reestablish the state government. At Camden, Arkansas, however, he found most of the state papers and records. He decided to establish his capital there, temporarily at least, away from the social life and confusion of Little Rock. He summoned the state officials who were scattered in Arkansas and Texas and began the long arduous task of sorting and systematizing official records as a prelude to determining future policies.

One of his most pressing problems involved finances. Legality of claims against the state, the order in which they should be paid, and possible sources of revenue all demanded attention. Creditors were clamoring for payment and seemed to expect the miracle of immediate satisfaction. Legal claims amounting to some two million dollars were finally recognized, with only a small portion of this sum covered by Confederate notes in the treasury. A system of priorities was set up, with first payment going to private soldiers in the army. Much of the money was expected to come from the Confederate government, which was officially liable for the actual military expenses.[29]

By June, Reynolds felt that affairs of state were well enough in hand for him to visit General Price in Little Rock, and by the 27th of the month, he had moved his capital to that city and was issuing official executive orders from there.[30]

The fall of Vicksburg and Port Hudson in July 1863 placed the entire Mississippi River under Federal control and cut the Confederacy in two, leaving the states of Texas, Arkansas, and Missouri, most of Louisiana, and the Indian Territory in virtual isolation from the government and armies east of the river. Recognizing that political as well as military power would have to be exercised locally in the Trans-Mississippi Department, President Davis suggested that General Smith take the western governors completely into his confidence, and together they might make the West self-sufficient, prevent the secession of the western states from the Confederacy, and successfully carry on the war until such time as the Mississippi could be retaken.[31] The general called a conference of the governors of the four western states, which met at Marshall, Texas, August 15-18, 1863.

They recommended that General Smith exercise executive powers in the department, with safeguards against interference with the states, and established a Committee of Public Safety with Governor Reynolds as chairman. It was to organize committees of correspondence in each county and parish to cooperate with itself and the departmental commander in the war effort.[32] Governor Reynolds played a leading part in the deliberations of the conference. It was an indication of his standing with his colleagues that he was chosen chairman of the Committee of Public Safety, which made him, next to General Smith, the most important official in the Trans-Mississippi Department.

After spending a few days in Shreveport with General Smith, the governor left for Little Rock, but had only reached Arkadelphia, Arkansas, when he received word of the surrender of the Arkansas capital on September 10 by General Price. This was a blow to Reynolds who had so recently brought order out of the chaos of his state government and its records, but he set up a temporary camp at Arkadelphia until he could locate a new site to establish his executive offices. He made a temporary transfer to Washington, Arkansas, where the Little Rock government had been moved.[33]

The Missouri Confederate Capitol in Marshall, Texas

Late in October he returned to Shreveport, planning to establish himself near the headquarters of the Trans-Mississippi Department. After considerable effort, he found it impossible to obtain suitable quarters because of the extent of General Smith's needs and the lack of healthful locations in the area.[34]

On November 5, 1863, he sent his officers and such records as he now possessed forty miles westward to Marshall, Texas, and followed them himself a few days later.[35] He had been favorably impressed by the little city during his visit in August and was now determined that it should be the state capital until he could return in triumph to Jefferson City.

Marshall was then a town of about two thousand inhabitants, located near the head of navigation of the Red River and Caddo Lake. It was already the headquarters for several bureaus of General Smith's command, but the governor was able to find accommodations among its friendly and hospitable people.

At the corner of South Bolivar and Crockett streets, he leased the home of Judge Asa Willie as a capitol building. Willie was then in Austin as a member of the Texas Supreme Court. A short time later, Reynolds rented the spacious home of Mrs. Mary Key for $225 in Confederate notes.[36] This home became the governor's residence and the focal point for all Missouri Confederates.

Once settled in Marshall, the governor found many problems to engage his attention. As chairman of the Committee of Public Safety, he was in

The Missouri Confederate Governor's Mansion in Marshall, Texas
[The Dallas Morning News]

frequent communication with General Smith and President Davis on questions of civil government. He suggested that a branch of the treasury department be established in the West, but Davis turned down the suggestion because of a shortage of trained treasury personnel in Richmond.[37] He concerned himself with financial problems on both state and national levels and asked General Smith to join him in requesting that the Confederate Congress provide for a war department with full powers to act in the trans-Mississippi states. Smith agreed to this in theory but suggested that the governor himself was the only man to whom Davis would be willing to delegate the great powers to be exercised by the head of such a department. Reynolds then dropped the idea, for, as he told Smith, he was much too busy as governor, and he believed himself constitutionally incapable of holding a Confederate government position while serving as governor of a state.

Reynolds did accompany General Sterling Price on his ill-fated Missouri campaign in the autumn of 1864, hoping to be inaugurated in Jefferson City. The large local Federal garrison made this impossible, however, and after the Battle of Westport on October 23, Reynolds returned to Marshall.

Marshall remained the seat of the fugitive government until May 1865, when, after a third governors' conference called by General Smith to consider the question of continued resistance, the general surrendered his command, the last organized Confederate troops to lay down their arms.

After the surrender, Reynolds, with a number of other Missourians, crossed the border into Mexico, determined then to live his life in exile.

In the spring of 1868, however, he returned to St. Louis and resumed the practice of law. On May 26, 1869, the story was completed when he returned to Governor [Joseph W.] McClurg the Great Seal of the state, taken from Jefferson City in 1861 and in his possession since 1863. He expressed a hope that it would be an "augury of the speedy oblivion of past strife, and of the complete restoration of fraternal feeling" in the state.[38]

NOTES

1. Thomas L. Snead, *The Fight for Missouri from the Election of Lincoln to the Death of Lyon* (New York: Scribner's Sons, 1888), 239-243.

2. *Little Rock Arkansas True Democrat*, 25 July 1861.

3. *Marshall Texas Republican*, 10 August 1861.

4. On May 14, 1861, General Sterling Price and General William S. Harney,

commanding U.S. troops in St. Louis, signed an agreement that no more U.S. troops would enter the state and that the Missouri State Guard under Price would maintain peace in the state, protect property of Unionists, and resist any Confederate move into the state. Governor Jackson had conceived this as necessary strategy to gain time for arming the state, but [Jefferson] Davis, whom Jackson had already asked for Confederate troops, considered it a complete breach of faith with himself.

5. Thomas C. Reynolds, "General Price and the Confederacy," 47, Thomas C. Reynolds Papers, Missouri Historical Society, St. Louis.

6. *Columbia Missouri Statesman*, 28 June 1861.

7. *Little Rock Arkansas State Gazette*, 6 July 1861.

8. Ibid., 20 July 1861.

9. U.S. Record and Pension Office, *Organization and Status of Missouri Troops (Union and Confederate) in Service During the Civil War* (Washington, DC: Government Printing Office, 1902), 242.

10. Reynolds to Thompson, 10 August 1861, quoted in Thompson to G. Pillow, 11 August 1861, U.S. War Department, *The War of the Rebellion: A Compilation of the Official Records of the Union and Confederate Armies* (Washington, DC: Government Printing Office, 1880-1902), ser. 1, vol. 3: 643 (hereinafter cited as *OR*); Reynolds to J. C. Frémont, 15 August 1861, ibid., ser. 1, vol. 3: 449-450.

11. Act of August 6, 1861, ibid., ser. 1, vol. 53: 721.

12. Jackson to E. C. Cabell, 8 August 1861, ibid., ser. 1, vol. 3: 639.

13. Jackson to J. Davis, 18 August 1861, ibid., ser. 1, vol. 3: 646.

14. C. F. Jackson, 26 September 1861, ibid., ser. 1, vol. 53: 751.

15. Act of August 20, 1861, ibid., ser. 4, vol. 1: 576-577.

16. *Journal of the Senate, Extra Session of the Rebel Legislature . . . Town of Neosho, Newton County, Missouri, on the Twenty-First Day of October, Eighteen Hundred and Sixty-One* (Jefferson City, 1865), 8, 10; Jackson to J. Davis, 5 November 1861, *OR*, ser. 1, vol. 53: 754-755.

17. Act of November 28, 1861, *OR*, ser. 1, vol. 53: 758.

18. Thompson to Price, 1 January 1862, ibid., ser. 1, vol. 8: 727. These bonds are still turning up, and there have been recent attempts to have some of them redeemed by the state treasurer. [Ed. Note: Written in 1950]

19. Jackson to Price, 30 December 1881, ibid., ser. 1, vol. 8: 725-726.

20. M. Jeff Thompson, diary, Meriwether Jeff Thompson Papers, Western Historical Manuscript Collection, University of Missouri–Columbia.

21. Act of January 27, 1862, *OR*, ser. 4, vol. 1: 882.

22. Act of February 15, 1862, ibid., ser. 4, vol. 1: 939.

23. Davis to Jackson, 21 December 1861, ibid., ser. 1, vol. 8: 717.

24. Thompson, diary, 62-65; Thompson to Jackson, 3 March 1862, *OR*, ser. 1, vol. 8: 765.

25. *Little Rock Arkansas Patriot*, 11 December 1862.

26. Reynolds to Price, 25 May 1863, *OR*, ser. 1, vol. 53: 871-872; statement of Reynolds, unidentified clipping, 27 May 1863, Reynolds Papers.

27. *Marshall Texas Republican*, supplement, ca. 6-13 September 1862.

28. *Little Rock Arkansas Patriot*, 11 December 1862.

29. Clipping, 27 May 1863; Reynolds to Price, 25 May 1863, *OR*, ser. 1, vol. 53: 871-872.

30. Thomas C. Reynolds, Military Special Orders No. 12, 27 June 1863, *OR*, ser. 1, vol. 22, pt. 2: 889-890.

31. Davis to Smith, 14 July 1863, ibid., ser. 1, vol. 22, pt. 2: 925-927.

32. Proceedings of Governors' Conference, 15-18 August 1863, ibid., ser. 1, vol. 22, pt. 2: 1005.

33. Reynolds, "General Price and the Confederacy," 132.

34. Reynolds to Price, 4 December 1863, *OR*, ser. 1, vol. 53: 918.

35. Ibid.

36. A photostat of this lease is in the possession of Mrs. J. F. Lentz, Marshall, Texas. The "Capitol" is still standing, but the "Governor's Mansion" was wrecked early this year [ca. 1950] to make way for a lumberyard.

37. Davis to Reynolds, 10 December 1863, in *Jefferson Davis, Constitutionalist: His Letters, Papers, and Speeches*, ed. Dunbar Rowland (n.p.: J. J. Little and Ives, 1923), 6: 130.

38. Reynolds to McClurg, 26 May 1869, Reynolds Papers.

Military Prisons of St. Louis, 1861-1865

W. B. HESSELTINE

During the Civil War in the United States and for many years after its close, the people of the country were interested in the stories which the veterans of that gigantic conflict had to relate. Stories of "How I Lost My Leg," "How We Fooled the Yanks," and "The Capture of a Johnny General" were listened to with eagerness by the stay-at-homes and by those whose valor or imagination was so defective that they had no scars to show and no breathtaking experiences to relive. But among the storytellers which the conflict brought forth as a sort of accidental by-product, the one who was always sure of a sympathetic audience was the veteran who had served his country in the "prison pens" of the enemy. Erstwhile Confederates who regaled neighbors and friends with accounts of frigid winters on Johnson's Island and at Fort Delaware were paralleled in countless northern communities by wearers of the blue who brought from the recesses of their past gruesome tales of suffering on Belle Isle, in Libby prison, or under the torrid Georgia sun in the stockade at Andersonville. And in the stories which these returned soldiers told there was a surprising unanimity; they were all convinced that their enemies, whether Federal or Confederate, had deliberately subjected their captives to such harsh treatment that they would be unfit for further service in the field.

A critical examination of the facts relating to the treatment of prisoners of war reveals that there was enough suffering in even the best military prison to lend color to this allegation. But even at Andersonville, where almost thirteen thousand graves were dug for Federal prisoners in less than one year, the charges cannot be substantiated. At best, a military prison was a makeshift affair, designed for temporary exigencies, and by this fact entailing unintentional hardships upon the unfortunates who were taken prisoners of war. The prisons which were located in St. Louis during the Civil War are excellent examples of the makeshift character of such institutions.

Almost the first prisoners of war taken in the War Between the States were the men who were assembled at Camp Jackson under General [Daniel] Frost for their annual drill under the militia laws of the State of Missouri. These prisoners were not confined, probably because there were no suitable buildings, but were released on their oath not to bear arms during the approaching conflict.[1] Following upon this coup by Captain [Nathaniel] Lyon, riots broke out in the city and revealed to the military authorities that there was a considerable secession sentiment in St. Louis. In order to deal with this sentiment, arrests of Confederate sympathizers were begun, and these captives, combined with prisoners of war taken from the forces of Sterling Price and Governor [Claiborne] Jackson, made necessary the establishment of prisons under the control of the military authorities. Not all of the sympathizers with the South were arrested by the military government, for some of them, correctly interpreting the condition of affairs as inimical to their safety, fled to the confines of the seceding states. The property of such exiles was subject to confiscation, and the buildings owned by two of the fugitives were seized for military prisons.

At the corner of Fifth and Myrtle streets, a Mr. [Bernard M.] Lynch, hated by the abolitionists of the city for his business, conducted an institution known in the vernacular of the time as a "slave pen." With the beginning of the war, "the traffic in human beings suddenly ceased," and Mr. Lynch departed for the Confederacy. "No little colored boy or girl was ever again to be sold there. The place hallowed by the sighs and tears of bondmen and of motherless children was for a time to become a prison house for those who had bought and sold their fellowmen." A sort of poetic justice, thought the abolitionists.[2] The building seized, a two-story brick structure, was occupied in the early part of September 1861 by a contingent of twenty-seven prisoners. Among these prisoners was a young Max McDowell, son of Dr. Joseph McDowell, the founder of the McDowell Medical College on Gratiot Street.[3]

May 30, shortly after the attack on Camp Jackson, several small detachments of Home Guards arrived before the McDowell Medical College and began a search of the building for boxes of munitions which had come from Baton Rouge just before the "capture" of the militia camp. The search was thorough but "no arms of any kind were discovered—not even in the dissecting room."[4] Dr. McDowell, a tall and imposing man, had been active in politics for a number of years and was known to be a staunch proslavery advocate and a bitter secessionist. The activities of the military authorities impressed

Gratiot Street prison in St. Louis was formerly McDowell Medical College.

upon him, as they had upon his neighbor, Mr. Lynch, that his period of usefulness in St. Louis was on the verge of a decline, and he followed his neighbor's example in emigrating to the Confederacy.[5]

Two sons shared this exodus: the one, Max, returning to the environs of St. Louis to gather recruits for the army of Price, fell into the hands of the military and soon found himself an inmate of Mr. Lynch's quondam slave pen.[6] The other son, Drake, accompanied his father to the South and later to Europe from whence the report came that he had been appointed physician to the Emperor Maximilian of Mexico.[7] After his departure, the Republican press of the city suggested that the bust of Dr. McDowell in the city library be thrown from the window in order that the good Union members could read at ease.[8] This bust was the last reminder of Dr. McDowell, for in December 1861 the McDowell Medical College was confiscated by the provost marshal and converted into a military prison.[9]

The former classrooms of the medical college were hastily reconditioned to meet their new uses, bunks were constructed, cooking stoves installed, and with a realistic disregard for possible squeamishness among the inmates, the dissecting room was transformed into a mess hall.[10] It was agreed that "if a skeleton should now and then be revealed" the nerves of the prisoners would probably not be greatly shocked.[11] It was estimated by the press that the prison would hold two thousand prisoners, but General [Henry] Halleck, commanding the department, realized that this figure was too high, and at the same time that the McDowell building was reconditioned, he notified the authorities in Washington that a larger building was needed. The most available building was a new penitentiary being constructed at Alton, Illinois, and Halleck asked authority to fit it up as a military prison if he could get the consent of the governor of the state.[12] The necessary permission was given, and the latter part of January 1862, Halleck sent an agent to build fires in the new penitentiary for a couple of days in order to dry out the walls.[13] During the first week of February, prisoners were moved from St. Louis to the Illinois prison, and by the twelfth of the month, it was reported crowded.[14]

From this time the prisons in St. Louis differed in character from the usual military prison. The prisons at Johnson's Island, Fort Delaware, Point Lookout, Camp Chase, Camp Morton, Camp Douglas, and others were devoted almost exclusively to prisoners of war while in the prisons of St. Louis, political prisoners were confined with Confederate soldiers, Federal deserters, and Northern soldiers awaiting trial for crimes. Only when Alton was too full to admit more prisoners of war were Confederate soldiers held for any length of time at the Gratiot Street prison. However, since most captives were transferred through St. Louis, the prisons always had a number awaiting transfer to the regular prison at Alton. Political prisoners after a hearing were either released on bond, exiled to the Confederacy, or sentenced to death or imprisonment. Those sentenced to prison terms were usually transferred to Alton where they were confined in the cells of the penitentiary.

General Henry Halleck asked that the new penitentiary at Alton, Illinois, be used as a military prison.

Immediately after the occupation of McDowell's College, General Halleck placed Colonel J. W. Tuttle in charge of the prison and gave him the necessary instructions for dealing with his charges. Tuttle was authorized to make arrangements for the internal police of the prison, and for this purpose, he was instructed to divide the prisoners into squads of twenty, separating officers and men. These squads were to be made responsible for the cleanliness of their quarters. As for the cleanliness of their persons, Halleck instructed Tuttle to make provisions for washrooms. Brooms might be requisitioned by the commander. Friends of the prisoners, it was decided, might send them unmarked clothing but no articles of luxury or adornment. Combs and brushes might be sent, but pipes and tobacco sent into the prison were to be placed in a general fund for the benefit of all the prisoners. Colored prisoners were to do the washing for their fellows, while the white prisoners were to be detailed to bring in water under guard.[15]

In regard to the sick among the prisoners, Halleck instructed Tuttle to give them the regular diet of United States Army hospitals. The dangerously ill were to be removed to the nearest approved general hospital. Hospital attendants were to be detailed from among the prisoners. Learning a few days later that Colonel Tuttle was not satisfied with the treatment given to the sick, General Schuyler Hamilton, doubtless voicing the wishes of General Halleck, informed the medical director at St. Louis, "I deem it one of our first duties to see that every amelioration of the condition of the prisoners of war is rendered to their unhappy lot that enlightened humanity and a due regard to their safe keeping will permit."[16] The hospitals in the city where the most dangerously ill were cared for were the New House of Refuge, the City Hospital on Fifth Street, military hospitals on Fourth Street, Hickory Street, and at Jefferson Barracks, and the Sisters of Charity.[17] Most of the sick, however, were cared for in buildings adjoining the medical college, where they were under the care of Confederate surgeons taken prisoners of war. The surgeons volunteered for this duty and served under the direction of a Federal medical officer.[18] This arrangement, however, lasted but a short time, for in February 1862, it was decided not to regard medical officers as belligerents, and the Confederate surgeons were released from prison, contract physicians taking their place.[19] The sick were allowed to receive money and clothing from friends,[20] and visitors were permitted under the same conditions that Federal sick were visited—at the discretion of the surgeon in charge.[21]

Visitors to the well prisoners were more closely scrutinized than those to the sick—it was finally decided to administer the oath of allegiance to all callers—but they were allowed to send gifts. The story is told of certain ladies who sent in a Thanksgiving dinner to friends in the prison, the officer in charge promising to give it to the most needy. Looking over the prison, the officer decided that some of the guards from an Iowa regiment met this qualification and gave the dinner to them.[22] This story may have represented an actual occurrence, but it was not the deliberate purpose of the responsible authorities, at first at least, to prevent the friends of the prisoners from supplying them with food. In January 1862, General Hamilton authorized Colonel Tuttle to receive food which some sympathetic women had prepared for the prisoners. At the same time, Tuttle was instructed to announce in the papers the hours at which gifts would be received at the prisons. However, the implication that this involved could not be overlooked, and Hamilton hastened to state that he was well assured that the prisoners were well supplied, and he was constrained to receive such presents only to prevent the food being wasted.[23]

That the prisoners were not so convinced that the supply of food was adequate is shown by a protest from them in May 1862. This protest led to an official investigation. An inspector learned that the prisoners received two meals a day and were issued the full army ration. In the morning, they received coffee, fresh meat or bacon, and bread. There was always an abundance of coffee and bread, large pieces of the latter being thrown away by the prisoners. The second meal consisted of the balance of the pound of fresh meat or one-third pound of bacon allowed by the army regulations, soup, beans and rice or peas and hominy, and bread. All of this, except the beef, was wasted by the prisoners according to the inspector. Further, it was learned that Captain [P. H.] Bishop, in immediate command of the prison, had never heard a complaint. The inspector agreed that three meals a day would be better, but the cooking arrangements were inadequate for more than two.[24] Later in the year, a prisoner, doubtless hoping for favors from the officers whom he described as "the gentlemanly keepers," reported to General [John] Schofield that during five months the ration which he received in prison was superior to any he had obtained in Price's army. Being of an economical turn of mind, the sight of the overflowing slop barrels about the prison filled him with horror, and he suggested that three meals might easily be served if the prisoners did not waste so much.[25]

The latter part of May 1862, the prisoners in Lynch's former slave pen were moved up to McDowell's College, and the Myrtle Street prison was closed. This was done as a sanitary measure, as the slave pen was considered greatly inferior to the college.[26] In fact, it was believed by loyal Unionists and the military authorities in St. Louis that their prison was the best in the United States. An inspector in June found minor faults such as the confinement of the political and military prisoners together, the fact that citizens were allowed to

General John Schofield served as commander of Union troops in Missouri and northern Arkansas during late 1862 to early 1863.

speak to prisoners, and the lack of religious services, but he pronounced the culinary and sanitary arrangements "most admirable" and the system of policing the prison "perfect."[27] "Among Military men, Gratiot Street prison is now pronounced superior as regards management and accommodations, to every other place of confinement in the West except that at Alton, and the latter is larger and somewhat more convenient for prison uses," declared the *Missouri Republican*.[28] Captain [H. W.] Freedley, an inspector sent from the office of the commissary general of prisoners, was quoted as authority for such a statement. The prisoners were "properly and kindly" cared for by Captain Bishop and his assistants and had never had reason to complain of their treatment. Their wants were carefully considered and provided for. The result, according to this paper, was that the prisoners all had the highest respect for the officers over them.[29]

An inspection from the office of the local provost marshal general did not bear out the laudatory character of this opinion in all respects. It was found that the officers' quarters were equipped by the inmates. In the "Square Room" of the prison, seventy by sixty by fifteen feet, there were 250 men, which filled the room to the utter disregard of the rules of hygiene. "From this room, sir—all from this room," replied Captain Bishop when asked whence the sick in the hospital came. The "Round Room," sixty feet in diameter, held 250 men but was better ventilated than the square room. But despite the unfavorable character of portions of this report, the chauvinistic press assured its readers that it proved that "nothing has been left undone by the management of the prison to secure the health of its inmates."[30]

With the approach of winter, it became impressed upon the military authorities and the Western Sanitary Commission that conditions were not as praiseworthy as they had believed. Early in November 1862, Gratiot Street prison had 800 prisoners, when its maximum capacity should have been 500. Colonel Thomas Gantt took possession of the old Myrtle Street prison and put it into condition for receiving prisoners. It was planned to acquire still another building on Fourth Street.[31] November 5, Lieutenant Colonel F. A. Dick became provost marshal general and moved 150 prisoners to Myrtle Street. The capacity of the old slave pen was 100, but the influx of prisoners into the college made this action necessary. This relief was but temporary, for within a few days, there were 1,100 prisoners at the McDowell's College. About the middle of the month, sickness began to increase in Gratiot Street at an alarming rate. Two hundred and thirty-five cases of sickness broke out in one week, and sick and dying men lay upon the floors unable to gain admission to the hospitals. Each morning men were found dead on the floor who had had no medical attention because of the large number of the sick. Despite the fact that the Alton prison was also overcrowded, Colonel Dick relieved the pressure in St. Louis by sending there his excess, until by the end of the first week of December he had reduced the number in Gratiot to 570.[32] Because of these conditions, a board was appointed to inquire into the necessity for additional prison accommodations. The board found 471 prisoners in McDowell's College and 145 in Myrtle Street. Since they estimated that 750 could be held in the one and 150 in the other, and they learned that there was room at Alton for over 500, they agreed that there was no need for an additional prison. The sanitary commission measured the rooms in the prisons and decided that Gratiot Street would not hold more than 625 and Myrtle 100, but they agreed that there was no immediate need for another building.[33]

Throughout this first year of the prison's existence, the inmates had attempted to relieve the crowded conditions by removing themselves at every opportunity. The officials of the prisons, however, were unappreciative of these efforts, and the vigilance of the guards kept the number of escapes to a small number. Various means were used by the prisoners in their efforts to avoid the crowded conditions of the prisons. In July several prisoners disguised themselves as Negroes and made good their egress. Orders were immediately given to prohibit members of this race from entering the prison.[34] The most feasible method of escape lay from the McDowell College building to the adjoining structure, which was occupied by the "Christian Brothers" Academy. The basements of the buildings were connected, and prisoners occasionally managed to get into the prison basement and from there into the academy vaults; others attempted to cut through the walls with jackknives, shovels, bricks tied in shirttails, and other crude tools. An easier way of escape lay across the roofs of the buildings, but this route exposed them to the view of the guards who at no time showed any hesitancy in shooting prisoners. The guards had instructions to shoot any person who put head or members out of the windows and did not immediately withdraw them when commanded to do so.[35]

However much the relief from the condition of the prison might have been appreciated by the prisoners who were successful in escaping, the number of these was too small to have any effect within the prison. After the reoccupation of the Myrtle Street prison in November, the prisons were not so crowded. In the old slave pen, new bunks were installed, and a reporter visiting the prison shortly after it was occupied found that it was quite clean. A more sanitary system of police was inaugurated, beds were aired each morning before breakfast and the prisoners forced to wash themselves. After breakfast, the inmates were allowed to exercise in the yard. According to this visitor, the prisoners were well fed, healthy, and grateful for the humane treatment which they received.[36]

To the prisoners, the excellent character of their surroundings was not so obvious as to the casual visitor. Captain Griffin Frost of the Missouri State Guard spent the months from January to May 1863 in the Gratiot Street prison and wrote an account of his experiences which show conditions through the

Captain Griffin Frost wrote about his experience as an inmate in the Gratiot Street prison.

eyes of an inmate of the prison. Captain Frost and his companions arrived in St. Louis by way of Springfield after having been captured in Arkansas. He arrived on the last day of 1862 on a bitter cold afternoon after having been without food for twenty-four hours. One prisoner chilled and died as the new arrivals stood in the street to be searched for money, knives, and valuable papers. When this was done, they were escorted to their quarters in the round room, "a very dark, gloomy place, and very filthy besides." The prisoners found that Gratiot Street prison was a hard place and "the fare so rough, it seems an excellent place to starve." The rations consisted of one-fifth loaf of baker's bread, a small portion of bacon, and a "tin cup of the stuff they called coffee" for breakfast and the same amount of bread, a "hunk" of beef and a "pint of the water the beef was boiled in which is called soup," and a "couple of boiled potatoes" for dinner. "All dished up and portioned out with hands; knives, forks and spoons not being allowed." Frost heard that the rations intended for the prisoners were being sold and the officers pocketing the money. Of the officers, Frost was willing to believe much. One of them informed the prisoners that all Southern women were prostitutes, and to men who prided themselves on their "chivalry," this was an unbearable insult. "The officers of the regiment now guarding us are perfect devils—there is nothing too low, mean, or insulting for them to say and do." After a few days of this portion of the prison, Frost was removed to the officers' quarters, which he found a great improvement over his former room. It was cleaner and less crowded, as there were only eight in a room sixteen feet square. They slept on bunks instead of the floor, and the fare was better and more plentiful. The officers were allowed to walk in the halls and look out of the windows into the street.

In these quarters, the officers were able to forget some of their hardships and obtain a more pleasant perspective on life. Being young, the incongruity of the place of their confinement appealed to their sense of humor, and they spoke of their college and college life. They gleefully hailed new "students" who brought them word of the outside world while they deplored the passage of those who "graduated" by taking the oath of allegiance. These "practiced their profession" in the state militia. But after a month at McDowell's College, Frost confessed that he had learned little in the way of dissecting human bodies, "not from the want of subjects, however," he hastened to explain, "as there are three or four deaths every day."

This more pleasant outlook on life was marred by the proximity of the men in the lower quarters of the prison. Complaints of the scarcity of food came to the officers, and "all through the night can be heard coughing, swearing, singing and praying, sometimes drowned by almost unearthly noises, issuing from uproarious gangs, laughing, shouting, stamping and howling,

making night hideous with their unnatural clang. It is surely a hell on earth."
In March smallpox broke out among the prisoners, causing the involuntary
students to wonder that "every disease under heaven does not break out in the
lower quarters; half starved and crowded together as they are in their dirt and
rags."[37]

Captain Frost was sent east for exchange in April. Just before he left
St. Louis, a committee of two physicians appointed by the sanitary commission made a report which agreed with the prisoners on the bad conditions of
the prisons. The physicians declared the prisons to be a disgrace "to us as a
Christian people." In the barracks, they found bunks, designed for two people
and three tiers high, placed so close together that there was scarcely space to
pass between. In the hospitals, no bedding was furnished to the prisoners, who
kept themselves warm with blankets and bits of carpets. The floors were so
incrusted with dirt as to resemble earthen floors. "In these rooms the prisoners
spent day and night, for the small yard of the prison is scarcely sufficient to
contain a foul and stinking privy. The day we visited this prison was warm so
that all the windows were open and the air was more tolerable on that account,
but it is difficult to conceive how human beings can continue to live in such
an atmosphere as must be generated when the windows are closed at night or
in stormy weather. Here were persons lying sick, with pneumonia, dysentery
and other grave diseases awaiting admission to the hospital."[38] A contradic-
tory report was made a few weeks later by a medical officer who declared
the police arrangements and the whole internal management of the prison
were well conducted. Colonel [William] Hoffman, the commissary general of
prisoners, informed Secretary [Edwin] Stanton that the conditions found by
the sanitary commission had been remedied, but he asked the secretary for a
medical officer to be assigned to his office in order that he might check up on
conditions in the various prison camps.[39]

It was not until October that an inspector was sent from Hoffman's
office, but in the meantime, a surgeon sent by the Department of the Missouri
visited the prisons and reported that the police of Gratiot Street prison was
as good as the dilapidated floors and ceilings would allow. When scrubbed,
the water leaked from one floor to the next. The inspector also recommended
repairs looking toward securing the prisoners better and suggested that more
vegetables be added to the diet to prevent scurvy.[40] Hoffman authorized the
necessary expenditures for these improvements.[41] In October the inspector
from Hoffman's office found the prison and hospital in satisfactory condition.
There were 960 prisoners in the Gratiot and Myrtle Street prisons, many without
bunks, but since adequate washing facilities were provided, the prisoners were
clean. Myrtle Street was lacking in ventilation.[42] A less conservative report

came from General W. W. Orme, who had been sent by Secretary Stanton to inspect the prison. General Orme found that the buildings were excellent, conveniently arranged, and kept in a good state of police, although there was a lack of personal cleanliness among the prisoners. The prisoners received "an abundant supply of good food," had splendid facilities for cooking, and were generally in good health.[43]

The policy of the administration in regard to improvements in the prisons was revealed by Hoffman in instructions to his medical inspector. Since prison camps were of a temporary character, he explained, and might not be occupied but for a few months or a year or two, it was only intended to put hospitals and prisons in such condition as to meet the demands of humanity. It was not expected that the hospital would be fitted with all the comforts of a well-organized and permanent establishment. "At best it must fall far short of perfection, but it is hoped the essential will be sufficiently attained to insure that there shall be no want of comfort," but the inspector was cautioned to have due regard for economy in any suggested improvements.[44]

During the winter, the Gratiot Street prison began to fall below even the low criterion set forth in these instructions. In February 1864 the inspector urged Hoffman to transfer the prisoners to Benton Barracks. Neither of the prisons was satisfactory. The hospitals were ill ventilated, the beds, clothes, and persons of the patients in the hospitals were foul, and wards and barracks were dirty. The sanitary condition of Myrtle Street was said to be a disgrace to its commander. It was cleansed by dragging a hose which flooded the room, washed the debris into the halls, and left the room standing in water, which leaked through to rooms below. In one room, a red-hot stove boomed over a wet floor and filled the room with steam. "The only prison yard, or place where the prisoners can exercise in the open air, is on the west side of the north wing, and is about 70 by 20 feet in dimensions. It is surrounded by a 15-foot fence, and contains the sinks, the supply of fuel on hand, and a variety of rubbish."[45] Another surgeon concurred in the statement that the buildings were unfit for prisoners, pointing out that in the largest room of Gratiot, there was only 230 cubic feet of air for each man, while in the smaller rooms, there was as little as 180 cubic feet. He too recommended abandoning the prison for barracks.[46] A month later, the excess prisoners were removed from Gratiot to Alton[47] and the McDowell College building patched up, but General [William S.] Rosecrans, commanding the department, began the construction of buildings at Jefferson Barracks to which the prisoners could be removed.[48]

During the summer of 1864, no steps were taken toward moving the prisoners, partly because a new provost marshal began to improve conditions. In June he reported that improvements had been made in every respect; the walls

General William S. Rosecrans began construction of buildings at Jefferson Barracks that could be used if the Gratiot Street prison closed.

which had been cracked and falling had been braced, and changes made in the direction of better sanitation. An inspector was appointed to pass through the prisons daily, and a weekly report was sent in to the office of the commissary general of prisoners.[49] An early report from this daily inspector revealed the state of his mind better than the condition of the prisons. He reported the buildings were clean, "kitchen and mess-room . . . are scrubbed daily, and no dirt is allowed to accumulate." The quarters were clean and healthy, had good ventilation, and the beds were equipped with new straw ticks. "The food, consisting of the prisoners' ration, while it does not suit the taste of some who have been so unfortunate as to become the recipients of our Government's bounty inside of stone walls and iron bars, is of good quality, the allowed quantity, well cooked, and to all but a few, who would be content with nothing short of liberty and hotel fare, it gives satisfaction. . . . In brief, the Gratiot Street Prison is kept, in every way, outside as well as in, clean and wholesome, and the prisoners are as comfortable as their condition as prisoners admits. . . . Myrtle Prison, in all its details, is but the rival of the Gratiot. . . . These . . . prisons . . . present more the appearance of public charitable institutions where the needy are cared for and no labor asked in return than they do of prisons. I can see nothing materially which can add to the safety or comfort of the prisoners."[50] The provost marshal, however, continued to demand that the prisoners be removed to Jefferson Barracks.[51]

Perhaps because of this laudatory report, Hoffman took occasion to declare that "it is not expected that anything more will be done to provide for the welfare of the rebel prisoners than is absolutely necessary. . . . Structures which may be ordered for them must be of a temporary and cheap character, though suitable to give protection against inclement weather and to serve the war."[52] With the approach of winter, the condition of the prisons steadily became less satisfactory. The weekly inspection reports, made now by a more critical officer than at first, pointed out more and more defects.[53] In September it was declared that "This old negro stall [Myrtle] is a nuisance in every respect and will not do for the coming winter."[54] In October estimates for a new prison were ordered, and the next month, the crowded condition of the prisons seemed to make a new prison imperative. A nearby foundry was fixed upon as a suitable place for housing the excess of prisoners.[55] With this suggestion, the repairs on the Gratiot Street prison were stopped to await the decision of the commissary general of prisoners.[56] The estimates for the new prison came to $4,900 and were submitted to Hoffman. In January 1865 the commissary general informed the provost marshal the estimates had been submitted to General Halleck and had not been approved. "I think it very doubtful whether any change will be authorized unless it is clearly shown that the buildings which have been occupied up to this time are no longer tenable."[57] After this rebuff, the weekly inspector informed his superior that the Gratiot Street prison, after certain repairs "will, in my opinion, as far as cleanliness and general management is concerned, favorably compare with any prison in the West, taking into consideration the many disadvantages this prison, as a prison, is possessed of."[58]

In the latter part of January, however, there was a momentary danger that a new prison would have to be occupied. The night of January 24 was quite cold, and one of the guards, just before going on duty, sought to fortify himself against the chill of the watch by heavy draughts of alcoholic stimulants. An officer detected the soldier's foresight and, with a lack of appreciation for his motives, confined him to a cell. But the cell was little preferable to the sentinel post, and within a short time, a cry of fire arose from the prisoners. Answering officers found quantities of smoke issuing from the cell of the recently incarcerated soldier. When the fire was extinguished, it was perceived that the guard had built a bonfire in the middle of the floor to warm himself. Tried by court-martial for being drunk and attempting to set the prison afire, he was found guilty of the first charge and sentenced to solitary confinement for five days with rations of cold bread and water.[59]

During these months when the officials who administered the prisons were advocating the removal of the prisoners to better quarters, the prisoners were suffering from the prison equipment, but they suffered more from other changes in the prison system. Captain Frost, sent for exchange in April, was captured again in October 1863—"vacation having expired, we find ourselves once more matriculated in McDowell's college, and it may be our lot to become useful members of society."[60] His second winter in school was harder than the first. Shortly after his arrival, orders came from the commander of the department to prohibit sale of fruits and edibles through the gates of the prison, and all intercourse between citizens and prisoners was forbidden.[61] The reason assigned for this action was that the Confederate authorities refused to allow visitors to their prisons, and this prohibition was made in retaliation.[62] In a short time, orders came from the commissary general of prisoners prohibiting the prisoners to make purchases of any kind,[63] and the prisoners were informed that gifts of clothing and provisions could not be sent by their friends.[64] This stringent policy was modified to some extent in December 1863 by an order from the secretary of war which permitted sutlers to sell tobacco and stationery to the prisoners. The prisoners correctly ascribed this modification to Stanton's fear that they would become ill if deprived of tobacco.[65] For most of their luxuries after this, the prisoners were indebted to those subterranean channels known as the Underground Railroad and the Underground Express Company. These lines of communication were kept open by new arrivals, particularly citizens who were confined for short periods while awaiting investigation. When a citizen entered the prison, the military prisoners thought themselves fortunate: "It is the best show we have to keep the U.G.R.R. in repair."[66]

Within two months the result of restricting purchases and gifts became noticeable in the increase of scorbutic diseases. The tendency to scurvy thus created was hastened by the failure to issue any vegetables to the prisoners from December 1863 to the following February.[67] Early in March, Colonel

Hoffman permitted the sutler to sell all kinds of vegetables, sugar, and meats to the prisoners.[68] Late in the summer, a circular from the commissary general of prisoners permitted purchases of sugar and tea for the sick and vegetables for the prisoners generally on the recommendation of the surgeon at the prison.[69]

This change brought about an amelioration of conditions for a time, but the winter of 1864-65 again brought out the worst features of the makeshift prisons of St. Louis. From November to February, there were 818 sick in the hospitals and 134 deaths, "showing the fearful mortality at the rate of nearly 50 per cent. for the year; over 16 per cent. for the four months, and over 4 per cent. per month." Many of the prisoners were in such bad condition when they entered the prison that they were admitted to the hospitals within a few days. Often they were mere boys who entered the Confederate service when their country was on the verge of collapse. Unable to withstand the hardships of a campaign, they fell captive easily, and the poor food and crowded conditions of the prison soon had their inevitable effect.[70]

But the approach of spring resulted in a decrease in sickness, and many prisoners were removed to other prisons while some were sent east for exchange. And spring brought liberty to the prisoners, for in Virginia, Richmond fell and Lee surrendered at Appomattox. Within a few weeks of this collapse of the Confederacy, a board of examiners was appointed to clear the prisons. Two hundred prisoners were released by this board from the Gratiot prison and the penitentiary at Alton immediately. Conscripts from Price's army and all prisoners of war who would take the oath of allegiance were released as rapidly as they could pass before the examiners. By the first of May the number of prisoners at Alton had been reduced from 3,000 to 853, and in the Gratiot Street prison there were only 150, including citizens, Federal soldiers, and a few prisoners of war.[71] June 13 there were only 112 citizens and Federal soldiers at Alton,[72] and on the twentieth, they were removed to Gratiot Street to await examination and release.[73] August 31 there was but one prisoner left in the Gratiot Street prison.[74]

The prisoners released from the slave pen and the medical college of St. Louis returned to their homes upon their release, but they did not forget their prison experiences. Unlike most of the memories of the war, the recollections of the prisoners seem to have become more bitter with the passage of time. During the war, the people of the North had become convinced that the Confederate authorities were deliberately mistreating the prisoners whom they held in Libby prison, Belle Isle, Andersonville, and other prisons. Within a few months of the end of the war, Henry Wirz, the commander of the Andersonville prison, faced a court-martial on charges of cruelty and murder in the Georgia prison. Witnesses at his trial told incredible stories of atrocities, and the commission, victims of a war psychosis which enabled them to believe the worst of their conquered enemies, sentenced the unfortunate victim to death. From this time Confederates vied with Federals in relating stories of atrocities which befell prisoners of war in the enemy's prisons. Captain Frost, writing in 1867, gave an account of his experiences in Gratiot and other prisons, alleging as he did so that he was revealing more cruelties than were told of Andersonville. But a careful analysis of the conditions in the prisons of St. Louis reveals only the natural defects of a makeshift prison.

NOTES

1. *The War of the Rebellion: A Compilation of the Official Records of the Union and Confederate Armies* (Washington, DC: U.S. Government Printing Office, 1880-1901), ser. 2, vol. 1: 106, 116 (hereinafter cited as *OR*; all references are to series 2). Cf. also William Bell, "Camp Jackson Prisoners," *Confederate Veteran* 31 (July 1923): 260.

2. Galusha Anderson, *The Story of a Border City During the Civil War* (Boston: Little, Brown, 1908), 186.

3. *St. Louis Missouri Republican*, 4 September 1861.

4. Ibid., 1 June 1861.

5. Anderson, *Border City*, 188.

6. *St. Louis Missouri Republican*, 3 September 1861.

7. Ibid., 6 June 1864.

8. *St. Louis Missouri Democrat*, 4 February 1862.

9. *St. Louis Missouri Republican*, 24 December 1861.

10. Ibid., 27 December 1861.

11. Ibid., 24 December 1861.

12. Halleck to Adjutant General Lorenzo Thomas, *OR*, 3: 169.

13. Ibid., 3: 216.

14. Ibid., 3: 245-246, 257-258; ibid., 1: 183; *St. Louis Missouri Republican*, 7 February 1862.

15. *OR*, 3: 185.

16. Ibid., 3: 194.

17. Ibid., 4: 95.

18. Ibid., 3: 209.

19. Ibid., 1: 164-166.

20. Ibid., 3: 211.

21. Ibid., 3: 221-222.

22. Anderson, *Border City*, 195. Anderson dates this incident in 1861, a month before the Gratiot Street prison where he locates the story was established.

23. *OR*, 3: 198, 199.

24. Ibid., 3: 574-575.

25. Ibid., 4: 454.

26. *St. Louis Missouri Republican*, 28 May 1862.

27. H. L. McConnel to B. G. Frarrar, *OR*, 4: 57.

28. *St. Louis Missouri Republican*, 6, 7 August 1862.

29. Ibid., 21 August 1862.

30. Ibid., 20 September 1862.

31. *OR*, 4: 673.

32. Dick to Hoffman, ibid., 5: 48-50.

33. Ibid., 5: 75-76.

34. Ibid., 4: 154.

35. *St. Louis Missouri Republican*, 2 September, 16 October, 8, 25 November 1862; *OR*, 5: 113.

36. *St. Louis Missouri Republican*, 25 November 1862.

37. Griffin Frost, *Camp and Prison Journal* (Quincy, IL: n.p., 1867), 27-42.

38. Executive Committee of the Sanitary Commission to Stanton, *OR*, 5: 588.

39. See Major T. I. McKenny to Lieutenant Colonel A. V. Colburn, ibid., 5: 564-565, and Hoffman to Stanton, ibid., 5: 686-687.

40. Ibid., 6: 150-151.

41. Ibid., 6: 199-200, 264.

42. A. M. Clark to Hoffman, ibid., 6: 406.

43. Ibid., 6: 662.

44. Ibid., 6: 773.

45. Ibid., 6: 982-983.

46. Surgeon B. B. Breed to Lieutenant Colonel Marsh, 26 February 1864, *OR*, 6: 992-993.

47. Ibid., 6: 1106.

48. Ibid., 6: 1113.

49. Colonel J. P. Sanderson to Hoffman, ibid., 7: 201.

50. Lieutenant Isaac Gannett to Sanderson, ibid., 7: 224-225.

51. Ibid., 7: 455-456.

52. Ibid., 7: 468.

53. Ibid., 7: 699-700, 772, 800, 862, 880, 1108-1109, 1128, 1150, 1202, 1285-1286.

54. Ibid., 7: 845.

55. Ibid., 7: 1115.

56. Ibid., 7: 1005, 1036, 1181.

57. Ibid., 8: 85.

58. Ibid., 8: 116-117.

59. *St. Louis Missouri Republican*, 25 January, 15 February 1865.

60. Frost, *Camp and Prison Journal*, 75-76.

61. *OR*, 6: 518-519.

62. Frost, *Camp and Prison Journal*, 83.

63. *OR*, 6: 640.

64. Frost, *Camp and Prison Journal*, 92.

65. *St. Louis Missouri Republican*, 21 December 1863; Frost, *Camp and Prison Journal*, 96.

66. Frost, *Camp and Prison Journal*, 96-97.

67. *OR*, 6: 992.

68. Ibid., 6: 1014-1015; *St. Louis Missouri Republican*, 11 March 1864.

69. *OR*, 7: 521.

70. Ibid., 8: 376-377.

71. *St. Louis Missouri Republican*, 1 May 1865.

72. Ibid., 13 June 1865.

73. Ibid., 23 June 1865; *OR*, 8: 661.

74. *OR*, 8: 1004. There is no record of the release of this last Confederate.

Order No. 11 and the
Civil War on the Border

ALBERT CASTEL

Order No. 11 was the most drastic and repressive military measure directed against civilians by the Union army during the Civil War. In fact, with the exception of the hysteria-motivated herding of Japanese Americans into concentration camps during World War II, it stands as the harshest treatment ever imposed on United States citizens under the plea of military necessity in our nation's history.

Issued August 25, 1863, by Brigadier General Thomas Ewing Jr., commander of the District of the Border with headquarters at Kansas City, Order No. 11 required all the inhabitants of the western Missouri counties of Jackson, Cass, and Bates not living within one mile of specified military posts to vacate their homes by September 9. Those who by that date established their loyalty to the United States government with the commanding officer of the military station nearest their place of residence would be permitted to remove to any military station in the District of the Border or to any part of Kansas except the counties on the eastern border of that state. Persons failing to establish their loyalty were to move out of the district completely or be subject to military punishment.[1]

The general public at the time, as well as most historians since, regarded the order as an act of retaliation for the destruction of Lawrence, Kansas, and the massacre of 150 of its citizens by William Clarke Quantrill's Missouri guerrillas on August 21, 1863. Critics of the order both then and thereafter condemned it as being cruel, unjust, and unnecessary.[2] Its defenders, on the other hand, while admitting its severity, maintained that it was fully warranted by the military situation and that it achieved the results intended—the forcing

of Quantrill's bushwhackers out of the border region of Missouri and the ending of guerrilla raids into Kansas.[3]

Both parties to the controversy over Order No. 11 have usually dwelt
upon the circumstances immediately preceding its promulgation and upon the
short-range impact of its execution. Rarely, if at all, have they examined its
full background or its ultimate operation. Yet it is only through such an examination that a valid evaluation of the order can be made. Once this is done,
then perhaps a definite answer can be given to the question: Was Order No. 11
a justified act of military necessity or an unjustified deed of military tyranny?

The territorial conflict of the 1850s left a legacy of hatred between Kansas
and Missouri. Kansans resented the invasions of the Missouri "border ruffians," and the Missourians bitterly recalled the incursions of John Brown,
James Montgomery, and other Kansas "jayhawkers." The outbreak of the
Civil War intensified this mutual animosity. Kansas jayhawkers and Red Legs
made devastating raids into Missouri during which they plundered and murdered, burned farmhouses and crops, and liberated hundreds of slaves. These
forays in turn caused pro-Southern guerrilla bands to retaliate against Kansas.
Led by Quantrill, the Missouri bushwhackers sacked Kansas border settlements and shot down unarmed civilians "like so many hogs." At the same
time they waged a deadly partisan warfare against Federal troops and Union
adherents in Missouri itself.

The efforts of the Federal army to put down bushwhacking were frus-
trated by the skill of the guerrillas, the difficult nature of the countryside, and
above all, the assistance rendered the bushwhackers by the civilian population. Most of the people of western Missouri looked upon the guerrillas as
their avengers and defenders, and a large portion of them had friends and kins-
men riding with Quantrill. Consequently, they aided them in every possible
way, from feeding and sheltering them, to smuggling them ammunition and
acting as spies. Even anti-Confederates assisted the partisans out of fear of
reprisals. Thus in effect, the Federal forces in western Missouri were opposed
by an entire people.[4]

By the spring of 1863, Union officers serving along the border had concluded that the bushwhackers could never be suppressed by ordinary tactics.
"Good men and true," wrote one of them, "have been for months trying to
catch the bushwhackers, and I know it is, as they declare, almost an impos-
sibility."[5] And declared another, "If any one . . . can do better against bushwhackers than we have done, let him try this country, where the people and
bushwhackers are allied against the United States and its soldiers."[6]

In June 1863, Brigadier General Thomas Ewing Jr. took command of
the District of the Border. Ewing, aged thirty-four, was a prominent Kansas

Republican, former chief justice of Kansas, and the brother-in-law and one-time law partner of General William T. Sherman. A man who believed that he had "few equals in mental vigor," he was intensely ambitious and hoped to secure election to the United States Senate. With that goal in mind, he was at this period seeking the favor of Senator James H. Lane, the "king" of Kansas politics.

By the end of July, Ewing decided that unless his forces were tripled, the only possible way to destroy the guerrillas was to strike at the root of their power, the support they received from the civilian population. Therefore, on August 3 he wrote his departmental commander, Major General John M. Schofield, stating that since two-thirds of the families in western Missouri were kin to the bushwhackers and were "actively and heartily engaged in feeding, clothing, and sustaining them," several hundred families of the "worst" guerrillas should be transported to Arkansas. This would not only deprive the guerrillas of their aid, but would cause the guerrillas whose families had been removed to follow them out of the state. Surrender terms could then be offered to the less offensive bushwhackers remaining.[7]

Schofield approved the plan, and on August 18, Ewing put it into effect by issuing General Order No. 10.[8] Then, three days later, Quantrill and 440

Brigadier General Thomas Ewing issued the controversial Order No. 11 on August 25, 1863.

bushwhackers destroyed Lawrence. This deed, which was not only the climax of the Kansas-Missouri border war but also the most horrible atrocity of the entire Civil War, shocked, frightened, and enraged Unionists in both Kansas and Missouri and caused them to demand that the bushwhackers be crushed once and for all so as to prevent further raids of this kind. Ewing, who likewise believed that drastic action was needed, responded to their clamor by promulgating Order No. 11 on August 25.

Immediately, large numbers of pro-Southern and Conservative Union Missourians denounced the order as "inhuman, unmanly, and barbarous."[9] Most prominent and vehement among the critics was George Caleb Bingham, the famous artist. Although a Unionist, Bingham hated all Kansans in general and Ewing in particular. After Order No. 11 was announced, he went to Ewing's headquarters in Kansas City and demanded that it be rescinded. Ewing refused, and the interview became highly acrimonious. Finally, as he departed, Bingham warned, "If you persist in executing that order, I will make you infamous with pen and brush as far as I am able."[10]

Bingham carried out his threat in both respects. First he produced a painting entitled *Order No. 11*. It showed Ewing astride a horse complacently supervising his troops as they expel a Missouri family from its home. A Kansas Red Leg has just shot down a young man, and another is about to shoot the elderly head of the family, oblivious to the pleas of a beautiful young woman kneeling at his feet. The house is being pillaged by Union soldiers, one of whom bears a likeness to the noted jayhawker, Colonel Charles Jennison. In the background, columns of smoke rise from burning fields, and a long, funereal line of refugees wends its way along the road. The painting was mediocre art but excellent propaganda, and it did more than anything else to create the popular conception of Order No. 11.[11]

What he depicted in the painting, Bingham also expressed in various writings which may be regarded as representative of all the criticisms of Order No. 11. According to him, the order was "an act of purely arbitrary power, directed against a disarmed and defenseless population" in violation of "every principle of justice." It was inspired by vengeance and was issued by Ewing in order to curry favor with the Kansas "mob" and advance his political ambitions. It resulted in "barefooted and bareheaded women and children, stripped of every article of clothing except a scant covering for their bodies," being "exposed to the heat of an August sun and compelled to struggle through the dust on foot." Under it, men "were shot down in the very act of obeying the order, and their wagons and effects seized by their murderers." Union soldiers and Red Legs burned dwellings and sent long wagon trains of plunder into Kansas. Refugees "crowded by hundreds upon the banks of the Missouri

George Caleb Bingham

River, and were indebted to the charity of benevolent steamboat conductors for transportation to places of safety where friendly aid could be extended to them without danger to those who ventured to contribute it."

There was neither need nor cause for Order No. 11, asserted Bingham. Most of the real bandits on the border were not Quantrill's bushwhackers but Kansas Red Legs who carried on their "nefarious operations under the protection and patronage of General Ewing." The bushwhackers were but small in number, "at all times insignificant in comparison with the Federal troops." The guerrillas could "at any time have been exterminated or driven from the country had there been an earnest purpose on the part of the Federal forces in that direction, properly braced by a willingness to incur such personal risks as become the profession of a soldier."

Finally, the order did not accomplish its professed purpose. Instead of driving them out, it gave up the country to the bushwhackers, "who, until the close of the war, continued to stop the stages and rob the mails and passengers, and no one wearing the Federal uniform dared to risk his life within the desolated district."[12]

Much of Bingham's pictorial and verbal condemnation of Ewing and Order No. 11 was false and unfair and motivated by personal malice. It is extremely unlikely, for instance, that Ewing, as the painting *Order No. 11* would imply, ever sat about on his horse callously watching the Red Legs slay defenseless men. The charge that the Red Legs enjoyed Ewing's "protection and patronage" was viciously absurd, since Ewing, while in command of the District of the Border, made constant and earnest efforts to suppress the Red Legs and stop jayhawking.[13] As for the assertion that bushwhacking did not become widespread until after Order No. 11, this is so obviously contrary to facts as not to require refutation.

Other of Bingham's accusations, however, had at least some basis in fact. Thus, in issuing the order, Ewing was motivated in part by a desire to satisfy the clamor for revenge in Kansas. In addition there can be little question that he was also concerned about his political prospects. Many Kansans criticized his conduct of affairs along the border and declared that he should be removed from command. Senator Lane warned him that unless he took harsh measures against the guerrillas, he would be a "dead dog" politically.[14]

However, these were not the sole motives, nor even necessarily the main ones, behind the issuance of Order No. 11. Other important considerations were Ewing's desire to reassure the badly frightened people of Kansas and to forestall a threatened mob invasion of western Missouri. Shortly after the Lawrence massacre, Senator Lane called on the men of Kansas to assemble on the border for the purpose of marching into Missouri and carrying out a campaign of "devastation and extermination." Had it not been for Order No. 11, this invasion probably would have taken place; as it was, even after issuing the order, Ewing had a great deal of difficulty heading off Lane's proposed expedition.[15] Thus it can be argued that however drastic Order No. 11 was, it helped prevent much worse.

Still another reason for Order No. 11, and probably the main one, was the military situation. The Lawrence massacre made it obvious that all previous efforts to combat the guerrillas had been unavailing and that they threatened to drive all Unionists from the border. Therefore the only thing that could be done, for it was the only thing left to be done, was to direct measures against the civilian population which contributed so much to the success of the bushwhackers. Although the timing and circumstances of the order made such an assumption natural and plausible, it was not, except in a limited sense, a retaliation for the massacre. It had been presaged by Order No. 10 and was essentially an extension of a policy already in effect, a policy suddenly made more drastic as a result of a shockingly horrible event.[16]

Finally, even if Ewing had not issued Order No. 11, a similar program would have gone into effect. For on the very same day that Ewing published the order, Schofield sent him the draft of an almost identical order. The major difference between the two was that Schofield's draft was much harsher than Ewing's order. Schofield believed that "nothing short of total devastation of the districts which are made the haunts of guerrillas will be sufficient to put a stop to the evil." Unlike Order No. 11, Schofield's proposal established no method of differentiating between Union and Confederate adherents.[17] All in all, Bingham's criticism of Ewing's motives in issuing Order No. 11 were for the most part either erroneous, pointless, or both. In any case, Schofield must share the responsibility for the order with Ewing.

Bingham was on much firmer ground in denouncing the severity of the order. There can be no doubt that its execution resulted in a great deal of hardship and suffering. H. B. Bouton, a Unionist living near Kansas City, told of seeing large numbers of "poor people, widows and children, who, with little bundles of clothing, are crossing the river to be subsisted by the charities of the people amongst whom they might find shelter."[18] Colonel Bazel Lazear, Federal commander at Lexington, Missouri, wrote his wife, "It is heart sickening to see what I have seen. . . . A desolated country and women & children, some of them allmost [*sic*] naked. Some on foot and some in old wagons. Oh, God."[19]

Marauding by Union troops increased the misery of the refugees. Most of the soldiers enforcing the order were vengeance-minded Kansans who welcomed such a splendid opportunity to punish the Missourians. Ewing, to be sure, repeatedly ordered his men not to engage in wanton pillaging, but

Order No. 11 *by George Caleb Bingham*

his efforts were largely in vain.[20] By the end of September, the depopulated district was a silent, forlorn land of stark chimney standing over charred ruins.[21]

But if Bingham had some justification for denouncing the hardships caused by Order No. 11, he was almost totally wrong in contending that it was unnecessary and that the inefficiency and cowardice of the Federal forces were alone responsible for the success of the bushwhackers. Schofield, a competent professional soldier who ultimately became the commanding general of the United States Army, personally investigated the situation in western Missouri after the issuance of the order and concluded that it was "wise and just—in fact a necessity."[22] For over two years, the guerrillas had been attacking Federal posts and patrols, terrorizing Unionists, and raiding border settlements, and doing so with ever-mounting intensity. As anyone familiar with the nature and history of partisan warfare knows, not only are guerrillas extremely exasperating but also terribly difficult to combat, and that one of the most effective ways (sometimes the only way) to defeat them is to deprive them of their civilian support as Orders No. 10 and 11 contemplated.[23] Such tactics, for example, were employed successfully in South Africa by Lord Kitchener against the Boer commandos, partisans who had many characteristics in common with the Missouri bushwhackers. According to the British military historian Cyril Falls, Kitchener resorted to "destroying farmhouses and their stores . . . and placing the inhabitants, mostly women, old people, and children, in camps, wherein the death-toll from sickness was high."[24] And along the same line, it should be noted that [Ulysses] Grant in 1864 became so annoyed by [John] Mosby's raids that he instructed [Philip] Sheridan to send a cavalry division through Loudon County, Virginia, "to destroy and carry off the crops, animals, Negroes, and all men under 50 years of age capable of bearing arms."[25]

Order No. 11, moreover, was imposed on a predominantly enemy population, which was willingly aiding and abetting the bushwhackers. Neither Bingham nor any of the other critics of the order maintained otherwise. The most they claimed was that "hundreds" of the people subjected to the order were "true and loyal" to the Union.[26] But even if this were true, the loyalists constituted only a small fraction of those affected by the order. Ewing, it will be recalled, estimated that two-thirds of the families in Jackson, Cass, and Bates counties were voluntarily helping the bushwhackers. This contention is supported by the *Kansas City Western Journal of Commerce*, which declared that most of the inhabitants of these counties were disloyal and that the few remaining Unionists were terrorized by the guerrillas into aiding them.[27] The Reverend George Miller, who lived in Kansas City during most of the war and opposed Order No. 11, stated in his memoirs that over four-fifths of the people in that region were secessionists.[28] In connection with this last statement, it is interesting to note that a Federal officer engaged in carrying out the order wrote in his diary that only one person in five was being permitted to remain in the district as being loyal to the Union.[29]

As a final answer to this particular criticism of Bingham's, it should be pointed out that under the laws and practices of war, whenever enemy civilians willingly assist guerrillas, then they must expect to take the consequences, and that among the consequences is forced evacuation of their homes.

The last, and in a way the most important, of Bingham's strictures on Order No. 11 was that it utterly failed to attain its avowed objective: the destruction of the guerrillas. This charge, to the extent it referred to the immediate effect of the order, was well founded. On this matter we have the testimony of one of the bushwhackers, who later recalled that despite the order, "Quantrill was in no hurry to leave the country for the South. The farmhouses were nearly all vacated as required by Order No. 11, but in every smoke house there hung from the rafters hams and bacon, and the country was full of stray hogs, cattle, and chickens which the owners had been forced to leave behind. There was plenty of feed for horses, and the men gathered the food at night."[30] When Quantrill left Missouri early in October, he did so only because of the approach of cold weather.

Thus, the immediate effectiveness of Order No. 11 was practically nil. What, then, was its ultimate result? To this question, unfortunately, there can be no definite answer, for the simple reason that the order was not allowed to function as originally intended. First, Ewing himself relaxed its terms by issuing, on November 20, Order No. 20. This provided for a limited resettlement of the depopulated district by "loyal persons" under a strict system of screening and accountability.[31] Then in January 1864, as part of a general reorganization of military affairs in the West, the border counties came under the command of Brigadier General Egbert B. Brown, a Missouri militia officer who disapproved of Order No. 11. Acting without prior consultation with Schofield or his approval, Brown on January 14 issued an order permitting all persons not "disloyal or unworthy" to return to their homes in the district.[32] Although nominally similar to Order No. 20, Brown's order set up a very loose procedure for determining loyalty and disloyalty, and it seemingly ignored the existence of Ewing's resettlement program, under which, according to the *Kansas City Western Journal of Commerce*, "nine-tenths of all the really loyal who intend to return have done so."[33] Ewing at once protested the new order to Schofield, declaring that it would undo all that Order No. 11 had accomplished and that "General Brown will let disloyal refugees return, and following them will return the guerrillas."[34] But Schofield soon ceased to command in Missouri, and Brown's policy remained in effect.

As a consequence, Ewing's prediction was fulfilled. By May, Colonel James H. Ford, commander of Union forces in Jackson County, was writing that "the country is full of bushwhackers, and . . . they have friends all through the country who furnish them with food. . . . I am satisfied that there are many families that are feeding them that have proved their loyalty."[35] And in June, following a scout through Jackson County, another Federal officer reported that "wherever we found settlements there we found signs of bushwhackers, and vice versa. Around Hickman Mills, Pleasant Hill, and the Sni Hills there are a good many farmers returned under the orders of General Brown, all of them bearing protection papers, either from General Brown's headquarters or headquarters Saint Louis."[36]

Significantly, not one of the bushwhackers in his memoirs indicates that Order No. 11 in any way handicapped their operations in 1864. On the contrary, one of them related that Quantrill's band, when it returned to Missouri in the spring, stopped off at a farmhouse and "got a good breakfast of biscuits and bacon . . . prepared by the woman of the house."[37]

To be sure, it might be argued that Order No. 11 was successful since there were no more guerrilla raids into Kansas from Missouri following its issuance. But it is extremely doubtful that the order as such was more than a minor and indirect factor in achieving this result. Of greater importance were the strengthened border defenses of Kansas following the Lawrence massacre, an improved home guard system in that state, and above all, the fact that the bushwhackers during the summer of 1864 concentrated their operation in northern and central Missouri so as to prepare the way for Sterling Price's invasion that fall.[38] If the guerrillas had wanted to make another foray into Kansas, they could have done so at almost any time. Certainly all through 1864 and even in 1865, Kansas communities were in a constant fret over being raided, a good indication that they placed little faith in the effectiveness of the badly watered-down Order No. 11.[39]

Regarded objectively from the standpoint of historical perspective, Order No. 11 was a natural and perhaps inevitable response on the part of the Federal military authorities to a situation which had become intolerable. It was, by mid-Victorian if not by modern standards, very cruel. Yet this cruelty, in the final analysis, merely reflected the cruelty of the Kansas-Missouri Border War, without doubt the most savage and bitter phase of the entire Civil War.

NOTES

1. *The War of the Rebellion: A Compilation of the Official Records of the Union and Confederate Armies* (Washington, DC: U.S. Government Printing Office, 1880-1901), ser. 1, vol. 22, pt. 2: 473 (hereinafter cited as *OR*; all references to series 1). The terms of the order also included a narrow strip of the northern part of Vernon County. In all, the region affected by the order had a population of about 40,000 at the beginning of the war.

2. For example, see Jay Monaghan, *Civil War on the Western Border* (Boston: Little, Brown, 1955), 287; Carl W. Breihan, *Quantrill and His Civil War Guerrillas* (Denver: Sage Books, 1959), 133-139; Darrell Garwood, *Crossroads of America: The Story of Kansas City* (New York: W. W. Norton, 1948), 320-321; John N. Edwards, *Noted Guerrillas: or The Warfare of the Border* (St. Louis: Bryan, Brand, 1877), 205; Charles Robinson, *The Kansas Conflict* (Lawrence, KS: Journal Publishing Co., 1898), 447-448.

3. See Lt. Col. R. H. Hunt, *General Order No. 11* (Topeka: Kansas Commandery of the Military Order of the Loyal Legion of the United States, 1908), 3-7; Henry E. Palmer, "The Lawrence Raid," *Kansas Historical Collections* 6 (1897-1900): 317-325; Shalor W. Eldridge, *Recollections of Early Days in Kansas* (Topeka: Kansas State Historical Society, 1920), 197.

4. *Kansas City Western Journal of Commerce*, January 23, 1864, estimated that in 1863 nine-tenths of the people in Jackson, Cass, and Bates counties "supplied and aided" the guerrillas.

5. Ibid., 13 June 1863.

6. Ibid., 2 May 1863.

7. *OR*, vol. 22, pt. 2: 428-429.

8. Ibid., 450-451, 460-461.

9. *Kansas City Western Journal of Commerce*, 5 September, 3, 10 October 1863, quoting the *Lexington Union* and the *St. Louis Republican*.

10. C. B. Rollins, ed., "Letters of George Caleb Bingham to James S. Rollins," *Missouri Historical Review* 33 (October 1938): 62.

11. Bingham completed the painting in November 1868. The original hangs in the [Cincinnati Art Museum. A similar version, completed in 1870, hangs in the] art gallery of the State Historical Society of Missouri, Columbia.

12. The above statements and quotations are from a public letter written by Bingham in 1877, most conveniently found in William L. Webb, *Battles and Biographies of Missourians: or, The Civil War Period in Our State* (Kansas City: Hudson-Kimberly, 1900), 256-264.

13. Albert Castel, *A Frontier State at War: Kansas, 1861-1865* (Ithaca, NY: Cornell University Press, 1958), 111-112.

14. William E. Connelley, *Quantrill and the Border Wars* (Cedar Rapids, IA: Torch Press, 1910), 417-418.

15. Castel, *Frontier State at War*, 146-149.

16. *Kansas City Western Journal of Commerce*, 5 September 1863; Schofield to Ewing, 25 January 1877, in Webb, *Battles and Biographies*, 265.

17. *OR*, vol. 22, pt. 2: 471-472. John N. Edwards, *Noted Guerrillas*, 205-206, who got most of the material for his book from former guerrillas, even stated, mistakenly, that the order actually originated with Schofield, who in turn got his instructions from Washington.

18. *Kansas City Western Journal of Commerce*, 19 September 1863.

19. Vivian K. McLarty, ed., "The Civil War Letters of Colonel Bazel Lazear," *Missouri Historical Review* 44 (July 1950): 390.

20. *OR*, vol. 22, pt. 2: 570-571, 591; ibid., vol. 34, pt. 2: 326, 375; *Kansas City Western Journal of Commerce*, 19 September, 23 November 1863, 30 January 1864. John N. Edwards, who rarely missed an opportunity to berate the Kansans, declared that Ewing executed Order No. 11 "mercifully." Edwards, *Noted Guerrillas*, 206.

21. About one-half of the refugees crossed into north Missouri, while most of the other half went south. *OR*, vol. 22, pt. 2: 753. Only about six hundred of the ten thousand some inhabitants of Cass County remained there by September 9. Richard S. Brownlee, *Gray Ghosts of the Confederacy: Guerrilla Warfare in the West, 1861-1865* (Baton Rouge: Louisiana State University Press, 1958), 126.

22. John M. Schofield, *Forty-six Years in the Army* (New York: Century, 1897), 83.

23. Theodore Ropp, *War in the Modern World* (Durham, NC: Duke University Press, 1959), 77; Cyril Falls, *A Hundred Years of War* (London: Duckworth, 1953), 278, 282, 288-289.

24. Falls, *Hundred Years of War*, 148, 279.

25. Virgil Carrington Jones, *Gray Ghosts and Rebel Raiders* (New York: Holt, 1956), 279.

26. *OR*, vol. 22, pt. 2: 484; ibid., vol. 34, pt. 2: 242-243; Webb, *Battles and Biographies*, 261.

27. *Kansas City Western Journal of Commerce*, 5 September 1863.

28. George Miller, *Missouri's Memorable Decade, 1860-1870* (Columbia, MO: E. W. Stephens, 1898), 36.

29. Sherman Bodwell, diary, 29 August 1863, Kansas State Historical Society, Topeka.

30. Frank Smith, memoirs, copy in possession of author.

31. *OR*, vol. 22, pt. 2: 693-694, 702-703, 713-714; *Kansas City Western Journal*

of Commerce, 21 November 1863.

32. *OR*, vol. 34, pt. 2: 79-80.

33. *Kansas City Western Journal of Commerce*, 23, 30 January 1864. About 250 families were allowed to resettle under Order No. 20, according to Ewing's chief quartermaster. *The History of Jackson County, Missouri* (Kansas City: Union Historical Co., 1881), 290-291.

34. *OR*, vol. 34, pt. 2: 81, 89.

35. Ibid., vol. 34, pt. 3: 623.

36. Ibid., vol. 34, pt. 1: 1022.

37. Smith, memoirs.

38. Brownlee, *Gray Ghosts*, 206-209.

39. *Kansas City Western Journal of Commerce*, 18 June, 2 July 1864; *OR*, vol. 34, pt. 3: 401, 502; ibid., vol. 34, pt. 4: 25, 54-55; Charles Robinson to Mrs. Charles Robinson, 5 February 1865, Charles Robinson Papers, Kansas State Historical Society.

The Recruitment of Negro Troops in Missouri during the Civil War

JOHN W. BLASSINGAME

During the early months of the Civil War, President Abraham Lincoln declared that if Missouri, Maryland, and Kentucky seceded, "the job on our hands . . . [would be] too large for us, we would as well consent to separation at once."[1] Lincoln probably despaired most of losing Missouri for it was located at the confluence of the nation's mightiest rivers—the Missouri, the Ohio, and the Mississippi—and had the largest white population of the slave-holding states. His anxiety resulted from an awareness that Missouri's varied topography of prairies, alluvial plains, and Ozark uplands had long divided its people, its economy, and its political interests along sectional lines. As a consequence of these forces, when Edmund Ruffin fired the first shot on Fort Sumter, Missourians were unsure of their state's mission in the impending war, but they realized that it had played a major role in precipitating that war. Missouri's admission to the Union in 1820 was perhaps the most important catalyst in arousing latent sectional animosities, Missourians led the South's fight for "Bleeding Kansas" in 1854-1858, and Dred Scott was a Missouri slave. At his inauguration in January 1861, Governor Claiborne F. Jackson, a Confederate sympathizer, called for a state convention to decide if Missouri would cast its lot with the embattled Confederacy. Surprisingly, with the solid support of the antislavery, foreign-born residents in and around St. Louis, the convention rejected secession. Subsequently, in July 1861 the convention deposed Jackson and chose Hamilton R. Gamble (the state supreme court judge who dissented in Dred Scott's first suit for freedom) for governor. Later, in an attempt to "save" the commonwealth for Lincoln and the Union, General

The first Negro regiments were accepted into the service of the United States on September 27, 1862.

Nathaniel Lyon captured the militia encamped in St. Louis, chased Jackson from Jefferson City, and halted the Confederates at Wilson's Creek.[2]

To save Missouri for the Union was a relatively "simple" military matter involving the confrontation of a foe expected to act in a certain manner. On the other hand, Lincoln's most intricate problem was to prosecute the war successfully without alienating the Union sentiment in indispensable Missouri. Accordingly, with his support, in July 1861, Congress declared the war aim to be the restoration of the Union and not the destruction of slavery. To prevent Missouri and Kentucky from fleeing to the arms of the enemy, Lincoln publicly disavowed any intention to abolish slavery. He demonstrated his determination not to interfere with slavery when he rescinded the tactless August 30, 1861, proclamation of General John C. Frémont which freed slaves in Missouri. Under the prod of circumstances, however, steps were taken which led to the extinction of slavery.[3] Recognizing that necessity eventually would lead to the freedom of the slaves and to insure the permanent loyalty of Missourians, Lincoln counseled them, to no avail, to accept compensated emancipation as embodied in the act he had convinced Congress to pass on April 10, 1862. On September 22, 1862, Lincoln issued his preliminary emancipation proclamation, but he implicitly excluded the loyal slaveholding states from its purview. On September 27, 1862, redoubtable Benjamin F. Butler accepted the first Negro regiments into the service of the United States. Confident that he had mollified the border states, Lincoln issued the Emancipation Proclamation on January 1, 1863.[4]

The promulgation of the Emancipation Proclamation gave impetus to the movement for gradual emancipation in Missouri. Such prominent Missourians as Senator B. Gratz Brown, Congressman Henry T. Blow, and State Representative John D. Stevenson led the fight which culminated with the Missouri legislature's enactment of a law in June 1863 which provided for gradual emancipation. The widely publicized campaign for "immediate" emancipation led to an exodus of slaves, the magnitude of which was not equaled in any other state. Many of the slaves sought out their masters and boldly informed them that they were leaving, then they took horses, wagons, stock, and tools and departed for Kansas. In several instances, the slaves of a neighborhood formed wagon trains and "in the light of day" departed for the land of freedom. Others armed themselves to discourage any contest over their exit. In counties where there were few slaveholders there was little opposition to this hegira.[5]

Logically, it would seem that the passage of the ordinance for gradual emancipation would have decreased the intensity of internal strife in Missouri. Instead, it accentuated the conflict between the various factions. Partially to bring order out of the chaos in the state, Lincoln appointed General John M. Schofield, a West Point graduate and Lyon's chief of staff at Wilson's Creek, to command the Department of the Missouri. Because of the large number of disloyal slaveholders in Missouri, Schofield found it very difficult to wage war vigorously in the Southwest. In an effort to break the power of the disloyal slaveowners, Schofield authorized Colonel William Pile, Thirty-third Missouri Volunteers, to recruit colored troops in the most disloyal areas of the state, provided he could obtain the consent of the governor.[6] Because there was a controversy then ranging in the state over whether the slaves of disloyal persons should be "confiscated," Governor Gamble demanded that each prospective recruiter apply to him for permission to recruit Negroes. With Schofield's refusal to accede to this, Gamble "unhesitatingly" gave his consent to the recruitment of Negroes, provided that the slaves of the loyal owners would not be taken and that the colored regiments raised would not be credited to the State of Missouri. Consequently, Pile designated the troops he recruited as "Arkansas Volunteers (colored)."[7] Pile found it very difficult to comply with Gamble's demand to refrain from enlisting the slaves of loyal masters as the recruiters made few attempts to differentiate the slaves of loyal masters from those of disloyal owners. By the end of September, practically all of the slaves of identifiably disloyal masters had been enlisted, and recruiting agents had begun a general policy of enticing or forcing the slaves of loyal

A graduate of West Point, John Schofield was teaching in St. Louis in 1861 when the war began.

owners into the service. Particularly in northern Missouri this practice caused great consternation among the slaveholders. Coincidentally, Brigadier General Thomas Ewing Jr., former chief justice of the Supreme Court of Kansas, commanding the District of the Border and faced with widespread disloyalty and guerrilla warfare on the Kansas-Missouri border, put into operation a plan calculated to break the spirit of the rebel sympathizers. On August 18, 1863, he ordered the commanders of army posts in his district to provide a military escort for all slaves who wished to escape to Kansas. Any slave who enlisted was sent to Kansas City, Missouri. The plan was so effective that in a few weeks the border counties were practically devoid of slaves.[8]

As a result of the dwindling number of slaves subject to confiscation according to the Act of July 17, 1862, Schofield wrote the War Department on September 29, 1863, that it would be necessary to recruit the slaves of loyal owners. He thought those masters of undoubted loyalty should be paid a set sum (to be determined by the secretary of war) out of the substitute fund. Payment would be made immediately upon the slave's enlistment, leaving the doubtful cases for future settlement. Schofield informed the secretary of war that he would eagerly carry out such a policy. In his opinion, which he believed most slaveholders also held, the slaves would be of more value to the Union as soldiers than to their masters as laborers. Schofield's confidence in them notwithstanding, many of the slaveholders found the suggested enlistment of their slaves unpalatable, and when they appealed to Lincoln for succor, he ordered Schofield to prevent the enlistment of colored troops except upon presidential approval.[9]

Although Lincoln had ordered a curtailment of recruitment, there was an increased desire for slave enlistments. On October 1, 1863, Senator John B. Henderson indited a letter to Schofield in which he counseled him to urge upon the president the propriety of enlisting all of the able-bodied Negroes in the state. To pacify the loyal owners, he suggested paying them $300 the moment one of their slaves enlisted. The senator offered to use his influence with Lincoln when Schofield expressed his support of the plan.[10] Despite continual pressure from Henderson, Schofield, and Stanton during the month of October, Lincoln refused to sanction the recruitment of all Missouri slaves. Conversely, on October 1, 1863, Lincoln approved Stanton's suggestion to recruit slaves in Maryland, and on October 3, 1863, approved a "confidential" order (which was not published) to regulate the recruitment of slaves in Maryland, Tennessee, and Missouri (General Orders No. 329). Later, when he contemplated the possible adverse effects of the enlistment of slaves on the upcoming election of state judges in Missouri, he excluded that state from the operation of General Orders No. 329.[11]

Forcing Negro Slaves Into Union Service

ABOLITION OFFICERS DRIVING NEGROES FROM THE PLANTATIONS.   Page 29

The strong showing of the Unconditional Unionists in the election for state circuit and supreme court judges convinced Lincoln of the political desirability of recruiting Missouri slaves, and therefore, he sanctioned such a step. Accordingly, on November 14, 1863, Schofield issued General Orders No. 135, which authorized state provost marshals to recruit Negroes, slave and free. All loyal owners whose slaves were taken or who consented to their enlistment could receive as much as $300 compensation upon filing a deed of manumission. The owner had to file an oath of allegiance with his claim. The president would appoint a board to determine the validity of claims made for compensation. (The members subsequently appointed were General [Joseph B.] Douglass of Boone County, Mr. Schofield of St. Joseph, and a Mr. Miller of Ohio, who was a friend of Stanton's.) All colored recruits were to be sent to St. Louis where Colonel Pile commanded the general rendezvous camp.[12] In spite of the appreciable increase in the number of Negroes enlisted, many Missourians expressed dissatisfaction with the results of the order. The order was ineffectual because state provost marshals, who were largely conservative in outlook, were in charge of recruitment. Furthermore, the slaveholding state provost marshal general, James D. Broadhead, opposed the policy of enlisting slaves.[13]

As it became clearly apparent that Schofield's order would not bring about a sizeable increase in the number of Negroes enlisted in the Union army, Missourians began to doubt his sincerity. While the Conservative Unionist faction inveighed against Schofield's "vigorous" recruitment of slaves, the radicals railed against his "apathy." Viewing Schofield's actions and motives in the light of historical perspective, it appears first that he was at heart anti-slavery, and second, he was a Conservative and intimate friend of the leader of the Conservatives, Governor Gamble. Finally, and of overshadowing importance, Schofield was unable to perform the gargantuan task of walking the middle road between the state's political factions. As a result, the discontent over Schofield grew to such proportions that there was a general outcry for his removal from the department. At first Lincoln refused to remove him, but agreed to do so when Missouri's congressional delegation threatened to block his confirmation as major general. In January 1864, Lincoln placed General William S. Rosecrans in command of the Department of the Missouri.[14]

Apprised of the mistakes of his predecessor, Rosecrans avoided political party struggles and entered vigorously upon the task of recruiting slaves. To insure the availability of slaves for the draft (Congress had made slaves liable to the draft on February 24, 1864), Rosecrans issued General Orders No. 35, March 1, 1864, prohibiting the exportation of slaves from Missouri. Since the state needed its slaves "to fill up the quotas of the various Districts required

ONE GOOD TURN DESERVES ANOTHER.

Old Abe. "WHY I DU DECLARE IT'S MY DEAR OLD FRIEND SAMBO! COURSE YOU'LL FIGHT FOR US, SAMBO. LEND US A HAND, OLD HOSS, DU!"

The English periodical PUNCH lampooned Lincoln regarding his Negro recruitment policy.

by the draft," any person who violated the order was subject to arrest.[15] At the outset, Rosecrans continued to use provost marshals to recruit Negroes, for he believed recruiting agents would foment disorder and violence and that it would be better to use provost marshals, because they were spread uniformly over the state and, therefore, could easily detect attempts to hinder enlistments and preserve peace. However, subsequent recruiting activities were so ineffectual that Rosecrans began to question the advisability of continuing his system of recruitment. Consequently, on August 5, 1864, he rescinded all orders relative to the recruitment of colored troops and empowered General Thomas Ewing Jr. to supervise parties sent out to recruit for colored regiments. This order brought pressure upon Rosecrans from state officials, and on August 19, 1864, he again gave provost marshals sole authority to recruit Negroes but placed them under Ewing's superintendence.[16]

At first, Missourians expressed little interest in the question of slave enlistments. Instead, railroad construction and how to attract immigrants were their principal preoccupations. Later, when they realized that the slaves, who would eventually be emancipated, could be used to fill Missouri's draft quota, there was much deliberation on the possibility of Negro enlistments. Many Missourians reasoned that inasmuch as Missouri's quota was based on congressional representation, which in turn was based on three-fifths of the slave population, at least three-fifths of the slaves should be drafted.[17] The

William S. Rosecrans became the commander of the Department of the Missouri after Schofield's removal. [*Dictionary of American Portraits*]

populace divided into two factions on the question of slave enlistments. The Conditional Unionists (Conservatives) were reluctant to upset the social order while the Unconditional Unionists (Radicals) were desirous of destroying the old relations between master and slave. Most Missourians supported the broad outlines of the Radical policy in this sphere, although not to the same extreme as the Radicals. The Unconditional Unionists conducted a vigorous campaign to inaugurate the recruitment of slaves. They supported the enlistment of slaves because it would have increased the pace of emancipation in the state.

The Radicals clearly expressed their position on the question of slave enlistment at a convention which opened in Jefferson City on September 1, 1863. At the beginning of the first day, the convention put itself on record in favor of immediate emancipation. Indefatigable Charles D. Drake, learned St. Louis lawyer and member of the Missouri legislature, then rose and delivered the most significant speech of the convention. After discoursing on various aspects of secession, Drake boldly stated his attitude about arming the slaves:

> I have no squamishness about arming the negro. I am no half-breed Unionist, sensitive about seeing white men alongside of the "American citizen of African descent." No traitor is too good to be killed by a negro, nor has any traitor a right to insist on being killed by a white man. If for the sake of slavery he turns traitor, let former slaves be his executioners;

Negro Soldier

it is a just and fit retribution. Disaffection, if not disloyalty, lurks in him who opposes the arming of the negro.[18]

Subsequently, Union sympathizers circulated Drake's speech widely in Missouri, Maryland, and Tennessee as an argument for slave enlistments. At the end of the first day, the convention adopted a resolution presented by Mr. McClurg of Caldwell County. Because the slaves in the state were escaping to, and enlisting in Iowa, Kansas, and Illinois, and a draft was imminent in Missouri, the convention resolved to demand permission from Schofield to recruit slaves of disloyal persons in the state.[19]

On the second day, several persons spoke of their loyalty, dilated on the immorality of slavery and some of them called for the enlistment of slaves. General George R. Smith of Pettis County, a former slaveholder, drew a rousing cheer from the delegates when he told them that it had warmed his heart to see the Negro enlisted to serve against the rebels.[20] Among other things, the convention resolved to tender its thanks "to President Lincoln for his action in arming and organizing the colored citizens of African descent for the purpose of killing rebels," called for the recruitment of the slaves of disloyal owners, immediate emancipation, and dispatched a committee of seventy to present their demands to Lincoln. When the delegates appealed to Lincoln to intervene in the state's political affairs and to enlist slaves, he politely refused.[21]

The delegates returned to their respective homes determined to make the enlistment of slaves a campaign issue in the state elections. Meetings were held in several counties, endorsing the resolutions of the convention. On September 19, 1863, the people of Perry County met and resolved: "We are in favor of the General Government arming the Negroes, or using them in any way that may inure to the benefit of the loyal white man, or to the injury of the rebels."[22] At an election victory celebration in Otterville, the Unconditional Unionists endorsed the enlistment of slaves because they felt it was "a death blow to the rebellion."[23] Missourians supported the enlistment of Negroes because of the small number of slaveholders in its white population (1,069,509) and the small number of slaves—19,185 whites owned 114,931 slaves in 1860.[24]

Slaveholders in Missouri, although in a decided minority, stubbornly resisted all attempts to enlist their slaves. In the large slaveholding counties, the slaveowners used several devices to circumvent the order authorizing slave enlistments. First of all, the Conservative provost marshals either spoke out against the recruitment of Negroes or did nothing to inform the slaves that they could enlist. The provost marshals either refused to accept the slaves or enlisted them only if they came to the recruiting stations on their own initiative. The provost marshal of Boone County refused to enlist Negroes, and when they began to run off to other counties to enlist, he issued an order prohibiting the enlistment of Boone County slaves elsewhere and provided a patrol of militia to enforce the order. Second, in such counties as Monroe and Macon, patrols of slaveowners and guerrillas blocked attempts of the slaves to enlist. In several instances in Callaway County, a band of owners followed companies of Negroes going to enlist, "shooting among them, killing and wounding some," and carrying back to slavery all they could capture. In Randolph, Chariton, and Howard counties, the Negroes were told that if they enlisted dire calamities would befall them—that they would be placed in front in battle and would receive no pay, that their masters would turn their families out to starve, and furthermore, that after the war, Lincoln would sell them into slavery.[25] The slaveholders of Lafayette County kidnapped the families of those slaves who enlisted and sold them in Kentucky or took them into rebel-held territory. Rosecrans attempted to halt the practice in March 1864 with his prohibition against the removal of slaves from the state.[26]

The system described above made recruitment of slaves in Missouri rather haphazard in nature, depending primarily upon the slave's personal desire and knowledge. Because the Conservative provost marshals would not encourage them to enlist, the slaves often took matters into their own hands; if a slave decided to enlist, he endeavored to convince others to do the same. The few

Negroes in the Union Army Serving as Hostlers

Radical provost marshals led armed Negro troops through their districts to obtain recruits and to protect those slaves who wished to enlist. To make their task easier, several masters voluntarily agreed to the enlistment of their slaves. Appalled at the pace of enlistment, many Radicals, such as Felix Bandissin of Franklin County, actively recruited slaves. Many Radicals advocated the passage of a congressional act freeing the families of slaves when they enlisted to increase the desire of slaves to enlist. (Congress passed such an act on March 3, 1865.)[27] Inasmuch as the provost marshals made no appeal to their patriotism, the Negroes in [Kansas City] met on [March] 22, 1864, to consider ways to promote the enlistment of colored persons in the army. After "Reverend Arnold" opened the meeting, "Dr. Nevill" made a "brilliant war speech" in which he impressed upon the minds of his audience "the necessity of enlisting in the service of their country, the result of which would be the total abolition of slavery throughout the United States." Upon adjournment, the colored "citizens" issued a call for volunteers.[28]

Despite repeated efforts to discourage them, the slaves expressed great interest in military service.[29] On November 5, 1863, the *Kansas City Daily Journal of Commerce* reported, "Everywhere throughout the State . . . the Negroes are coming forward with alacrity to enroll themselves in the service of the Government." On December 1, 1863, the *St. Louis Daily Missouri Democrat* observed, "The patriotic fever is running high among Africa's sable sons." Some of the slaves, aware that their masters might attempt to prevent them from enlisting, marched in arms to the recruiting station in St. Louis.[30] The slaves viewed army service as an avenue to immediate emancipation and their contribution to the destruction of the manacles that held them in bondage for so long. The Negroes were extremely proud of their uniforms (often they adorned their caps with miniature flags) because they symbolized the realization of their dream of freedom.[31]

Their noble dream was tarnished by Lincoln's indecision, the machinations of the slaveholders, and an ineffectual recruiting system. Consequently, Missouri furnished only 8,344 Negroes to serve in five regiments (665 were substitutes for whites who had been drafted). However, it should be noted that a majority of the Negroes recruited in Kansas, Illinois, and Iowa were runaway Missouri slaves.[32] The slaveholding minority, through various devices and some influence in the state government, was relatively successful in thwarting the desires of the majority of Missourians. The demand for the enlistment of slaves was great and challenging. In the choice of the elevation of the slave to the honorable position of a soldier or his subjugation as chattel, there was a startling contrast between popular desire and official performance; between the wide and valid support for the recognition of the slave as a warrior and the inability of governmental instruments and leaders to implement this desire.

NOTES

1. Lincoln to O. H. Browning, 22 September 1861, quoted in J. G. Randall, *Lincoln and the South* (Baton Rouge: Louisiana State University Press, 1946), 63.

2. William B. Hesseltine, *Lincoln and the War Governors* (New York: A. A. Knopf, 1948), 216; Hans C. Adamson, *Rebellion in Missouri, 1861: Nathaniel Lyon and His Army of the West* (Philadelphia: Chilton, 1961), vii-xii, 261-285; Lucien Carr, *Missouri: A Bone of Contention* (Boston: Houghton, Mifflin, 1888), 139-148, 241-342; James A. Woodburn, "The Historical Significance of the Missouri Compromise," *American Historical Association Annual Report, 1893* (Washington, DC: U.S. Government Printing Office, 1894), 251-297; *Dictionary of American Biography*, s.v. "Jackson, Claiborne Fox"; ibid., s.v. "Gamble, Hamilton Rowan."

3. Randall, *Lincoln and the South*, 49-80; Benjamin Quarles, *The Negro in the Civil War* (Boston: Little, Brown, 1953), 137-138; John G. Nicolay and John Hay, *Abraham Lincoln: A History* (New York: Century Co., 1886), 4: 416-420.

4. *Frankfort (KY) Commonwealth*, 16 March 1864; *Official Army Register of the Volunteer Force of the United States Army for the Years 1861, '62, '63, '64, '65*

(Washington, 1867), pt. 7: 246; Galusha Anderson, *The Story of a Border City During the Civil War* (Boston: Little, Brown, 1908), 218.

5. *St. Louis Daily Missouri Democrat*, 31 July, 17 August 1863; *Kansas City Daily Journal of Commerce*, 21, 29 August 1863; Perry S. Rader, *The Civil Government of the United States and the State of Missouri, and the History of Missouri* (Columbia, MO: E. W. Stephens, 1898), 357; Thomas W. Herringshaw, *Herringshaw's Encyclopedia of American Biography of the Nineteenth Century* (Chicago: American Publisher's Assoc., 1904), 124, 155, 889; William E. Parrish, *Turbulent Partnership: Missouri and the Union, 1861-1865* (Columbia: University of Missouri Press, 1963), 135-136.

6. The editors have chosen to continue the author's use of colored, instead of African American or black, in this article. Benjamin P. Thomas and Harold M. Hymand, *Stanton: The Life and Times of Lincoln's Secretary of War* (New York: Knopf, 1962), 263; General Orders, No. 143, 22 May 1863, *The War of the Rebellion: A Compilation of the Official Records of the Union and Confederate Armies* (Washington, DC: U.S. Government Printing Office, 1880-1901), ser. 3, vol. 3: 215 (hereinafter cited as *OR*).

7. Schofield to Adjutant General Lorenzo Thomas, 10 June 1863; Thomas to Colonel E. D. Townsend, 28 September 1863, both in "The Negro in the Military Service of the United States, 1639-1886," 3, pt. 1: 1311, 1626, Adjutant General's Office, Record Group 94, National Archives and Records Administration; Thomas to Pile, 13 June 1863, *OR*, ser. 3, vol. 3: 356; *St. Louis Daily Missouri Democrat*, 31 August 1863; Anderson, *Border City*, 218-219; John M. Schofield, *Forty-Six Years in the Army* (New York: Century, 1897), 69-76.

8. The Confiscation Act of July 17, 1862, provided that the slaves of persons engaged in, or in sympathy with, the rebellion within the jurisdiction of, escaping to, or captured by military authorities should be freed. The theory was that some of the slaves would be enlisted as soldiers. James G. Randall, *Constitutional Problems Under Lincoln* (Urbana: University of Illinois Press, 1951), 357-365; Schofield to Thomas, 26 September 1863, "Negro in the Military Service," 3, pt. 1: 1637-1638; *St. Louis Daily Missouri Democrat*, 24 August 1863; Thomas Ewing Jr. Papers, Library of Congress.

9. Schofield to Townsend; Lincoln to Schofield, 1 October 1863, both in "Negro in the Military Service," 3, pt. 1: 1631-1635, 1640; *Kansas City Daily Journal of Commerce*, 21 October 1863.

10. *St. Louis Daily Missouri Democrat*, 8 December 1863.

11. Stanton to Lincoln, 1 October 1863; Schofield to Stanton, 12 November 1863, both in "Negro in the Military Service," 3, pt. 1: 1642-1644, 1656, 1733-1734; Stanton to Schofield, *OR*, ser. 3, vol. 3: 1009; *Appletons' Annual Cyclopedia, 1863* (New York: Appleton, 1863), 3: 615.

12. Stanton to Schofield, 13 November 1863; General Orders, No. 135, Department of the Missouri, both in *OR*, ser. 3, vol. 3: 1032, 1034-1036; *St. Louis Daily Missouri*

Democrat, 16 November 1863; *Kansas City Daily Journal of Commerce*, 28 May 1864.

13. *St. Louis Daily Missouri Democrat*, 25 November, 22 December 1863; Samuel B. Harding, "Missouri Party Struggles in the Civil War Period," *American Historical Association Annual Report, 1900* (Washington, DC: U.S. Government Printing Office, 1901), 1: 85-103.

14. *St. Louis Daily Missouri Democrat*, 6, 11, 18, 24 January 1864; Schofield, *Forty-Six Years*, 69, 73-76, 108-110.

15. "Negro in the Military Service," 4: 2398; *Kansas City Daily Journal of Commerce*, 10 March 1864; *OR*, ser. 3, vol. 4: 499; Anderson, *Border City*, 319.

16. Rosecrans to Stanton, 23 March 1864; Thomas to Townsend, 29 April 1864; General Orders, Nos. 139 and 150, Department of the Missouri, all in "Negro in the Military Service," 4: 2424, 2740, 2749.

17. *St. Louis Daily Missouri Democrat*, 18 November, 7 December 1863; *Kansas City Daily Journal of Commerce*, 19 November, 22 December 1863.

18. *St. Louis Daily Missouri Democrat*, 4 September 1863.

19. Ibid., 2 September 1863.

20. Ibid., 5 September 1863; Samuel B. Harding, *Life of George R. Smith, Founder of Sedalia* (Sedalia, MO: privately printed, 1904), 343-353.

21. *St. Louis Daily Missouri Democrat*, 3 September 1863; *Appleton's Annual Cyclopedia, 1863*, 3: 655-657; Carl Sandburg, *Abraham Lincoln: The Prairie Years and the War Years* (New York: Harcourt, Brace, 1954), 425-429.

22. *St. Louis Daily Missouri Democrat*, 29 September 1863.

23. Ibid., 28 November 1863.

24. Walter Williams and Floyd Calvin Shoemaker, *Missouri: Mother of the West* (Chicago: American Historical Society, 1930), 2: 13-15.

25. *St. Louis Daily Missouri Democrat*, 5 January 1864.

26. Ibid., 22 December 1863, 5 January 1864; *Kansas City Daily Journal of Commerce*, 24, 28 January 1864; "Negro in the Military Service," 4: 2332-2336; Walter B. Stevens, *Missouri, The Center State, 1821-1915* (Chicago: S. J. Clarke, 1915), 1: 31.

27. *St. Louis Daily Missouri Democrat*, 5 January, 20 February, 16 July 1864; *Kansas City Daily Journal of Commerce*, 8 January 1864; Schofield to Thomas, 26 September 1863, Major General J. M. Palmer to Stanton, 3 April 1865, both in "Negro in the Military Service," 3, pt. 1: 1637-1638, 6: 3605-3606; Descriptive Books of the 18th, 62nd, 65th, 67th, and 68th U.S. Colored Troops (these were Missouri regiments), Adjutant General's Office, Record Group 94.

28. *Kansas City Daily Journal of Commerce*, 24 March 1864.

29. Ibid., 4 December 1863; Schofield to Thomas, 10 June 1863, Schofield to Townsend, 29 September 1863, Thomas to Townsend, 7 October 1863, all in "Negro in the Military Service," 3, pt. 1: 1311-1313, 1631-1635, 1662.

30. *Kansas City Daily Journal of Commerce*, 13 November 1863; *St. Louis Daily Missouri Democrat*, 21 January 1864.

31. *St. Louis Daily Missouri Democrat*, 5 January 1864; *Kansas City Daily Journal of Commerce*, 8 January 1864; Anderson, *Border City*, 181.

32. C. W. Foster, Chief, Bureau of Colored Troops, to Townsend, 20 October 1865, "Negro in the Military Service," 6: 3696-3718. Negro recruits were credited in varying numbers to the following towns: St. Louis, 670 (general rendezvous to which most slaves escaped); Jefferson City, 399; Louisiana, 356; Troy, 343; Macon, 292; Lexington, 272; Tipton, 267; Mexico, 213; Hannibal, 206; Glasgow, 193; Fayette, 172; Sedalia, 169; Marshall, 167; Carrollton, 165; Boonville, 231; Brunswick, 140; Fulton, 136; Wellsville, 110; Chillicothe, 105; Columbia, 103; Liberty, Potosi, Ironton, Kingston, St. Charles, Cape Girardeau, Springfield, Pilot Knob, and Washington had 40 or more. Descriptive Books, 18th, 62nd, 65th, 67th, and 68th U.S. Colored Troops.

Black Education in
Civil War St. Louis

LAWRENCE O. CHRISTENSEN

The Civil War inaugurated a period of change that greatly influenced patterns of life among St. Louis blacks. During the conflict, thousands of African Americans within zones of intense military activity found their lives disrupted. Many of them fled to St. Louis—some to stay, others to leave again.[1] All became free of slavery's restrictions. New organizations were established to help the victims of war, including wounded soldiers and refugees, both black and white. Various agencies concerned themselves with educating and Christianizing the freedmen. Unfortunately, the vast majority of the efforts, by their design, concentrated primarily on the immediate needs of the freedmen rather than on easing their transformation from slavery to freedom. With organizational aid, African American leaders created a system of free schools despite division within the black community. An absence of systematic planning, however, marred that and other wartime efforts on behalf of the freedmen.

The Western Sanitary Commission coordinated the work of the benevolent associations functioning in St. Louis during the war.[2] Although General John C. Frémont appointed the organization's commissioners and they worked closely with the military, the commission remained a private, charity-dispensing agency. As its name implied, it attempted to improve medical and dietary facilities for people affected directly by the war. The commission established hospitals to care for the wounded and the refugees, recruited nurses, inspected sanitary facilities in army camps, outfitted hospital ships and railroad cars, raised money to finance its operations, distributed tons of medical supplies

and clothing, and even dispensed jams and jellies contributed by concerned Unionists.[3]

According to its historian, J. G. Forman, the commission's efforts to aid freedmen were only incidental to its other varied activities. Commission agents naturally came into contact with freedmen through their investigations of army camps and during their numerous trips through the countryside transporting ill and wounded soldiers from the front to St. Louis hospitals. By the summer of 1863, the commission found itself transporting black refugees from southern camps to the city. Many of these freedmen soon became either Union soldiers or hired laborers in states farther north. Men rejected by the army and the families of African American soldiers, however, remained in St. Louis. With the aid of other agencies, the commission assumed some responsibility for those left behind. For example, it hired teachers and helped finance schools to educate the freedmen's children. In 1864 the Western Sanitary Commission purchased a site and financed construction of the Freedmen's Orphan Home in St. Louis. One contemporary estimated that the commission contributed a thousand dollars a month to the aid of freedmen living in the city.[4]

Two women's voluntary organizations cooperated closely with the commission's efforts on behalf of the freedmen. Both the Freedmen's Relief Society of St. Louis, organized in 1863, and the Ladies Union Aid Society helped the commission manage a refugee and freedmen's home established in the Lawson Hospital. The women made clothing, nursed the ill, prepared food, conducted a school, arranged transportation for the dislocated, and generally tried to assuage suffering. The Lawson Hospital project closed in July 1865, but the Freedmen's Relief Society continued operating through 1866.[5]

Additional aid for black St. Louisans came from the American Missionary Association. Founded in 1846 as an abolitionist organization, the AMA devoted itself to Christianizing and educating African Americans during the Civil War and Reconstruction periods. Although professing to be nondenominational, the association recruited most of its agents and received the largest amount of its financial support from Congregationalism. With most AMA agents adherents to Calvinistic faiths, they criticized the emotionalism of Episcopal Methodists and Baptists but reserved special disapprobation for Catholics.[6] At least one AMA agent had come to St. Louis prior to the war.[7]

White AMA missionaries encountered difficulties in Christianizing black immigrants to St. Louis. In 1863, for example, George Candee, a white AMA leader, noted that he had to compete for newly arrived blacks with three black Methodist and three black Baptist churches. According to Candee, the Second Baptist Church owned property valued at $15,000; the Second Methodist Church owned its property free and clear; and two other black churches owned their own buildings on leased land. The black preachers of each of these churches opened their doors to the new arrivals, and the black refugees obviously preferred to worship with their congregations. Mrs. E. A. Candee, who represented the AMA, reported a decided black prejudice against whites conducting their religious services. She discussed a black

Methodist congregation that, in order to retain its black pastor, disobeyed a denominational law that required each church to change its minister every two years. Mrs. Candee wrote that the church's congregation had once divided because it was supplied with a white preacher. In addition, AMA agents complained that African American refugees tended to scatter throughout the black community, making them difficult to identify and virtually impossible to assemble for missionary activities.[8]

Later, in 1863 and 1864, after the establishment of specific depots for black refugees, some AMA missionary activity became possible, but other work occupied the time of association agents. For example, George Candee accompanied a group of black refugees to Keokuk, Iowa, for the Contraband Relief Society, which was involved in a relocation program.[9] As it developed, the most important AMA efforts involved educating the freedmen.

Schools for St. Louis blacks predated the Civil War period. Although a city ordinance prohibited the education of African Americans, John Berry Meachum, a black minister, organized a school in the basement of his church during the 1820s. In 1845, St. Louis Catholics established a school for black girls that was forced to close not long after it began. After 1847, state law as well as city ordinance prohibited the teaching of black children, but in 1856 the Sisters of Mercy opened a school for them that, evidently, caused no ad-verse white reaction. Also, African American teachers organized subscription schools during the 1850s. In 1863, George Candee commented that four or five such schools had been operating in St. Louis for six or eight years.[10]

When Candee arrived in St. Louis, Hiram R. Revels was teaching one of the most successful subscription schools. Born in Fayetteville, North Carolina, perhaps in 1827, Revels became a barber as a teenager before at-tending Quaker schools in Indiana and Ohio during the 1840s. Between 1845 and 1847, Revels received ordination as an African Methodist Episcopal min-ister. He came to St. Louis to serve as the pastor of St. Paul's Chapel in 1854, but a dispute with the bishop resulted in Revels leaving the church for a Presbyterian church in Baltimore, Maryland. He stayed in Maryland for two years before enrolling in Knox College in Galesburg, Illinois. When J. L. Richardson came to St. Louis in 1863, Revels taught the largest of the city's subscription schools for African Americans. He continued to teach a subscrip-tion school during a part of 1864, but then he apparently moved to Mississippi. In 1870, Revels won election to the U.S. Senate from Mississippi, becoming the first African American elected to that body.[11]

Although subscription schools, including the one conducted by Revels, remained an avenue for black education, the first organized efforts to reach all of St. Louis's black children involved the combined, but not always congenial, participation of the AMA, the Western Sanitary Commission, other benevolent agencies, and the African American community.[12] These endeavors encountered several difficulties along the way. Teachers who had already established subscription schools naturally objected to the development of a system of free schools, and black parents expressed a preference for black teachers in their schools.[13] Some whites objected to blacks receiving an education, and those interested in establishing schools for African Americans found it difficult to obtain the necessary quarters. Tensions developed between long-standing black residents and more recent arrivals. Moreover, poverty plagued efforts to create black schools. The school board for free black schools lacked sufficient funds to support their schools adequately, and the children sometimes stayed home because they had no clothes to wear. Although such difficulties continued to hinder the development of a viable system of black education, progress did occur between 1863 and 1865.

Much of the progress can be attributed to the cooperation among those people and organizations interested in the future of African Americans. For example, in 1863 the first AMA school opened at the contraband headquarters in the Missouri Hotel. According to the AMA school's teacher, J. L. Richardson, money and books came from the women of the contraband society (probably

The Missouri Hotel, built and opened prior to statehood, was an important landmark in St. Louis. The state's first legislature convened there.

the Freedmen's Relief Society of St. Louis).[14] Later, Richardson located a large room that would accommodate three hundred to four hundred students. The Switzerland Penny Society, a European aid society established to promote black education, paid the rent on that room and another. In addition, the Western Sanitary Commission supported a school taught by a soldier's wife at Benton Barracks.[15] A combined military and civilian concern for the freedmen was also evident in Major Lucien Eaton and his wife, Emily. As a member of the military, Lucien served as a liaison between the army and various civilian agencies, and Emily supervised the Freedmen's Relief Society in the city.[16] A pattern eventually emerged in these cooperative efforts: the Western Sanitary Commission provided funds for rent and, occasionally, for teachers' salaries; the AMA recruited and paid the teachers; and the army frequently supplied rations and housing for people connected with the black schools.[17]

At the end of 1863, as a means of coordinating efforts, black ministers, AMA representatives, members of the Western Sanitary Commission, and other whites created a school board. Through contributions from benevolent associations and individuals, the board hoped to establish a system of free schools for African American children. Since earlier attempts at organization had proved frustrating, individuals concerned about black education held a public meeting and appointed ten African Americans to a board, who in turn had the power to select three white men to act with them. The board's membership reflected the importance of black and white ministers in working with St. Louis blacks. M. M. Clark, a black African Methodist Episcopal minister, served as president of the board. Three other black members and two of the three white members also preached either full-time or part-time. Truman Post, the white minister of the First Congregational Church, and Galusha Anderson, the white minister of the Second Baptist Church, both served on the board. Candee, the chief AMA representative in St. Louis and also a white minister, reluctantly accepted appointment as the superintendent of the black schools.[18]

Organized as an interim, voluntary body to recruit teachers, raise money, and dispense available funds until the Missouri General Assembly could create a school system for African Americans, the school board had little power and few funds with which to carry out its responsibilities. A shortage of money remained critical throughout the board's life. In March 1864, Candee, who had hired only two teachers because of a shortage of funds, solicited the AMA for money. By February 1865 the board had been in existence for a year. In that time it had organized only four schools. Support for these schools had come from the Western Sanitary Commission, miscellaneous contributions, and AMA assistance. Total expenditures averaged only $350 per month.

The Reverend J. F. Boulden, a member of the African American school board, served as a pastor in St. Louis from 1863 to 1865.

Recognizing its problems, the board petitioned the city board of education to take over the black schools, or at least to contribute funds for their support. The city board responded with $500 later in 1865, but the funds came too late to prevent the black schools from closing temporarily both in February and March. Sara G. Stanley, a salaried AMA teacher in a board-controlled school, reported in late March 1865 that operating expenses would have to be paid by her students if the school remained open.[19]

The lack of funds further complicated another board problem. While the AMA was attempting to organize schools, four subscription schools operated by African American teachers continued to function. In addition to Hiram Revels, who taught the best-attended school, the black teachers included Josephine Bailey, Virginia Green, and Georgia L. Buckner. According to AMA teacher J. L. Richardson, all three women had attended Oberlin College.[20] Perhaps his information was accurate, but none of them had graduated from Oberlin. The first black woman to graduate from that school, Jane Patterson, did so in 1862. Not until 1867 did another black woman earn a degree from Oberlin. According to Oberlin records, a Georgia L. Buckner from St. Louis was a student in the Preparatory Department from 1857 through 1860.[21] Perhaps the other two women had also attended Oberlin's Preparatory Department.

The subscription schools held their classes in black churches and could operate on a tuition of about one dollar a month. To organize a system of free schools, the board thought it advisable to incorporate these private establishments into its organization. Although the teachers expressed a cooperative attitude, the board failed to raise sufficient money to pay salaries equivalent to what the teachers earned in their private endeavors.[22] The free schools tended to attract students away from the subscription schools without the board being financially able to employ the private teachers at adequate remuneration. The teachers of subscription schools thus became opposed to the board, and in October 1865 three of the pay schools continued to operate.[23]

This successful competition from tuition schools can be partially explained on the basis of color. Until Bailey and Buckner agreed to work for the school board, all of the AMA teachers were white. George Candee, who recognized black St. Louisans' preference for black teachers, called it a great obstacle and advised that the AMA try to find an African American to assume the superintendent's position. On another occasion, he requested that the AMA pay the salary of a black preacher at Benton Barracks, another contraband center. Although Revels initially agreed to come under the board's auspices, he wanted more money than the board could or would pay. He later agreed to accept the board's offer, but because friends objected, he reversed his previous decision. Candee reported on the negotiations with Revels, but he failed to elaborate further on the outcome.[24] Enough black St. Louisans obviously had the financial means to send their children to schools taught by black teachers to keep the subscription schools in operation.

The black-controlled board resolved that "the educational interests of the colored children in this city and state require that the schools be taught by colored teachers as far as practicable."[25] Nevertheless, according to Candee and Galusha Anderson, with well-educated black teachers such as Revels able to do better financially by operating subscription schools, the board experienced difficulty in hiring good black teachers.[26] Candee apparently evinced little prejudice against hiring black teachers, since he had attempted to persuade Revels to come under the board's supervision and advocated hiring a black superintendent to replace himself. The board's desire to hire blacks led to the replacement of a white teacher, who later taught in the St. Louis public school system, with an African American. Candee expressed dissatisfaction with the board's action and wrote that his hopes of establishing schools with first-class teachers of whatever color had disappeared.[27]

Although the board had early stated its preference for black teachers, it invited A. K. Spence, a white AMA teacher, to interview for the superintendent's position. Only one board member dissented from extending the invitation. On the night scheduled for Spence's interview, however, too few board members attended to provide the necessary quorum for a legal meeting. With

Hiram Revels, later the first African American U.S. senator, taught a subscription school in St. Louis during the early years of the Civil War. [*Dictionary of American Portraits*, Library of Congress, Brady Collection]

the board comprising ten blacks and three whites, obviously a large number of black members did not want a white superintendent. Candee advised the AMA to withdraw from the city because of the incident. Optimistically, he reported, "By a united effort I think the Board can run the schools of this city after a fashion even on an exclusively colored basis."[28]

While blacks worried about whether white or black teachers taught their children, some whites actively opposed any black schools. Since the state legislature waited until February 1865 to repeal legislation prohibiting the teaching of African Americans, those hostile to black education had the law on their side during much of the Civil War.[29] When officials failed to enforce the prohibition, activists took matters into their own hands. In the spring of 1863, unknown persons burned an AMA school only three days after it began holding classes.[30] During 1864, AMA teachers received military protection for their schools and students. The guards prevented "such annoyances as having our schollars [*sic*] stoned on their way home, our windows broken and hideous noises in our basement if the door was [*sic*] not kept locked." The Protestant teacher, Lydia Hess, blamed Irish Catholics for the harassment.[31]

The white AMA teachers, who described St. Louis as providing a hostile working environment, did encounter difficulties. One asserted that professed Union people opposed teaching African American children. Another wrote that even antislavery people objected to educating blacks. Antagonistic white attitudes perhaps caused one AMA teacher to experience problems in finding an available schoolroom.[32] Another teacher refused to hold classes in a dilapidated room provided by the independent board.[33] Sara G. Stanley described one of the board's rooms:

> The day after my arrival here, I found my way to the school to which I had been assigned. It was in the basement of one of the colored churches, and perhaps not more disagreeable and unattractive in its surrounding and appointments than might have been expected from its subterranean location; yet when I first beheld it, I recoiled with a shiver that could not be repressed. . . . On opening the door nothing was immediately perceptible, but as the eye gradually became accostomed [*sic*] to the darkness, I was enabled to discern a long low room, furnished with ungainly moveible [*sic*] seats and containing perhaps one hundred and fifty children. It was bare and dreary, the smoked and blackened wall unrelieved by a single map . . . or black board. Through the dusty windows the dim light struggled for admission, and the chill March wind found entrance through numberless broken panes.[34]

Stanley called this the best of the three black schoolrooms.[35] While a shortage of funds for the rental of adequate quarters and the city's great increase in African American population partially accounted for the inadequate school facilities, white prejudice against black education must also have been a factor.[36]

Often young, quite idealistic, and strongly Protestant, the AMA teachers may have magnified their problems.[37] Even when those factors are taken into consideration, however, the teachers in St. Louis's free black schools needed a strong commitment to face their tasks. Facilities and students offered them little. A lack of clothes and of money for tuition fees prevented the poorer African American students from attending the subscription schools. During May, enrollments sometimes increased in the free schools because the students who had "been housed up during the winter months, for want of proper clothing, especially shoes," could attend during the warmer weather.[38] In the fall of 1865, Lydia Hess conducted a house-to-house survey of black homes and reported over one hundred families too poor to send their children to school. The financially embarrassed black school board could not furnish free books, and many black families used all their available money to feed, clothe, and house themselves.[39]

More prosperous African Americans sent their children to either the subscription schools or Catholic schools. Estimated enrollments in the subscription schools varied from 350 in December 1863 to 187 in February 1864. This large reduction within a few months may be attributed to the attraction of tuition-free schools the black school board had organized in December

*Poverty prevented numerous African American children from
attending the free schools. Many were forced to work to help
support their families; others lacked essential clothes and shoes.*

1863.[40] In October 1865, however, sufficient students paid one and one-half
dollars a month to support three black pay schools.[41]

Black Catholics formed a small but prosperous group in St. Louis.[42]
Candee called them "some of the wealthiest colored men in the city." Most
Catholic students attended parochial schools, but at least one Catholic parent complained that the Catholic schools gave African American students
only a limited education, and he asked that the AMA establish a school in his
neighborhood.[43] A year later, however, another AMA teacher reported that
the black Catholics utterly opposed the free schools, perhaps partly because
of their strong Protestant flavor.[44]

In addition to Catholic opposition to free schools, subscription schools
continued to exist because of the distaste that many African American residents of long standing expressed for the newer arrivals. Children of recent
migrants composed a large portion of the free-school population. According
to one observer, these students manifested little cultivation and had "rough
uncouth habits." The more affluent black population did not want contact
between their children and the sons and daughters of the newcomers.[45] In his
1858 book, *The Colored Aristocracy of St. Louis*, Cyprian Clamorgan, a free
African American barber, described the aristocratic pretensions of prosperous
black St. Louisans: "A bare suspicion of former disregard of the proprieties
of life should exclude a family from familiar intercourse with an aristocratic

circle." Clamorgan also suggested that the black aristocrats followed a stricter code than white society, which frequently allowed a "full purse" to cover a "multitude of sins."[46]

During the period of transition from slavery to freedom, with such diverse elements brought together, conflicts and deep frustrations over the first efforts to educate African American children on a massive scale naturally occurred. Clamorgan's book suggests one basis for conflict within the black community. Moreover, white antagonism toward blacks assuming new roles in society added another dimension of conflict.[47] Some of those most intimately involved in educating the freedmen thought of their efforts as a failure.[48] AMA teachers may have expressed such frustration because of chronic absenteeism or a constantly changing student body in their schools. One teacher estimated the student population in board-controlled schools at 700 in January 1865. One month later the board president calculated that 600 students were attending the schools. In 1865 the white St. Louis Board of Directors of Public Schools estimated that 1,500 students had attended the non-tax-supported, free black schools.[49]

Whatever the actual number, despite the conflicts among blacks, among whites, and between blacks and whites resulting from the sometimes frustrating situation, progress occurred between 1863 and 1865. The cooperative efforts of the various white organizations and the African American community furnished more black students with the rudiments of an education than would otherwise have been possible. As a provider of teachers and a catalyst within the white community, the American Missionary Association must be credited with making a great contribution to this progress. Through the combined work of leading African Americans, the AMA, and other whites, the independent education board was created. It served as a focus for those concerned with black education. It facilitated the coming together of blacks and whites who confronted the problems, debated solutions, and finally united to pressure the city board of education to first support black schools and then, in 1866, to assume responsibility for them.[50]

NOTES

1. J. G. Forman, *The Western Sanitary Commission: A Sketch* (St. Louis: R. P. Studley, 1864), 110; James W. Goodrich, ed., "The Civil War Letters of Bethiah Pyatt McKown, Part I," *Missouri Historical Review* 67 (January 1973): 247.

2. Galusha Anderson, *The Story of a Border City During the Civil War* (Boston:

Little, Brown, 1908), 295. The commission's semiofficial standing and ability to raise huge sums of money gave it this status.

3. Forman, *Western Sanitary Commission*, 5-10; J. Thomas Scharf, *History of St. Louis City and County* (Philadelphia: Louis H. Everts, 1883), 1: 541-543.

4. Forman, *Western Sanitary Commission*, 5, 95, 134; Scharf, *History*, 1: 548-549; Anderson, *Border City*, 314.

5. Forman, *Western Sanitary Commission*, 132-134; Scharf, *History*, 1: 547; Anderson, *Border City*, 294; *St. Louis Directory* (St. Louis: Holland and Thorp, 1866-1867), 193-194.

6. Clifton H. Johnson, *American Missionary Association Archives as a Source for the Study of American History* (New York: Division of Higher Education of the United Church Board for Homeland Ministries and American Missionary Association, 1964), 1-5. See also Clifton H. Johnson, "The American Missionary Association, 1846-1861: A Study of Christian Abolitionism" (PhD diss., University of North Carolina, 1958).

7. G. H. Pool to S. S. Jocelyn, 4 May 1859, American Missionary Association Archives, Amistad Research Center, Tulane University, New Orleans. Unless otherwise noted, all letters cited in this article are found in the AMA Archives. See Joe M. Richardson, "The American Missionary Association and Black Education in Civil War Missouri," *Missouri Historical Review* 69 (July 1975): 433-448, for more information about statewide AMA activities.

8. George Candee to Jocelyn, 26 March, 7 April 1863; J. L. Richardson to Jocelyn, 9 November 1863; Mrs. E. A. Candee to Jocelyn, 31 July 1863.

9. Candee to Jocelyn, 26 March, 18 September 1863. Candee reported that a Miss McBeth had established an AMA mission at Jefferson Barracks.

10. N. Webster Moore, "John Berry Meachum (1789-1854): St. Louis Pioneer, Black Abolitionist, Educator, and Preacher," *Bulletin of the Missouri Historical Society* 29 (January 1973): 99-100; George E. Stevens, *History of the Central Baptist Church* (St. Louis: King Publishing, 1927), 7; Daniel M. Hogan, "The Catholic Church and the Negroes of Saint Louis" (master's thesis, Saint Louis University, 1955), 18; William Bar[na]by Faherty, *The Catholic Ancestry of St. Louis* (St. Louis: Bureau of Information, Archdiocese of St. Louis, 1965), 25; George Candee to Jocelyn, 7 April 1863; William E. Parrish, *Missouri Under Radical Rule, 1865-1870* (Columbia: University of Missouri Press, 1965), 118.

11. *American National Biography* (New York: Oxford University Press, 1999), s.v. "Revels, Hiram Rhoads"; *Indianapolis Freeman*, 7 March 1891; J. L. Richardson to Jocelyn, 29 October 1863; George Candee to Jocelyn, 16 March 1864.

12. Other investigators have overlooked the AMA's full contribution to black education in St. Louis during this period. Pauline Dingle Knobbs, "The Development of the Separate System of Education in Missouri" (PhD diss., George Peabody College for Teachers, 1946), 93-94, noted the association's presence but devoted little space to its work. Most writers have credited the AMA's work to the Western Sanitary

Commission. See Parrish, *Missouri Under Radical Rule*, 118-121; Scharf, *History*, 1: 548-549; J. W. Evans, "A Brief Sketch of the Development of Negro Education in St. Louis, Missouri," *Journal of Negro Education* 7 (October 1938): 540-551; George L. Mann, "The Development of Public Education for Negroes in Saint Louis, Missouri" (PhD diss., Indiana University, 1949), 101; Robert I. Brigham, "The Education of the Negro in Missouri" (PhD diss., University of Missouri-Columbia, 1946), 80-81.

13. Jobs for African American teachers figured prominently in this preference.

14. J. L. Richardson to Jocelyn, 10 April 1863; Forman, *Western Sanitary Commission*, 133.

15. J. L. Richardson to Jocelyn, 16 May, 21 October, 9 November 1863; George Candee to Jocelyn, 2 November 1863.

16. Katherine A. Dunning to George L. Whipple, 1 October 1864. Emily Eaton served as a vice president of the organization and became president in 1866. See also Forman, *Western Sanitary Commission*, 133; Lucien Eaton to Whipple, 28 December 1864.

17. George Candee to Jocelyn, 16 March 1864; M. M. Clark to Whipple, 17 November 1864; George L. Booth to Secretaries of the AMA, 26 November 1864.

18. George Candee to Jocelyn, 5 February, 16 March 1864; "The St. Louis Board of Education for Free Colored Schools," AMA Archives. In addition to Clark, the other black board members were Reverend J. F. Boulden, Second Baptist Church; Reverend Jordan W. Early, a part-time minister and tavern keeper; Reverend James A. Jones, a part-time minister and laborer; William P. Brooks, owner of a woodyard; Preston G. Wells, a barber; William N. Evans, a drayman; H. McGee Alexander, a storekeeper; William Robinson, a porter; and E. Pines, a bank porter. The other white member was Samuel Davis, of whom nothing further is known. For the occupations of the black members, see *Edwards' St. Louis Directory for 1864* (St. Louis: Richard Edwards, 1864), 117, 159, 180, 219, 227, 317, 438, 458, 555.

19. George Candee to Jocelyn, 30 November 1863, 16 March 1864; "St. Louis Board of Education for Free Colored Schools"; M. M. Clark to Whipple, 2 February 1865; D. N. Goodrich Jr. to M. E. Strieby, 17 February 1865; *Eleventh Annual Report of the Board of Directors, St. Louis Public Schools* (St. Louis: R. P. Studley, 1865), 26; Green Wilkerson to Strieby, 28 February 1865; Sara G. Stanley to Whipple, 27 March 1865.

20. J. L. Richardson to Jocelyn, 19 December 1863.

21. W. E. Biggleston, archivist of Oberlin College, to the author, 18 August 1969.

22. J. L. Richardson to Jocelyn, 29 October 1863; Lydia A. Hess to Jocelyn, 12 September 1863; George Candee to Jocelyn, 16 March 1864; George Candee to AMA Secretary, n.d. Revels chaired the meeting to establish the board.

23. George Candee to Jocelyn, 5 February 1864; Lydia A. Hess to Strieby, 3

October 1865.

24. Lydia A. Hess to Jocelyn, 29 March 1864; George Candee to Whipple, 1 June 1864; George Candee to Jocelyn, 18 September 1863, 16, 25 March, 8 April 1864.

25. George Candee to Whipple, 1 June 1864.

26. George Candee to Jocelyn, 8 April 1864; George Candee to Whipple, 1 June 1864; Anderson, *Border City*, 335. J. L. Richardson described the four black subscription schoolteachers, Revels, Green, Bailey, and Buckner, as "good as a class" and commented that Revels in particular was well educated. Richardson to Jocelyn, 29 October 1863.

27. George Candee to Jocelyn, 2 May, 1 June 1864. Candee reported that Lizzie Montague had been replaced. According to the *Fourteenth Annual Report of the Board of Directors, St. Louis Public Schools* (St. Louis: George Knapp, 1868), lxvii, Montague had been employed, and according to the *Eighteenth Annual Report of the Board of Directors, St. Louis Public Schools* (St. Louis: Democrat Litho. and Printing, 1873), cli, she continued to teach in the St. Louis public schools.

28. George Candee to Whipple, 8, 22 June 1864. White board members T. M. Post and Galusha Anderson wanted African Americans to teach and administer the black schools, but they wanted the quality kept high. T. M. Post to A. K. Spence, 2 May 1864.

29. Evans, "Development of Negro Education," 551.

30. J. L. Richardson to Jocelyn, 22 May 1863. Richardson attributed the act to "low wicked boys most likely backed by secesh men."

31. Hess to Jocelyn, 29 March 1864.

32. J. L. Richardson to Jocelyn, 5 June 1863; Lydia A. Hess to Jocelyn, 29 August, 12 September 1863.

33. D. N. Goodrich Jr. to Strieby, 17 February 1865. Goodrich said the rejected room was the worst in the city but added, "None of their school rooms are very good, though I presume they are as good as they can obtain."

34. Stanley to Whipple, May 1865; David M. Reimers, *White Protestantism and the Negro* (New York: Oxford University Press, 1965), 20. Reimers describes many of the southern AMA schools as flimsy.

35. Stanley to Whipple, 25 March 1865.

36. *Jefferson City People's Tribune*, 8 August 1866. The paper reported that a "just completed" St. Louis census showed a black population of 9,827. In 1860 the city's black population had numbered 3,297. U.S. Bureau of the Census, *Ninth Census of the United States: 1870* (Washington, DC: Government Printing Office, 1872), 1: 194.

37. Sara G. Stanley to Whipple, 25 March 1865. Stanley, a white woman, came to St. Louis from Oberlin College, where she had been a student.

38. Lydia A. Hess to Jocelyn, 12 September 1863; Hess to Samuel Hunt, 28 May 1866; Sara G. Stanley to Whipple, May 1865. In May 1865, Stanley recorded a decrease in attendance because her students worked as servants to aid their indigent families. Whether the enrollment increased or decreased, the indigence remained.

39. Hess to Strieby, 3 October 1865; Lucien Eaton to Whipple, 28 December 1864; J. G. Forman, secretary of the Western Sanitary Commission, to Strieby, 22 February 1865. Both Eaton, whose wife headed the Freedmen's Relief Society, and Forman, who served as superintendent of refugees and freedmen, asked that AMA workers remain in the city to help ease the African Americans' destitution. Forman said, "The care of these people is not half provided for by the W. S. Commission, by the Government, or by Voluntary Associations."

40. J. L. Richardson to Jocelyn, 19 December 1863; George Candee to Jocelyn, 5 February 1864. Candee listed enrollments in the following subscription schools: Mrs. Green, 27; Mr. Revels, 100; Mrs. Bailey, 35; and Miss Buckner, 25. Buckner had told Candee she had recently lost 25 students. Candee also wrote that J. L. Richardson had induced tuition-paying students to attend his free school.

41. Lydia A. Hess to Strieby, 3 October 1865. Tuition fees rose from a dollar per month in 1863 to one and one-half dollars per month in 1865.

42. Cyprian Clamorgan, *The Colored Aristocracy of St. Louis* (St. Louis: n.p., 1858), 7, 13, 15. Clamorgan noted that three of his aristocrats were Catholic. According to him, the richest St. Louis African American, Mrs. Pelagic Rutgers, belonged to that church, as did Louis Charleville and Mrs. Nancy Lyons. Others with French names listed by Clamorgan may have also been Catholics, including Antoine Labadie, Mrs. Margaret Beauvais, and Antoine Crakin.

43. George Candee to Jocelyn, 30 November 1863.

44. George L. Booth to Secretaries of the AMA, 2 October 1864; Reimers, *White Protestantism*, 21. Reimers said that the AMA schools conveyed a denominational flavor: "The primary schools themselves taught a heavy dose of religion; the teachers used the Bible to teach Christianity along with spelling."

45. L. A. N. Montague to Jocelyn, 30 March 1864.

46. Clamorgan, *Colored Aristocracy*, 16.

47. Even all the AMA people did not cooperate. At one point, J. L. Richardson refused to accept the black school board's direction, and at the same time, he came into conflict with the pay schools by inducing students away from them. George Candee to Jocelyn, 25 March, 5 February 1864; M. M. Clark to Jocelyn, 15 March 1864. Clark, president of the black school board, said that Richardson's removal would facilitate the free school movement.

48. Green Wilkerson to Strieby, 28 February 1865; Lydia A. Hess to Strieby, 1 August 1865; Sara G. Stanley to Whipple, 25 March 1865. Stanley said her first task upon arriving in St. Louis was to "remove the pernicious influence of incompetent teachers." Hess wrote that Major Lucien Eaton and the Reverend Galusha Anderson

thought that "colored schools taught last winter came near being a failure."

49. George L. Booth to Whipple, 8 January 1865; M. M. Clark to Whipple, 2 February 1865; *Eleventh Annual Report of the Board of Directors*, 26.

50. Anderson, *Border City*, 336.

"This Noble and Philanthropic Enterprise": The Mississippi Valley Sanitary Fair of 1864 and the Practice of Civil War Philanthropy

ROBERT PATRICK BENDER

By the summer of 1863, civilian morale in the North had suffered serious setbacks. Although the Union armies achieved important strategic victories at both Gettysburg and Vicksburg, the war's tremendous human cost began to tax Northern patience. Resentment over the draft, as both an intrusive governmental action and a blatant example of class bias, caused public demonstrations to increase in both frequency and violence. In addition to the infamous draft riots in New York City, similar disturbances broke out in other Northern communities. The frustration and violence expressed in demonstrations at remote locations like Port Washington, Wisconsin, in November 1862 signified the public's war-weariness.[1]

At the same time, a number of volunteer civilian relief agencies began to run desperately low on the funds necessary to continue their philanthropic work. The executive committee of the Western Sanitary Commission, for example, seriously questioned their ability to continue operations beyond 1864, due to the considerable expense required to administer the many programs and facilities under their supervision. In addition, public misconceptions about the integrity of professional charity organizations led to mistaken suspicions about misappropriation of relief funds and other gifts.[2]

In the wake of these social, political, and financial considerations, philanthropic leaders across the North turned to a successful fund-raising tradition of the antebellum charity movement. They organized charity fairs, which immediately became known as "sanitary fairs" because of their association with various sanitary relief societies. The sanitary fairs of the Civil War served at least four purposes. First, the carnival-like atmosphere of the fairs provided a critical psychological diversion that helped restore morale among Northern civilians. Second, they raised enormous amounts of money, which funded the work of several relief agencies for the remainder of the war. Third, the events helped educate the public about the broad scope of work undertaken by relief organizations, which helped alleviate concerns about the misappropriation of funds and materials. Finally, sanitary fairs assisted relief agencies in the recruitment of sorely needed volunteers to serve in their programs.[3]

An examination of Civil War sanitary fairs also serves as a window through which the influence of larger ideological concepts on aspects of everyday life can be viewed. The debate between proponents of centralization and of localism, for example, found expression in many aspects of nineteenth-century life. In addition to the great political issues of the day, including the extension and expansion of slavery and the philosophy of states' rights, the debate that resulted from these conflicting concepts affected numerous facets of life. It was, as historian William E. Gienapp noted, an age in which all issues took on an increased political identity.

The political nature of this division was apparent in the contentious and competitive relationship that developed between the Western Sanitary Commission (WSC) and the United States Sanitary Commission (USSC). Although both organizations worked to improve medical care in support of the Union war effort, they differed greatly in their views about the nature of philanthropy and the future direction of public relief work. As the most public expression of each organization's beliefs about the essence of philanthropy, sanitary fairs exhibit how the debate over centralization and localism affected wartime relief work. In recent years, some very fine scholarship has focused on various aspects of the USSC's role in the development of modern philanthropic thought and practice. Jeanie Attie has researched how gender influenced both the success and internal divisions of the USSC. J. Matthew Gallman produced a thorough study of the USSC's Philadelphia branch office and its relationship with the central office. Aside from a fine article by historian William Parrish, however, the perspective of the WSC has largely been overlooked. Examining the issue from the perspective of the Western Sanitary Commission helps explain its persistent defense of autonomous work in the context of the wartime sanitary fair movement.[4]

In the fall of 1863, Chicago's "Northwestern" branch of the U.S. Sanitary Commission hosted the first sanitary fair of the war. Billed as the Great Northwestern Sanitary Fair, this twelve-day event cleared a net profit of "nearly eighty thousand dollars" before it ended. Although modest compared to the sums raised at subsequent fairs, the Chicago event demonstrated that sanitary fairs appealed to a broad segment of the Northern public. Participation in sanitary fairs offered Union citizens the opportunity to make a perceptible contribution to the war effort. Consequently, the fairs quickly became fashionable and developed national popularity. Communities from New York to Iowa soon planned similar events. Historians of Civil War philanthropy estimate that Northern communities organized as many as thirty charity fairs between 1863 and 1865. The pinnacle of the sanitary fair movement occurred between the spring and fall of 1864, when thirteen significant fairs took place.[5]

Whether hosted by a small community or a major metropolis, a national relief agency or state and local societies, all of the wartime fairs had similar characteristics. For example, many communities were influenced by prewar ideas about local philanthropic responsibility. Most wartime fairs closely re- sembled the local fairs that had proliferated before the war. Local authority remained an important theme, and local participation helped alleviate suspi- cions about the misappropriation of funds. Support came from all over and added to the sense of extended community. The city of St. Louis proved no exception. Taking their cue from the success achieved by cities in the East and upper Midwest, the leading philanthropists of St. Louis organized the Mississippi Valley Sanitary Fair in the spring of 1864.[6]

As with all such undertakings, the fair required a great deal of planning prior to the opening of festivities. The St. Louis Ladies Union Aid Society (LUAS) called for "a General meeting of the Loyal Men and Women of St. Louis." This gathering occurred on February 1, 1864, in the recently complet- ed Mercantile Library Hall to elect officers, appoint an executive committee,

Entrance to the Mississippi Valley Sanitary Fair [St. Louis Mercantile Library, University of Missouri-St. Louis]

William Greenleaf Eliot was a prominent nineteenth-century educator and religious leader in St. Louis. His accomplishments included publishing several books and founding Washington University.

and make other arrangements for "a Grand Mississippi Valley Sanitary Fair" that would take place in May of that year.[7]

Although initiated by the Ladies Union Aid Society, no single organization exercised more influence over the planning and execution of "this noble and philanthropic enterprise" than the St. Louis-based Western Sanitary Commission. The five-man executive committee of the WSC, which included James E. Yeatman, Carlos S. Greeley, Dr. John B. Johnson, George Partridge, and Rev. William Greenleaf Eliot, served as the fair's standing committee. The standing committee represented the interests of the WSC, the sole beneficiary of the fair's profits. Yeatman, a longtime leader among Missouri's philanthropic elite and president of the WSC since its inception in 1861, also served as chairman of the fair's thirty-one-member executive committee of gentlemen. This committee handled the planning, organization, and daily management of the event. Because of his social prominence and experience with benevolent work, Yeatman's leadership on both committees substantially increased the influence of the WSC. Individual departments were created to supervise specific elements of the fair and reported to the executive committee through their respective chairmen. Within this organizational structure, the WSC exercised a defining influence over the character and operation of the fair.[8]

As a result of this influence, the St. Louis fair inherited many of the characteristics of the WSC-USSC rivalry. The competition began immediately after the two agencies came into existence and intensified throughout the war, despite periodic public efforts intended to foster a more cooperative relationship. The U.S. Sanitary Commission, founded in June 1861, viewed its theories and practices as the most modern and efficient in the field of benevolence. Dominated by the social and intellectual elite of the East Coast, the USSC soon earned a reputation for self-righteousness, condescension, intolerance, and an underappreciation of relief needs beyond the Eastern theater. The philanthropic demands of the Trans-Mississippi and Western theaters grew significantly while the USSC paid little attention. As a result, several philanthropic leaders in St. Louis received permission from Major General John C. Frémont to form the Western Sanitary Commission in September 1861.[9]

To Eliot and Yeatman, the spiritual and practical leaders of the WSC, local authority over charitable matters represented a crucial facet of philanthropic work. It signified a community's acceptance of its Christian and civic duty to care for its less fortunate residents. To subordinate their organization to an outside influence amounted to a public admission that they either could not or would not provide the necessary aid. The USSC, however, viewed local or regional relief efforts as inefficient obstacles that interfered with the creation of a national program of centrally coordinated relief. The USSC sought to eliminate the WSC or force the upstart Missouri agency to serve under its authority. In the fall of 1861, the USSC convinced Secretary of War Simon Cameron to rescind Frémont's order. Eliot, however, persuaded Cameron and his successor, Edwin M. Stanton, to support the Western Sanitary Commission's independent status. The USSC then attempted to bring the St. Louis-based agency into its organization. Frederick Law Olmsted, general secretary of the USSC and its most stringent proponent of centralized administration, invited the Missouri agency to become a branch society with nominal independence. The WSC rejected this offer in a unanimous decision. "Whatever we could do as a sub-committee or branch of your Commission," Yeatman informed the USSC, "we can do equally well, or better, retaining our present organization." Although willing to cooperate with the national commission, the Western Sanitary Commission insisted on autonomy.[10] The U.S. Sanitary Commission publicly accepted this decision, but its members continued to express private indignation over the perceived threat to its mission. From this point onward, the two organizations remained suspicious of each other—especially concerning money.[11]

The Western Sanitary Commission soon found itself at the vanguard of resistance to the national commission and its concept of highly centralized public relief work. Animosity did not subside with the advent of sanitary fairs. In fact, the fairs quickly developed into a subtle battleground in this debate, as each agency sought to demonstrate the superiority of its own style of organization. The Mississippi Valley Sanitary Fair offered the WSC an opportunity to answer USSC criticisms and to publicize the broad and innovative scope of its work while highlighting the value of a relief operation that attempted to balance the ideas and practices of localism and centralization. With "a whole community at . . . work," Yeatman believed the St. Louis fair would demonstrate the value of the WSC and its vision of public relief work.[12]

While the Mississippi Valley Sanitary Fair remained the only such venture west of the Mississippi River sponsored by a major charitable relief agency, it proved to be one of the most successful fund-raising efforts of the war. Indeed, the St. Louis fair ranked third in terms of profits, behind only the Great Central Sanitary Fair of Philadelphia and the Metropolitan Sanitary Fair of New York.[13]

In addition to the leadership provided by the sanitary commission's executive committee, several prominent military, civil, and religious leaders from the community participated in planning the St. Louis fair. They included Brigadier General Clinton B. Fisk, former and current mayors Chauncey I. Filley and James S. Thomas, the Reverend Doctors Henry A. Nelson and T. M. Post, "and the other pastors of the city." Prominent national leaders, including President Abraham Lincoln and Vice President Hannibal Hamlin, were named honorary members of the fair, and Major General William S. Rosecrans served as president.[14]

Fair officials arranged with the city to secure sufficient grounds, including the use of the Mercantile Library Hall and the construction of temporary facilities. Officials established the fair's boundaries near the Mississippi River at Twelfth Street, between the north side of Olive Street and the south side of Washington Avenue. St. Louis architect William Rumbold designed the temporary structure that served as the fair's main building. Described as "a fine looking" cross-shaped structure, located on Twelfth Street between Olive and St. Charles streets, it measured 500 feet by 144 feet, with 314-foot east-west transepts and a ceiling that measured 50 feet at its apex. The building's main concourse, 28 feet in width, accommodated 47 separate departments. Some of the more popular departments included an art gallery, a "Floral Temple," the "Bower of Rest," and "a beautiful grotto" with a fountain. The "Delphic Oracle," a fortune-teller's booth decorated in black crepe, gold stars, and brass bells, proved to be one of the more novel and exotic attractions. The cruciform hall and its varied attractions left a memorable impression on those in attendance. Ella Gale, a young St. Louisan active as both a patron and a volunteer, had attended "every day and night since it opened." In a lengthy letter to her brother, Theodore, she described the building's lavish decorations, which included patriotic banners and bunting, a variety of floral displays, "large globes containing gold fish," and two Confederate cannons "which were taken at Vicksburg."[15]

Prominent attendees included Missouri's Unionist governor, Willard P. Hall, and several other Midwestern governors and regional political figures. Major General Alfred Pleasanton, recently transferred from the Army of the Potomac's Cavalry Corps, served as grand marshal of the elaborate and "magnificent" opening ceremonies on May 17. National political and military figures, including Lincoln, Hamlin, Speaker of the House Schuyler Colfax, and Lieutenant General Ulysses S. Grant, also received invitations to attend the fair. Unfortunately, official duties and the distance involved forced these individuals to decline, but nearly all sent photographs, autographed letters, and other salable items to demonstrate their support for the fair. Grant even arranged for his wife and family, who lived in St. Louis, to attend in his stead. The general's eight-year-old daughter, Nellie, proved particularly popular among the fair's patrons. Photographs of her selling dolls in the Children's Department, dressed as the nursery rhyme character "The Old Woman in the Shoe," sold for fifty cents and quickly became a favorite keepsake among fairgoers. Nellie Grant's work also inspired two poems that praised her patriotism and sense of public service; near the fair's conclusion, patrons subscribed small amounts of money to award Nellie a "beautiful $20 doll" in appreciation of her service. Other national figures, including authors James Russell Lowell

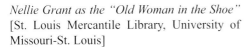

Nellie Grant as the "Old Woman in the Shoe"
[St. Louis Mercantile Library, University of Missouri-St. Louis]

and Ralph Waldo Emerson, lent their support by contributing essays and poems to the pages of the *Daily Countersign*, the fair's newspaper.[16]

Despite the Western Sanitary Commission's spirited defense of its independence and the U.S. Sanitary Commission's persistent efforts to distance itself from all forms of localism, numerous similarities existed between the St. Louis fair and the USSC fairs held between late 1863 and late 1864 in places like Chicago, New York, Cincinnati, and Philadelphia. For example, visitors to the St. Louis fair witnessed many of the same types of amusements as fairgoers in the East and upper Midwest. Attractions ranged from the latest technological and natural curiosities, such as the "stereopticon," a device that produced a three-dimensional image from dual images viewed simultaneously, and livestock to artistic displays and patriotic musical performances. In the tradition of other major sanitary fairs, composers Fred Beyer and T. Van Berg produced two original musical numbers in honor of the occasion. The "Sanitary Fair Polka" and the "Mississippi Valley Sanitary Fair Grand March" were both very popular. Patrons enjoyed a great variety of regional and ethnic cuisine at the fair's numerous refreshment facilities. They also purchased items at auction and general sale. Patrons paid one dollar per vote to award a $1,500 sword and a "fine young Silver Heels stallion" to the two most popular Union generals and "a beautifully embroidered" blue silk battle flag to the most popular Union regiment. This competition proved as successful in St. Louis as similar competitions held at USSC fairs.[17]

Subtle similarities, involving acknowledged assumptions about gender and class, continued to govern the way people participated in public relief work. Gender and class distinctions had characterized nineteenth-century philanthropic work before the war and remained influential during the sanitary fair experience. For example, both the WSC and the USSC drew heavily from a network of managers, workers, and fund-raising techniques from the charity organizations that existed before and during the war. Socially prominent people dominated the leadership roles in groups like the German Emigrant Aid Society, the St. Louis Provident Association, the St. Louis Freedmen's Association, and the Ladies Union Aid Society. Many of these same citizens also served on the Mississippi Valley Sanitary Fair's executive committee. In addition, the Executive Committee of Ladies supervised socially acceptable expressions of female public relief work, including the operation of the floral and millinery departments and publication of the *Daily Countersign*. *Daily Countersign* editor Anna C. Brackett and managers Mrs. E. W. Clark and Mrs. R. A. Ranlett, as well as the floral department's Minerva Blow and Mrs. A. S. W. Goodwin of the millinery department, all belonged to prominent local families with traditions of public service. Their leadership represented an established and acceptable public outlet for charitable-minded women of the upper class. Although the work involved a public expression of female authority and financial responsibility, nineteenth-century American society viewed activity of this type as a natural extension of a woman's stewardship over the household and family. The larger political implications of this service remained subdued.[18]

As with the USSC-sponsored fairs, members of the working class exercised no influence in planning the St. Louis fair. They were neither represented on the executive committee nor held the most important department chairs. Working-class residents primarily contributed through the physical labor necessary for the fair's preparation and operation. Skilled workers donated their labor and expertise to supply the fairgrounds with gas fittings and other essential utilities. Laborers performed manual tasks for wages "at the rate of $500 per annum." With the fair under way, employees and volunteers continued to carry out duties assigned to their class and gender. Working-class women worked exclusively as cooks and waitresses in the fair restaurants, while the leadership of the various feminine departments remained an upper-class function. Although some of the younger upper-class females, such as Ella Gale and her friend Susan Blow, served as waitresses at the fair restaurants, crossing class guidelines of participation remained an upper-class prerogative. Gender and class restrictions also combined to limit management of the fair's daily operation, with upper-class males continuing to make all of the decisions. This suggests an extension of many of the established guidelines about gender and class contributions rather than a dramatic expansion of public roles during the war. These proscriptions proffer that, at least in western areas, the war did not serve as a catalyst for swift change in gender and class roles within philanthropic endeavors.[19]

Arrangements made to reduce operating costs during the sanitary fairs proved another point of similarity between the WSC and the USSC. Despite the USSC's persistent, but unsubstantiated, claims of greater cost efficiency, the St. Louis philanthropists often proved their equal. Numerous St. Louisans, as well as residents of other cities, states, and even foreign countries, volunteered to serve as special agents assigned to procure materials of all description for the fair. Agents in Chicago purchased large quantities of building materials, including 400,000 feet of lumber, at reduced rates and arranged for free shipment to St. Louis. In exchange for published acknowledgment of their cooperation, numerous railroad and express companies eagerly provided free transportation for fair agents and materials designated for the fair. Arrangements of this nature had been established among relief organizations long before the phenomenon of sanitary fairs and helped reduce operating costs for such groups while providing a good public relations opportunity for the rail and express companies.[20]

Although several similarities existed between the Western Sanitary Commission and the U.S. Sanitary Commission fairs, other aspects blurred the distinction between localized and centralized relief and hint that a transition was under way in how people viewed and carried out philanthropy. As with other social issues of the period, debate over the proper direction of American philanthropy found many followers who advocated a more gradual approach to change. In the area of relief work, the WSC favored a gradual approach that balanced effective centralized practices with localized authority. Influenced by the success of their prewar benevolent efforts, as well as the divisive debate over an immediate or gradual end to slavery, its leaders emphasized slow social reform.[21]

The fund-raising efforts of the WSC illustrate a desire to balance local and centralized ideas. Although it limited its field operations to providing aid to soldiers and civilians in the Trans-Mississippi and Western theaters, the WSC did not hesitate to make use of personal, financial, and political associations in the East to raise funds. Its success in obtaining funds in eastern cities drew criticism from the USSC, which viewed the action as incompatible with the WSC's regional character. Olmsted worried that the St. Louis agency was "plowing our field" and complained bitterly about its fund-raising efforts in Boston. The USSC, mistakenly convinced that the WSC advocated strict localism, mocked the Missouri group's supposed lack of commitment to this principle. This practice continued during the St. Louis fair, which added to the already fierce WSC-USSC rivalry. The St. Louis officials, however, did not see a conflict and continued to raise funds from every available source. Although cast in the role of chief rival to the centralization of the USSC, the WSC did not portray itself as the rigid champion of strict localism. It instead emphasized both local and centralized methods of fund-raising. As a result, its members saw no contradiction in their efforts to raise funds in New England. "In spirit," the fair's February 5, 1864, circular proclaimed, the Mississippi Valley Sanitary Fair recognized "no State lines or sectional divisions or prejudices, but treats all soldiers alike." Soldiers from all regions served in the Trans-Mississippi and Western theaters and benefited from the work of the WSC and its fair. Managers of the St. Louis enterprise did not believe they should prohibit any citizen, irrespective of regional boundaries, from contributing to the welfare of Union soldiers.[22]

East Coast efforts to raise funds for the St. Louis fair proved very successful. New Bedford, Massachusetts, for example, established its own fund-raising department and contributed $4,615.21. The New Englanders

James Erwin Yeatman helped organize the Merchant Bank and incorporate what would become the Missouri Pacific Railroad. His civic enterprises included incorporating the Missouri School for the Blind and the St. Louis Mercantile Library.

even gained a special note of appreciation in the fair's general report for the "earnest sympathy and noble-hearted generosity" of their "valuable, timely and most welcome assistance." As a native of Massachusetts with both familial and professional connections across New England, Reverend Eliot proved particularly effective as a fund-raiser in the eastern states. On trips throughout New England and Washington, DC, Eliot fostered several important relationships to raise funds and maintain the WSC's independent status. His sister established a "Missouri room" in her Boston home, where she collected both goods and cash to be shipped to St. Louis. This single effort raised more than $17,000 in the Boston area. The executive committee authorized James E. Yeatman to make associations as "best calculated to promote the objects of this organization" during a spring journey to Washington, DC. By the fair's end, cash, material donations, and well wishes had come to the St. Louis fair headquarters from as far away as Cherryfield, Maine, San Francisco, and England.[23]

Even the USSC's branch offices could not be completely restrained from cooperating with the WSC and the St. Louis fair. Jessie Benton Frémont, an important early advocate of the WSC who was later active in the New York branch of the USSC, arranged to transfer "a very generous share" of unsold goods to St. Louis following the close of New York's Metropolitan Fair. St. Louis officials made similar arrangements to donate their excess to Philadelphia's Great Central Sanitary Fair, as well as other independent fairs in the Midwest. This practice of cooperation greatly annoyed USSC executives, who believed efforts of this nature impinged on their territory and encouraged further decentralization and inefficiency. To supporters of the WSC, however, these practices demonstrated the widespread appeal of a balance between centralization and localism. The different approaches blurred the distinction between localized and centralized charity and hint that a slow transition, rather than a swift change, was under way in the field of philanthropy.[24]

In several critical areas, the differences between the fairs of the WSC and USSC were more distinct and rooted in the rivalry between the two organizations. For example, the USSC remained unenthusiastic about sanitary fairs in general. Although its executive committee tolerated the fairs because of their undeniable financial success, officials continued to deride them as examples of philanthropic sectionalism that threatened to undermine their mission. USSC executives distanced themselves from the planning and operation of fairs sponsored by their own branch offices and instead concentrated on the acceptance of the central office's share of the fair profits. The executive committee of the Mississippi Valley Sanitary Fair, on the other hand, immediately encouraged the input and active cooperation of the citizens of St. Louis and other communities in the Mississippi River valley.

The tremendous variety of offers sent to executive committee headquarters at the Lindell Hotel demonstrates that St. Louis citizens and residents from across the Mississippi Valley region thought of the St. Louis fair in personal and community terms. Numerous individuals contributed ideas as well as cash and materials. Offers ranged from the ordinary to the ridiculous and included everything from the sale of apples and other produce to the exhibition of a performing act known as "The Happy Family Monkeys." The fair's executive committee debated the merits of all proposals and determined whether or not to accept them. Although the executive committee apparently never established set criteria for evaluating proposed contributions, committee minutes indicate the members' concern that no attraction or concession be at all controversial. Committee members also stressed the need for variety in the selection of attractions. They refused numerous duplicate applications. Such decentralized, community-oriented practices typified fairs throughout the war, but the WSC remained the only major relief agency to encourage this behavior.[25]

The main difference between the WSC and the USSC fairs is illustrated by the relationship each organization developed with their subordinate associates. These relationships exemplify the important contribution the WSC made as

General William Rosecrans, who presided over the fair, commanded the Army of the Cumberland before heading the Department of the Missouri.

a transitional force between local and centralized philanthropy. Whereas the USSC sought "absolute subordination," the WSC maintained more democratic relations. The hierarchy of the St. Louis fair allowed for greater distribution of responsibilities. Although subordinate to the executive committee, each department handled its own correspondence concerning prospective donations of cash, materials, and fair attractions. In addition, they were "empowered" to write and publish such circulars "as they may decide to be best productive of the objects of their department." The executive committee also authorized "local committees in various towns and cities" to act in the interests of the fair. Communities across the North established local councils to collect goods. Leaders of the USSC resented these attempts to control the decision-making process and viewed such efforts as an usurpation of authority.[26]

Cooperation between the WSC and its allied agencies, however, did not end with the collection of goods; it also extended into the heart of the decision-making process. Final decisions remained the responsibility of the executive committee, but it consistently sought the input of relevant departments. The controversy that followed the decision to allow the sale and consumption of "Native Wines" and beer, for example, illustrates the democratic nature of the St. Louis fair's decision-making process. This battle threatened to divide the fair's leadership along civic and religious lines. Clerics and other temperance advocates believed the sale and consumption of alcohol was inappropriate for a family-oriented charity event and called for citywide prohibition during the fair. Opponents feared that such activities would "promote or encourage" dangerous vice, attract a rowdy and ill-mannered element from St. Louis's large immigrant population, and, consequently, reduce the fair's profits. Advocates for wine and beer sales, however, believed the decision was a modest concession to the city's numerous immigrant populations, especially the thoroughly loyal Germans, from whom the fair's management hoped to draw a considerable portion of their attendance.[27]

The issue generated lengthy discussions during several executive committee meetings, with input from members of the general refreshment committee, religious leaders, and the Ladies Union Aid Society, as well as local merchants and saloonkeepers. Two executive committee votes failed to ban the sale of alcohol, but General Rosecrans soon interceded with a workable compromise. He issued General Order No. 6, which prohibited the sale and consumption of alcohol within five blocks of the fairgrounds. Municipal authorities also agreed to provide adequate police supervision to "immediately and summarily" subdue all instances of public impropriety. Rosecrans's solution kept the peace among the fair's organizers and also proved financially successful. A wine and beer hall, located in the Lucas Market section of town, soon reported "a thriving business." The wine and beer committee reported a net gain of $5,395.85. This figure exceeded all but two portions of the proceeds raised by the general refreshment committee, and none of the anticipated problems occurred.[28]

The only other controversy to arise during the fair's planning resulted from the decision to allow the raffling of prizes. Raffle prizes included a variety of small items, including a Singer sewing machine and a silver-plated tea set, and the grand prize, the Smizer Farm. Church leaders and women's groups again spearheaded an opposition movement with the support of the WSC executive committee. In an effort to secure "the best results" for the fair in both profits and public image, opponents denounced "the practice of raffling." Raffling, they believed, amounted to publicly sanctioned gambling. As with the conflict over the sale and consumption of alcohol, the executive committee solicited opinions from both sides and voted on the issue. The vote divided largely along religious-civic lines, but civic leaders again obtained the necessary simple majority to allow the practice. As with the sale of liquor, the raffle proved a great financial success. The Smizer Farm raffle alone accounted for $50,000 via the sale of one-dollar chances.[29]

Influenced by the animosity of the USSC toward the WSC, proponents of the St. Louis fair believed that the national organization failed to appreciate the special political, military, and philanthropic needs of the Trans-Mississippi and Western theaters. The USSC constantly questioned the necessity for a separate, Missouri-based relief organization. Because of its emphasis on centralized collection and distribution, the USSC failed to recognize any distinctive regional relief needs. It viewed any effort to define relief needs according to local or regional interests as rooted in sectionalism and secession. To the USSC, all regions shared the same needs, and problems could be solved by the same ways and means.[30]

Leaders of the Mississippi Valley Sanitary Fair, however, understood that Missourians had more to prove than residents of other Northern cities and communities and that philanthropic contributions played an important role in satisfying that sense of duty. Missouri's status as a border state, with a significant pro-Confederate population, caused a degree of suspicion to hang over the political loyalties of its residents. St. Louis, for example, even drew criticism from some members of the WSC. James Yeatman referred to it as a community on "the frontier of loyalty," where "the rebel ladies" remained "outspoken in their sympathies with Jeff Davis." The USSC further confused the issue of loyalty when it portrayed the WSC's care of Confederate prisoners of war, who were held mostly in St. Louis's Gratiot Street prison, as aid to the enemy. Because of these concerns, the Mississippi Valley Sanitary Fair needed to present something more than a standard demonstration of community pride and benevolence. The St. Louis fair's success quickly assumed a larger symbolic importance. It became an expression of St. Louisans' and Missourians' loyalty to the Union. Appeals for donations and volunteers picked up on the theme of loyalty. By equating contributions to the fair with patriotism, a competitive spirit soon developed among neighboring communities and states, as each sought to outdo the other.[31]

The Smizer Farm was one of several items raffled at the St. Louis fair. [St. Louis Mercantile Library, University of Missouri-St. Louis]

Speeches by political and military figures helped perpetuate the concept of competitive patriotism. Brigadier General James G. Blunt and Charles Anderson, the lieutenant governor of Ohio, spoke at the fair and celebrated local contributions as proof of strong Union sentiment—a sacrifice made in the name of the national cause—and challenged residents to surpass the accomplishments of other fairs.[32]

In addition to proving the loyalty of the region and raising funds for the relief of Union soldiers, their families, and orphans, the St. Louis fair addressed other important elements of Missouri's special philanthropic needs. Because the state served as a battleground for both regular and guerrilla forces, the refugee population grew quickly. St. Louis became a sanctuary for a nearly endless stream of refugees. The displaced included loyal Unionists, Confederate sympathizers who posed as loyalists, and free and escaped blacks, all of whom sought an escape from the poverty, chaos, and misery of war in the West.[33]

This migration commenced almost as soon as hostilities erupted and continued throughout the war, even after the main regular armies pushed south and east of Missouri. Refugees arrived in St. Louis from northern Arkansas and southern Missouri and the war-torn areas of Tennessee, Mississippi, Alabama, Texas, and Louisiana, and most arrived in a condition of "want and suffering." At the suggestion of Rev. W. H. Corkhill, hospital chaplain and superintendent of contrabands at Benton Barracks, and in response to Yeatman's extensive efforts to establish greater economic and educational

Civil War Refugees

opportunities for freedmen, the leaders of the St. Louis fair determined to address this growing problem.[34]

Fair officials established separate collections, under the administration of a freedmen's and refugees committee, to gather monetary and material donations for black and white refugees. Not surprisingly, the freedmen's portion of this fund was benefited by donations from eastern abolitionists. Gerrit Smith, for example, contributed $100. By the fair's end, the committee raised a total of $16,720.11, of which $6,115.36 benefited the freedmen.[35]

Despite the racially motivated separation of contributions to the fund, inclusion of blacks as beneficiaries of public aid represented a radical change in nineteenth-century public relief practices. In the mid-nineteenth century, even free blacks were rarely viewed as worthy of public aid. The St. Louis fair, therefore, became the only major sanitary fair to significantly address this controversial issue. Efforts to aid freedmen existed in eastern cities, but only in proportion to the relatively small number of black refugees in the area. With comparatively little direct contact with exiles of either color or the problems they posed, eastern efforts to aid this segment of the population remained abstract. The St. Louis endeavor to aid freedmen, although primarily motivated by the circumstances of war in the Trans-Mississippi and Western theaters rather than ideals of centralization or pure humanitarianism, represented a genuine and significant change in the distribution of relief materials.[36]

In addition to raising funds for the benefit of black and white refugees, the fair's managers employed a contingent of the Sixty-eighth U.S. Infantry, African Descent, to help construct fair buildings. For their labor the soldiers received fifty cents per day per man, plus free admission to the fair. In a striking move of unsolicited generosity, the men of the Sixty-eighth donated their pay, "together with a very considerable addition" taken from their "scanty monthly pay," to "the Freedmen's Department" of the fair. As with the distribution of relief materials, agencies often did not view African Americans as a source for donations. Through their contribution to this fund, the soldiers helped redefine ideas about the worthiness of blacks as both donors and recipients of public aid.[37]

The presence and participation of black soldiers and patrons did not go unnoticed by the white fair-going public. Although boundaries concerning blacks as donors and recipients of public aid began to expand somewhat because of the fair, other forms of "Negro equality" remained unacceptable to many St. Louis residents. For example, when Reverend Henry Nelson asked to be served at the Café Laclede while in the company of two black associates, a minor disturbance developed. Several of the white waitresses, "young ladies of the highest respectability," refused to serve the group. Authorities quickly removed Nelson and his party from the fairgrounds. A number of residents responded favorably to the group's prompt removal. Jane McDonald, an elderly St. Louis resident, thought the group's unceremonious removal "well done." The *Missouri Republican*, a loyalist St. Louis-based newspaper that espoused Democratic politics, ridiculed the incident as an "exceedingly repulsive" example of racial "fanaticism." Although displeasure over this "outrage" found expression in both public and private forums, it had no negative effect on the operation of the fair or donations to the black and white refugee funds.

These incidents demonstrate how certain aspects of the black experience underwent change due to the circumstances of war in the Trans-Mississippi and Western theaters while other aspects remained unchanged. The acceptable roles for African Americans at the fair involved some form of public subordination. Black workers and soldiers served under the supervision of white fair officials or white regimental officers and did not pose a challenge to the social status quo. Nelson's group, however, challenged the essential structure of the social relationship between blacks and whites by placing black male patrons in a position of authority over young, white, female volunteers. As reactions to this incident indicate, such a challenge went beyond what St. Louis society was prepared to tolerate.[38]

If the success of Civil War sanitary fairs is to be measured primarily in monetary terms, the Mississippi Valley Sanitary Fair was an enormous success. On August 16, 1864, the executive committee reported gross receipts of $618,782.28. After expenses, the St. Louis fair reported a net profit of

Café Laclede [St. Louis Mercantile Library, University of Missouri-St. Louis]

$554,591. Although this figure is considerably less than the net profits produced at the New York and Philadelphia fairs, it remains an impressive total because the St. Louis fair drew its attendance from a much smaller population base. When figured on a per capita basis, the Mississippi Valley Sanitary Fair exceeded its contemporaries by raising $3.50 per capita, compared to an average of $1.67 at both New York and Philadelphia. The St. Louis fair also reported a significantly higher net profit than USSC-sponsored events in Chicago and Boston. Chicago's Great Northwestern Sanitary Fair announced a profit of less than $80,000; Boston's two fairs netted profits of $146,000 and $247,056, respectively. Even on the fifteenth day of the St. Louis fair, the central treasury recorded daily receipts in excess of $12,000. The WSC, reinforced by the financial success of the Mississippi Valley Sanitary Fair, continued to operate as the main relief agency in the Trans-Mississippi and Western theaters for the duration of the war.[39]

Through examining the Western Sanitary Commission's sponsorship of the Mississippi Valley Sanitary Fair, a new picture of Civil War philanthropy begins to emerge. Ideas about philanthropy were entangled in the tumultuous mid-century debate over the respective merits of localism and centralization. Although members of the U.S. Sanitary Commission rightfully claimed many legitimate accomplishments and initiated several important innovations and sanitary reforms during the war, they often exaggerated their responsibility for the centralization and modernization of American philanthropic programs. The contribution of the Western Sanitary Commission and its fair suggests that fundamental change in the practices and beliefs of American philanthropists did not occur during the war. Significant alterations would not take root until at least a decade after it ended and, even then, would not come without strong opposition. The Western Sanitary Commission's balance of localism and centralization served an important transitional role in the evolution of nineteenth-century American philanthropy.[40]

The success of the Mississippi Valley Sanitary Fair also affected the WSC-USSC rivalry. Through its management of the St. Louis fair, the WSC served notice that it could operate efficiently and with innovation under its own authority. The success of the St. Louis fair suggests that its organizers were correct in their belief that they better understood the philanthropic practices and needs of their region's people. Although the USSC continued to be critical of the WSC for the remainder of the war, the St. Louis group proved to be the equal of its rival in the cause at hand.

NOTES

1. James M. Mcpherson, *The Battle Cry of Freedom: The Civil War Era* (New York: Ballantine Books, 1989), 609-611; Adam Kawa, "No Draft!" *Civil War Times Illustrated* 37 (June 1998): 54-60.

2. Jacob G. Forman, *The Western Sanitary Commission: A Sketch of its Origins* (St. Louis: R. P. Studley, 1864), 3-12, 129-138; Mary A. Livermore, *My Story of the War* (Hartford, CT: Worthington, 1889), 123-135, 409-449.

3. J. Matthew Gallman, *Mastering Wartime: A Social History of Philadelphia During the Civil War* (New York: Cambridge University Press, 1990), 146; Robert H. Bremner, *The Public Good: Philanthropy and Welfare in the Civil War Era* (New York: Alfred A. Knopf, 1980), 14-27; Beverly Gordon, *Bazaars and Fair Ladies: The History of the American Fundraising Fair* (Knoxville: University of Tennessee Press, 1998), 59-94.

4. William E. Gienapp, "'Politics Seem to Enter into Everything': Political Culture in the North, 1840-1860," in *Essays on American Antebellum Politics, 1840-1860*, ed. Stephen E. Maizlish and John J. Kushma (College Station: Texas A & M University Press, 1982), 14-69; Jeanie Attie, *Patriotic Toil: Northern Women and the American Civil War* (Ithaca, NY: Cornell University Press, 1998); Gallman, *Mastering Wartime*, 1, 9; William E. Parrish, "The Western Sanitary Commission," *Civil War History* 36 (March 1990): 17-35.

5. Gallman, *Mastering Wartime*, 146; Bremner, *Public Good*, 14-27; Gordon, *Bazaars and Fair Ladies*, 66-67; Livermore, *My Story*, 455; William Y. Thompson, "Sanitary Fairs of the Civil War," *Civil War History* 4 (March 1958): 51-68.

6. Jane Turner Censer, ed., *Defending the Union, 1861-1863*, vol. 4 of *The Papers of Frederick Law Olmsted* (Baltimore: Johns Hopkins University Press, 1986), 240, 337, 480, 495-497; Robert H. Bremner, "The Prelude: Philanthropic Rivalries in the Civil War Era," *Social Casework* 49 (February 1968): 79; Roland Usher, "Western Sanitary Commission," *Proceedings of the Mississippi Valley Historical Association* (n.p., 1908-1909), 219; Parrish, "Western Sanitary Commission," 17-35.

7. Mississippi Valley Sanitary Fair Executive Committee Meeting Minutes, 1 February 1864, box 1, St. Louis Protestant Orphan Asylum Records, Missouri Historical Society, St. Louis; *Final Report of the Western Sanitary Commission* (St. Louis: R. P. Studley, 1866), 1-5; Jasper Cross, "The Mississippi Valley Sanitary Fair, St. Louis, 1864," *Missouri Historical Review* 46 (April 1952): 237-239.

8. Western Sanitary Commission, *General Report of the Mississippi Valley Sanitary Fair* (n.p., 1864), 3-4; Executive Committee Minutes, 1 February, 30 June 1864.

9. "Western Sanitary Commission Circular," box 1, notebook 6; William Greenleaf Eliot to Tom Eliot, n.d., notebook 7, both in William Greenleaf Eliot Papers, Washington University, St. Louis; William Greenleaf Eliot, *Social Reform: A*

Discourse (St. Louis: George Knapp, 1857), 10-11; Gregory Eiselein, *Literature and Humanitarianism in the Civil War* (Bloomington: Indiana University Press, 1996), 13-14, 79-83; J. Matthew Gallman, *The North Fights the Civil War: The Home Front* (Chicago: Ivan R. Dee, 1994), 23-27, 86.

10. William Greenleaf Eliot, *Loyalty and Religion: A Discourse for the Times* (St. Louis: George Knapp, 1861), 10-12; Eliot, *Social Reform*, 1, 11-14; Censer, *Defending the Union*, 228-229; Executive Committee Minutes, 11 April 1864.

11. Censer, *Defending the Union*, 228-229, 306-309; Allan Nevins and Milton Halsey Thomas, eds., *Diary of George Templeton Strong: The Civil War 1860-1865* (New York: Macmillan, 1952), 188-189.

12. Censer, *Defending the Union*, 229, 240.

13. Gordon, *Bazaars and Fair Ladies*, 66-71; Alvin Robert Kantor and Marjorie Sered Kantor, *Sanitary Fairs: A Philatelic and Historical Study of Civil War Benevolences* (Glencoe, IL: SF Publishing, 1992), 167-171.

14. Executive Committee Minutes, 1 February 1864; *Final Report*, 1-18.

15. Executive Committee Minutes, 22-29 February, 3-7 March 1864; *St. Louis Daily Countersign*, 17 May 1864; *St. Louis Missouri Republican*, 17 May 1864; Ella Gale to Theo Gale, 22 May 1864, Gale Family Papers, Missouri Historical Society, St. Louis.

16. Roy P. Basler, ed., *The Collected Works of Abraham Lincoln* (New Brunswick, NJ: Rutgers University Press, 1953), 353-354; *Final Report*, 16-17; John Y. Simon, ed., *The Memoirs of Julia Dent Grant* (New York: Putnam, 1975), 76, 130-131; Executive Committee Minutes, 1 February, 17 May 1864; L. J. Cist to F. J. Dreer, 25 April 1864, Civil War Collection, Missouri Historical Society; *St. Louis Daily Countersign*, 17, 27 May, 4 June 1864; *Chicago Tribune*, 20, 22 May 1864.

17. Gallman, *Mastering Wartime*, 148-168; Thompson, "Sanitary Fairs of the Civil War," 55-64; Executive Committee Minutes, 18 April 1864; *St. Louis Daily Countersign*, 22 May, 4 June 1864. General Winfield Scott Hancock won the sword; the contest raised $4,517. The Tenth Kansas Infantry, which had served several months of garrison duty in St. Louis earlier in the war, won the battle flag, and General William T. Sherman won the horse. *St. Louis Missouri Republican*, 29 May 1864; *Kansas City Western Journal of Commerce*, 11 June 1864.

18. Jeanie Attie, "Warwork and the Crisis of Domesticity," in *Divided Houses: Gender and the Civil War*, ed. Catherine Clinton and Nina Silber (New York: Oxford University Press, 1992), 247-248; Jane E. Schultz, "Race, Gender, and Bureaucracy: Civil War Nurses and the Pension Bureau," *Journal of Women's History* 6 (Summer 1994): 45-48; J. W. McIntyre, *Third Annual Report of the St. Louis Provident Association* (St. Louis: St. Louis Provident Association, 1863), 2; Executive Committee Minutes, 1-10 February, 14, 25 April 1864; *Final Report*, 4; Minerva Blow to Henry Blow, 3, 11, 12 May 1864, Blow Family Papers, Missouri Historical Society; *St. Louis Daily Countersign*, 17 May 1864; Mary Elizabeth Massey, *Bonnet Brigades* (New York:

Alfred A. Knopf, 1966), 48-54.

19. Executive Committee Minutes, 3, 21, 31 March 1864; Schultz, "Race, Gender, and Bureaucracy," 45-69; Gallman, *The North Fights*, 181-186; Gallman, "Voluntarism in Wartime: Philadelphia's Great Central Fair," in *Toward A Social History of the American Civil War: Exploratory Essays*, ed. Maris Vinovskis (New York: Cambridge University Press, 1990), 112-113; Eiselein, *Literature*, 146; Massey, *Bonnet Brigades*, 32-33.

20. Sarah Henshaw, *Our Branch and its Tributaries* (Chicago: A. L. Sewell, 1868), 32-36; Charles J. Stillé, *History of the United States Sanitary Commission: Being the General Report of its Work During the War of the Rebellion* (Gansevoort, NY: Corner House Historical Publications, 1997), 82-83, 114, 138-165; "A Fortnight with the Sanitary Commission," *Atlantic Monthly* 15 (February 1865): 233-248; Executive Committee Minutes, 22-29 February, 10-24 March, 14-18 April, 2, 9 May 1864; Missouri Valley Sanitary Fair (MVSF) Circulars, 5 February-18 March 1864, Civil War Collection, Missouri Historical Society; Massey, *Bonnet Brigades*, 48-50; Travel Vouchers, 10, 17 February 1862; R. R. Hazard Sr. to A. W. Plattenburg, 11 February 1863, both in J. E. D. Couzins Papers, Missouri Historical Society.

21. Executive Committee Minutes, 6, 22, 29 February 1864; Censer, *Defending the Union*, 469, 471, 480, 495-497, 627; MVSF Circular, 5 February 1864.

22. Censer, *Defending the Union*, 306-308, 334-337; MVSF Circular, 5 February 1864.

23. *Final Report*, 9; Parrish, "Western Sanitary Commission," 21; Executive Committee Minutes, 28 April 1864; *St. Louis Daily Countersign*, 4 June 1864.

24. Executive Committee Minutes, 28 April 1864; Pamela Herr, ed., *The Letters of Jessie Benton Frémont* (Urbana: University of Illinois Press, 1993), 250.

25. Executive Committee Minutes, 4-29 February, 24-31 March, 21 April 1864; MVSF Circulars, 5 February-18 March 1864; Gallman, *The North Fights*, 78-83, 109-110.

26. Executive Committee Minutes, 22 February, 10-14, 21, 31 March, 18-25 April, 9 May 1864; Gallman, *Mastering Wartime*, 154-155; Nevins and Halsey, *George Templeton Strong*, 274-275; Attie, *Patriotic Toil*, 65, 71-75, 109, 198-202.

27. Executive Committee Minutes, 22 February, 10-14, 21, 31 March, 18-25 April, 9 May 1864; Gallman, *Mastering Wartime*, 154-155.

28. Executive Committee Minutes, 21 March, 18, 21, 25 April, 9 May 1864; *Final Report*, 8; *St. Louis Daily Countersign*, 31 May 1864.

29. Executive Committee Minutes, 10, 14, 21 March 1864; *St. Louis Daily Countersign*, 31 May, 4 June 1864.

30. Censer, *Defending the Union*, 260-268, 306-308, 334, 506; Nevins and Halsey, *George Templeton Strong*, 188-189.

31. Executive Committee Minutes, 1 February, 7 April 1864; William E. Parrish,

Turbulent Partnership: Missouri and the Union, 1861-1865 (Columbia: University of Missouri Press, 1963), xiii-xv; *General Report*, 3; Jacob G. Forman, *The Western Sanitary Commission* (St. Louis: Daily Missouri Democrat, 1864), 1-7; Merle Curti, "American Philanthropy and the National Character," *American Quarterly* 10 (Winter 1958): 421-432.

32. *St. Louis Daily Countersign*, 23, 31 May 1864; *St. Louis Missouri Republican*, 2 June 1864; Attie, *Patriotic Toil*, 147-149; Gordon, *Bazaars and Fair Ladies*, 48, 53.

33. James E. Yeatman, *Report to the Western Sanitary Commission in Regard to Leasing Abandoned Plantations* (St. Louis: Western Sanitary Commission, 1864), 3-15; James E. Yeatman, *Suggestions of a Plan of Organization for Freed Labor, and the Leasing of Plantations Along the Mississippi River* (St. Louis: Western Sanitary Commission, 1864), 2-16; Jacob G. Forman, *Report of the Western Sanitary Commission on the White Union Refugees of the South* (St. Louis: R. P. Studley, 1864), 3-11; John F. Bradbury, "'Buckwheat Cake Philanthropy': Refugees and the Union Army in the Ozarks," *Arkansas Historical Quarterly* 57 (Autumn 1998): 233-239; William Garrett Piston, "More than Bullets: The Social Impact of Guerrilla War in the Ozarks," *Ozarks Watch* 10 (1997): 164-166.

34. Forman, *White Union Refugees*, 3-44; Executive Committee Minutes, 7 March 1864; Yeatman, *Suggestions*, 2-16; Michael Fellman, *Inside War: The Guerrilla Conflict in Missouri During the American Civil War* (New York: Oxford University Press, 1989), 73-80; Bradbury, "'Buckwheat Cake Philanthropy,'" 244-245.

35. *Final Report*, 8.

36. Schultz, "Race, Gender, and Bureaucracy," 45-46; Curti, "American Philanthropy," 431-435; George M. Fredrickson, *The Inner Civil War. Northern Intellectuals and the Crisis of the Union* (New York: Harper and Row, 1965), 99-101; Gallman, *Mastering Wartime*, 124-125.

37. *St. Louis Daily Countersign*, 27, 31 May, 4 June 1864; Executive Committee Minutes, 14, 23 May 1864.

38. *St. Louis Missouri Republican*, 27 June 1864; Jane McDonald to Lizzie, n.d., Wilson P. Hunt Papers, Missouri Historical Society; *St. Louis Missouri Republican*, 27 May 1864.

39. *Final Report*, 13; Gallman, "Voluntarism," 95; Thompson, "Sanitary Fairs of the Civil War," 51-67; Cross, "Mississippi Valley Sanitary Fair," 245.

40. Important postwar works by members of the U.S. Sanitary Commission include Henshaw, *Our Branch*; Livermore, *My Story of the War*; Stillé, *History of the United States Sanitary Commission*; Jane Stuart Woolsey, *Hospital Days: Reminiscence of a Civil War Nurse* (Roseville, MN: Edinborough Press, 1996); Katharine Prescott Wormeley, *The Other Side of War on the Hospital Transports with the Army of the Potomac* (Gansevoort, NY: Corner House Historical Publications, 1998).

Charles D. Drake and the
Constitutional Convention of 1865

DAVID D. MARCH

The constitution of the state of Missouri adopted in 1865 was often called "Drake's Constitution." Its enemies, and there were many, referred to it as the "Draconian Code."[1] Both its proponents and opponents recognized that the guiding hand in the framing and adoption of the constitution was that of Charles D. Drake of St. Louis. Even a casual survey of the proceedings of the state convention of 1865 shows that Drake richly deserved to have his name associated with the document.

Charles D. Drake, son of the famous Dr. Daniel Drake of Ohio, came to St. Louis in 1834 to begin the practice of law.[2] After an unsuccessful experience in the collection of accounts for eastern firms doing business with St. Louis merchants,[3] and an even less remunerative participation in Whig politics during the 1840s, Drake eventually achieved recognition as an able lawyer and a crusader of no mean ability.[4] In 1854 his *A Treatise on the Law of Suits by Attachment in the United States* was published and soon became a standard work on the subject.[5] The Democrats of St. Louis elected him to the General Assembly in 1858 where, unfortunately, Drake succeeded only in alienating his colleagues by his overbearing and egotistical manner and in incurring the enmity of the Germans in St. Louis by attacking and attempting to prohibit by law certain social activities on Sundays in which they customarily engaged.[6]

When the clouds of secession and civil war darkened temporarily the roseate picture of Missouri's future, Drake contributed to the Union cause by rationalizing in public speeches and in the newspapers the position most Missourians wished to take on the question of secession, namely, continued adherence to the Union. As a member of the General Assembly, Drake had

Even though many delegates disliked him, Charles D. Drake successfully steered the 1865 convention to adopt a Radical constitution.

been a bitter opponent of abolition doctrines and "Black Republicanism," but this predilection for slavery did not cause him to waver in his devotion to the Union.[7] Beginning in the latter part of 1861, his attitude toward slavery changed progressively from defense of the institution of slavery to toleration of slave labor but not the institution, to gradual emancipation, and finally to immediate emancipation, culminating in the opinion that only traitors opposed immediate and unconditional freedom for the slaves.[8] Because of such views, augmented by a crusading spirit and an overweening desire for recognition, Drake became the most prominent of the Radical spokesmen in Missouri. He drew national attention to himself and the Radical movement when he led the famous Committee of Seventy to Washington in the fall of 1863 in a vain attempt to get President Abraham Lincoln to abandon administration support of Missouri's provisional government headed by Hamilton R. Gamble.[9]

Public sentiment favoring the immediate abolition of slavery and demanding the chastisement of secessionists grew rapidly during the latter part of the war. Early in 1864 the General Assembly, reflecting public dissatisfaction with the gradual emancipation ordinance adopted in 1863,[10] called for the election of delegates to a state convention to consider (1) amendments to the Constitution of 1820 necessary for the emancipation of slaves, (2) amendments necessary "to preserve in purity the elective franchise to loyal citizens," and (3) "such other amendments as may be by them deemed essential to the promotion of the public good."[11] In the sweeping Radical victory in November 1864, the voters of Missouri not only approved the calling of a convention, but also elected Radicals to approximately three-fourths of the convention seats. Drake, one of twenty candidates for the ten seats to which St. Louis was entitled, was elected easily despite some German opposition.[12]

On January 6, 1865, the delegates assembled in the Mercantile Library building in St. Louis. Arnold Krekel of St. Charles was elected president of the convention, and Drake was chosen vice president. Few of the sixty-six delegates were known outside of their local communities, the great majority being farmers and small-town lawyers, doctors, and merchants. Drake recalled that the delegates were almost without exception "sensible, upright, and worthy men, but only a very small number of them had ever had experience in lawmaking," and that few of the rural delegates could have written a single section that would have met the approval of "able legal minds."[13]

It was clear from the first days of the convention that a sufficient number of Radicals looked to Drake for leadership to enable him to exercise a predominate influence in the proceedings. Drake was well known over the state as a lawyer. His fight against the "forces of evil" in the General Assembly had probably found favor among rural people. Moreover, during the Radical campaigns, Drake had traveled over the state and into rural communities to address mass meetings in which he had protested passionately against the "bogus" emancipation ordinance of 1863 and attacked the Gamble administration for what the Radicals called a sympathetic attitude toward rebels. It is hardly surprising, therefore, that delegates who found themselves in unfamiliar surroundings and engaged in work for which they were not well prepared tended to follow Drake's lead. On every crucial roll call during the life of the convention, the farmers and small-town mechanics, almost without exception, voted with Drake.[14]

Drake's paramount influence in the convention was due also to his industry. Although he was not in good health at the time, Drake prepared diligently for the work he hoped to accomplish. He studied carefully the Missouri Constitution of 1820 and examined closely the constitutions of other states, particularly the constitution that had been recently adopted in Maryland. Before the convention convened, he had written a draft of a new constitution for Missouri and had made plans for the adoption of its essential provisions by the delegates.[15]

During the sessions of the convention, Drake was vice president, chairman of the committee on the legislative department, chairman of the revising committee and the enrolling committee, a member of a special committee on the elective franchise, and a member of the committee on boundaries.[16] In addition, he did a prodigious amount of work on the convention floor and in the committee of the whole. Drake was absent only two of the seventy-eight days in which the convention was in session, and those absences were due

Arnold Krekel, president of the Constitutional Convention of 1865, served as U.S. judge for the Western District of Missouri from 1865 to 1888.

to illness. It was he who planned the strategy that enabled the convention to complete its work in the face of much criticism both within and without the convention halls.

Drake's ability and industry, however, did not make him a popular man. He was a driver, not a leader, and his strong convictions and seeming confidence in his own infallibility were often irritating to his friends as well as to his enemies. It was not unusual for him to insist upon the adoption of his particular phraseology in a proposed section of an article, even though such obstinacy wounded the feelings of friends. He frequently offended delegates for no good reason by his cantankerous disposition and overbearing manner.[17]

The *St. Louis Daily Dispatch* carried the following item about Drake and the convention, which is not far from the impression that may be gleaned from the debates:

> It may be broadly stated that C. D. Drake is the most conspicuous member of the convention. His friends insist that he is, by all odds, the ablest. In debate he is a formidable antagonist. With a deep personal interest in the work of the convention, and with his habits of diligent and patient investigation, he is always ready to speak intelligently, and generally exhaustively, on whatever subject, from the disfranchisement of rebels to a point of order that may be brought up. It is difficult to take him by surprise. . . . He pursues his object with inflexible perserverance,

going straight forward like a mad dog looking neither to the right nor left.

He is dogmatical and not infrequently overbearing; and these traits have arrayed against him enemies in a body in which at the outset he was the admitted leader and teacher.[18]

In so far as the abolition of slavery and the crushing of the rebellion were concerned, the members of the convention, if not of one mind, were seeking the same goals. But on matters outside of these, wide differences of opinion existed. Hence, in order to secure a maximum affirmative vote on the emancipation ordinance, all proposed amendments were voted down, and a short, clear-cut measure abolishing slavery in Missouri was passed on January 11, 1865, with only four votes against it.[19] Three of the negative votes were cast by the "Conservative Triumvirate": Samuel A. Gilbert of Platte County, Thomas B. Harris of Callaway, and William F. Switzler of Boone, delegates from "rebel strongholds" where most Radicals were convinced no loyal man could be found. They were joined by William A. Morton of Clay County. The members of the "Triumvirate" were treated as little better than rebels by the Radicals. None was given an important committee assignment, and proposals offered by any one of them were likely to be quickly tabled. Indeed, the day after the emancipation ordinance was adopted, a committee was appointed to inquire into the loyalty of members of the convention. This committee did what was expected of it by bringing in a report which led the convention to declare Harris's seat vacant on the grounds that the delegate from Callaway had perjured himself when he took the oath required of all members that he had always opposed the enemies of the United States.[20]

The four negative votes, however, were not against emancipation per se, but rather against merely legalizing what to them seemed to be a deplorable condition that had been in existence for several months, without at the same time making provision for the guidance of the freedmen and protection of the whites. Switzler proposed that the convention require the General Assembly to provide for the apprenticeship of all slaves between the ages of twelve and twenty-one,[21] while Gilbert cried out during the debate, "In the name of God, if you are going to free negroes, send them from us!"[22] Certainly many people living in counties having a large number of Negroes wanted some plan adopted whereby the freedmen could adjust themselves gradually to their new condition. Many considered apprenticeship laws to be the best solution to the problem, just as Drake had in 1863.[23]

But all of the arguments against immediate and unconditional emancipation had been heard throughout the preceding two years. Those years of controversy had served to confirm the Radicals in the belief that men who advocated anything less than absolute and unqualified freedom for Negroes were scheming to keep slavery in fact, if not in name. Moreover, the experience of the border state of Maryland, which had been wrestling with problems similar to those in Missouri, was cited by Drake as an illustration of the tenacity of slaveholders. It had been necessary, he said, for the federal government to intervene in Maryland to prevent former slaveholders from flocking to the Orphans' Courts to have Negroes apprenticed to them.[24] Consequently, Drake offered a resolution, which the convention adopted as an ordinance, prohibiting any authority from apprenticing or binding for service any emancipated person, except in pursuance of such laws as the General Assembly might enact.[25] In addition, a resolution offered by William S. Holland of Henry County which forbade the General Assembly to compensate former slave owners for the loss of their property was later incorporated in the fourth article of the Constitution of 1865.[26]

Neither the act of the legislature providing for the convention nor anything said during the campaign for delegates indicated that the General Assembly or the people expected the convention to make an extensive revision of the Constitution of 1820. Indeed, Drake himself may have gone to Jefferson City

William F. Switzler, a member of the "Conservative Triumvirate," was a prominent Columbia journalist whose influence extended beyond mid-Missouri.

previously, when the legislature was considering the bill, in a vain attempt to obtain express authorization for drafting a new constitution.[27] In any case, he was determined to take advantage of the clause which authorized the convention to consider amendments which the delegates deemed "essential to the promotion of the public good," and a sufficient number of Radical delegates were willing to support Drake, or at least acquiesce in his plans as they unfolded. [28]

The convention had been in session thirty-two days before Drake formally moved that the Constitution of 1820 be revised.[29] Until then it had accomplished little more than the adoption of the emancipation ordinance. Meanwhile, Drake had been laying the groundwork for his revision motion. Immediately after the convention had organized, he had moved the appointment of eleven committees to "examine the parts of the present Constitution . . . and report to the Convention such amendments thereof as they may consider expedient."[30] The adoption of this motion implied, at least to Drake, that the constitution was to be subjected to thorough revision by amendment.[31] Drake, as chairman of the committee on the legislative department, had presented a report on the seventh day that contemplated an almost complete revision of the articles on the declaration of rights and the legislative department in the constitution.[32]

Drake anticipated a demand by persons within and without the convention that the delegates confine their work to the emancipation of slaves and the disfranchisement of those who had aided the Confederacy. Hence, his strategy was to oppose the adoption of special ordinances and to insist that they be presented as integral parts of revised articles of the constitution. He was even somewhat reluctant to free the slaves by ordinance. When that was done, he knew that if an ordinance disfranchising so-called rebels was also passed, the demand that the convention adjourn sine die would have been almost irresistible. For that reason no such ordinance was passed. Instead, disfranchisement provisions were placed in the revised constitution. This procedure made it necessary for the convention to adopt the dubious device of applying the disqualifying clauses in the proposed constitution to determine the eligibility of persons to participate in the ratifying process.[33] At another time Drake succeeded in postponing for three weeks the adoption of a proposal to declare vacant by ordinance the offices of judges and clerks of all courts of record, county recorders, and circuit attorneys.[34]

The question arises as to why Drake and most of the Radical delegates wished to revise the Constitution of 1820 so as actually to write a new one. The answer can be found in the tendency of the Radicals to distrust the General Assembly and in their fear that the Radical program would in some manner be sabotaged. They professed to believe, for example, that a mere declaration by ordinance that Negroes could no longer be held as slaves was not enough. There were various ways by which Negroes could be held in virtual slavery unless precautions were taken to protect them in their new freedom. Hence, safeguards should be "nailed down" in a constitution, or as Drake said:

> We intend to erect a wall and a barrier, in the shape of a constitution that shall be as high as the eternal heavens, deep down as the very center of the earth, so that they [Conservatives] shall neither climb over it nor dig under it, and as thick as the whole territory of Missouri so that they shall never batter it down nor pierce through it; and never shall put upon the colored race the disqualifications which have borne them down in times past.[35]

At Drake's instigation, or with his support, the convention made approval by the people an integral part of the amending process;[36] sought to limit the enactment of special laws;[37] forbade the creation of corporations by special acts, except for municipal purposes;[38] placed procedural restrictions on the legislature;[39] and endeavored to protect the credit of the state and the interests of those who owned state bonds.[40]

For these ends, and perhaps for others of less importance, most of the Radicals chose to interpret the convention call as a mandate for an extensive revision of the constitution, despite considerable opposition by those who thought that the convention was attempting to go far beyond anything the people had authorized. The most trouble was caused by the Germans who, although eager to abolish slavery and protect the freedmen, did not like the position of leadership which Drake had assumed. German opposition to him had never been far below the surface, for they did not forget his former Know-Nothing sympathies and his anti-German speeches in the General Assembly.

The first of a series of attacks on Drake occurred when he presented his draft of a "Declaration of Rights" which contained the statement that no one could be molested because of his religious persuasion or practice "unless under the color of religion, he . . . infringe the laws of morality."[41] This, said German spokesmen, was a clear manifestation of Drake's spirit of intolerance and puritanical notions. "Mr. Drake's views are well enough known," commented the *Anzeiger* of St. Louis. "He has been all his life a religious and political fanatic, and has never concealed his hatred against the German 'Infidels.'"[42] Krekel successfully led the move to strike out the offending clause and substitute "but the liberty of conscience hereby secured shall not be so construed as to excuse acts of licentiousness."[43]

Drake's stand against the extension of suffrage rights to aliens did even more to earn the opposition of the Germans than did the charge that he was attempting to insert his own ideas of morality into the organic law of the state. When the proposal was made that every alien who had declared his intention to become a citizen of the United States be allowed to vote if he could meet all other qualifications, Drake opposed the resolution. The loyalty of the Germans in Missouri had created a great deal of sentiment in favor of the proposition. Moreover, it was felt that a liberal policy toward aliens would stimulate immigration. Drake accurately predicted that his opposition would be heralded as a malignant assault upon the Germans and contended that the proposition was a cunning scheme to defeat the work of the convention. Whereupon Isidor Bush of St. Louis asked, "Who would defeat it because of this amendment? The Know-Nothings?" Drake replied sharply, "I thought that party was dead and buried." Bush retorted, "You are living proof that it is not."[44]

Opposition to the prolongation of the convention began to be strongly reflected among the delegates by the middle of February. The conservative Switzler, taking advantage of Drake's running fight with the Germans and the general opinion that the convention was not accomplishing anything, drafted a circular to be signed by the delegates stating their determination to resign and leave the body without a quorum. When almost a score of the members

Isidor Bush, a prominent German American businessman, viticulturist, and abolitionist, disagreed with Drake on restricting aliens' right to vote.

signed the paper, Drake called a caucus of Radical delegates at the home of Chauncey I. Filley. Among those present were several rural delegates who had signed the circular. Drake succeeded in convincing them that they had been duped by disloyalists, and a Radical phalanx was formed around Drake to thwart any further attempts to discredit the convention and to force adjournment sine die.[45]

In the convention the next day, Drake offered the following resolution:

> That the people of Missouri, in authorizing, by a majority of more than thirty thousand votes, the holding of this Convention, and in electing the members thereof, in our opinion, intended and expected not only that slavery should be abolished and disloyalists disfranchised, but that the Constitution of this State, framed nearly forty-five years ago, for a slave State of less than seventy thousand inhabitants, should be carefully revised and amended, so as to adapt it to a free State of more than a million of inhabitants.[46]

After an extensive debate, the resolution was adopted by a vote of twenty-nine to nineteen, with seventeen delegates absent.[47] The small affirmative vote served to stimulate, rather than end, the opposition to extensive revision. Bush said later that the resolution was adopted during a day "upon which barn-yard fowls pair off. A Drake set up the quack and there was an attempt to break up the Convention. Several geese, mistaking this drake for the real gander, followed him."[48] A mass meeting of Germans held at Turner's Hall on February 19 heard Gustavus St. Gemme, delegate from Ste. Genevieve, call for "a spirit that would have the force of a Cromwell and walk up in those halls and dissolve that long Parliament."[49]

The Drake forces were able to defeat all attempts to frustrate their determination to write a new constitution that would be in harmony with their conception of the new era into which Missouri was moving. In order to succeed, however, the rules of procedure had to be changed from time to time. When Drake thought that the opposition was trying to discredit the convention by delaying tactics, his forces shortened the time allotted for debate,[50] and the rule requiring a two-thirds vote to shut off debate was changed to require only a simple majority.[51] Toward the end of March, the Drake forces feared that the adoption of the new constitution might be defeated by absenteeism. Consequently, the rule which necessitated an affirmative vote by a majority of the total membership to revise or amend the constitution was changed so as to require the consent of only a majority of those present. Under the new rule, the proposed constitution could be adopted by one more than one-fourth of the total number of delegates.[52]

The minority was vociferous in opposition to Drake's tactics. George Husmann of Gasconade County said that since the minority no longer had any voice at all, those members might as well go home. Drake was accused of cramming his ideas down the throats of the delegates. The convention was being forced to swallow a large dose of "Drake's bitters."[53] Drake defended the changes in the rules on the grounds that the minority was engaged only in obstructionism, and that if the people did not approve of the work of the convention, they would have an opportunity to vote it down.[54] The people, of course, did not get a chance to vote on the various parts of the constitution over which there was so much acrimonious debate in the convention.

Lengthy arguments revolved around the question of the rights and privileges of the Negro. Drake was willing to insure Negro equality before the law with whites, but that was about as far as he was willing to go. That he did not believe the Negro equal to the white man was shown by the first clause of the "Declaration of Rights," which paraphrases the Declaration of Independence but substitutes "all men are created equally free" for "all men are created equal."[55] He believed that educational opportunities for Negroes equal to those for white children should be permitted under the law, but he did not oppose the evident desire of the committee on education to have separate schools established for Negroes and whites.[56] Drake opposed Negro suffrage at that time on the grounds that the freedmen were not capable of voting wisely and that to give them the privilege might prove detrimental to their well-being. He argued that freedom and the franchise were not inseparable, noting that without the right to vote, the Negro would be as free as a woman, a foreigner, or a minor.[57]

Regardless of Drake's personal attitude, expediency demanded that Negro suffrage be postponed until a later date when the question could be resolved with less bitterness. Drake feared that if such a provision were embodied in the constitution, the people would refuse to ratify it. Moreover, it would have been interpreted as bearing out the Conservative charge that the Radicals advocated racial equality. Newspapers, Radical and Conservative, had carried articles purporting to show the physical, mental, and moral superiority of the Caucasian races over the other races, especially the American Negro. Hardly a newspaper had failed to associate Negro suffrage in some illogical way with fancied horrible results of miscegenation.[58] Furthermore, the Negro vote was not essential for the Radicals to maintain control of the state if the "purity" of the elective franchise were preserved by the disfranchisement of enough white men. This the Radicals set about doing with a vengeance.

George Husmann, who represented Gasconade County in the 1865 convention, became an internationally known vintner.

The "iron-clad" or "kucklebur" oath incorporated in the Constitution of 1865 became the most notorious part of that instrument. Although David Bonham of Andrew County was chairman of the committee on the elective franchise, Drake was said to have written the entire section on disfranchisement, which was taken in large part from the new constitution of Maryland.[59] Article Two required that for at least the next six years every voter, officeholder, attorney, clergyman, teacher, and juror take an oath by which he swore that he had never been guilty of committing any one of a long list of disloyal acts.[60] Possibly the convention could have dealt with actual secessionists even more sternly without incurring very much criticism from Union men, but the oath was so all-inclusive that many loyal men could not take it with a clear conscience. The difficulty was that loyalty and Radicalism had become synonymous in the minds of many members of the convention. Radical delegates who represented areas of the state where guerrilla warfare was both a cause and effect of a deep hatred and distrust were hardly capable of dispassionate judgment. Stories of "rebel" cruelty which were related during the debate aroused some of them to a state that bordered on frenzy. Moreover, men who could recall times in 1861 and 1862 when it was not discreet to be militantly loyal were now eager to prove their devotion to the Union by chastising "traitors." Conservatives like Switzler and [Abner] Gilstrap, along with some German delegates, tried to get the section modified, but Drake and the Radicals would not be denied.[61]

The Radicals maintained that persons who had been guilty of the heinous crime of disloyalty had no scruples about committing perjury. Therefore, Drake proposed, and the convention adopted, a section requiring the General Assembly to provide for a complete, uniform, and biennial registration of all voters. Persons who declined to take the oath could not register. Moreover, registration officials were to have the power to hear and pass upon all evidence for and against the right of any man to have his vote counted. Thus, a person who had taken the oath and had voted might have his ballot summarily rejected on the grounds that he had sworn falsely.[62]

Political proscription of Confederate sympathizers was not sufficient punishment in the eyes of some of the Radicals. Ethan A. Holcomb of Chariton County wanted the convention to look into the expediency of taxing secessionists to replace property destroyed or stolen by Southern troops and guerrilla bands.[63] Others would permit the confiscation of property as punishment, not only for treason, but for a felony as well. Drake, who was not eager for the convention to countenance confiscation of property other than that held in slaves, succeeded in persuading most of the delegates to agree that treason should be the only crime for which the state could demand forfeiture of estate. However, two witnesses to the overt act were no longer necessary for conviction.[64] In order to meet the objections of many Radicals that it was virtually impossible to convict Confederate guerrillas in some of the counties, a provision was put in the constitution which allowed the state to secure a change of venue for the trial of persons charged with having committed a felony.[65] On the other hand, Union men who might have been guilty of bushwhacking could not be punished as long as their acts were committed under the military authority of the state or of the United States.[66]

On April 8, 1865, the new constitution was adopted by the convention by a vote of thirty-eight to thirteen. The affirmative vote was not an indication that the document was approved by all thirty-eight. Several members, like Holcomb, voted aye on adoption in order to get rid of the convention but announced they would fight ratification. Some of the members who voted against adoption explained the reasons for their action. Bush said that the convention had exceeded its instructions. Moses Linton, also from St. Louis, said the convention had not stopped at the disfranchisement of rebels, but had also disfranchised loyal men, and that the test oath would tear ministers from the pulpits and teachers from the classrooms. "May God and his good angels save us from this atrocious Constitution," were his concluding words. Husmann and a few other Germans opposed adoption because Negroes were not given equal political rights with white men.[67]

Some doubt existed during most of the life of the convention whether all of its work, a part of its work, or nothing at all should be submitted to the people. Many Germans believed quite correctly that Drake saw no necessity to provide for a popular referendum on the constitution. He believed this convention had as much authority as other conventions held since 1860, whose work was not made subject to popular approval.[68] Nevertheless, Drake feared that if he opposed the move to require the approval of the people before the proposed constitution could go into effect, he would be defeated. Should that have happened, his position in the campaign would have been seriously weakened.[69] Therefore, Drake offered no objection when it was finally decided to submit the document to the people on June 6, 1865. Instead, he turned his attention to the means of insuring, insofar as possible, victory in the campaign for ratification.

NOTES

1. The epithet referred specifically to the disfranchisement provisions in the constitution.

2. Charles D. Drake, *Autobiography of Charles D. Drake*, p. 469, folder 1003, Charles D. Drake Papers, Western Historical Manuscript Collection, University of Missouri-Columbia.

3. Ibid., 523.

4. Ibid., 585.

5. Charles D. Drake, *A Treatise on the Law of Suits by Attachment in the United States*, 3rd ed. (Boston: Little, Brown, 1866), preface, 5.

6. *St. Louis Tri-Weekly Missouri Republican*, 2 December 1859.

7. Ibid. In his autobiography, written almost thirty years later, Drake reluctantly admitted that in 1860 he had been a pronounced adversary of abolition doctrines. Drake, *Autobiography*, 693.

8. Charles D. Drake, *Union and Anti-Slavery Speeches Delivered during the Rebellion* (Cincinnati: Applegate, 1864).

9. Walter B. Stevens, "Lincoln and Missouri," *Missouri Historical Review* 10 (January 1916): 63-119.

10. *Proceedings of the Missouri State Convention Held in Jefferson City, June, 1863* (St. Louis: Knapp, 1863), 367-368.

11. *Laws of the State of Missouri, Passed at the Adjourned Session of the Twenty-Second General Assembly* (Jefferson City, 1864), 24-26.

12. *St. Louis Tri-Weekly Missouri Democrat*, 2 December 1864.

13. *Journal of the Missouri State Convention, Held at the City of St. Louis, January 6-April 10, 1865* (St. Louis: Missouri Democrat, 1865), 3-4, 6, 9; Drake, *Autobiography*, 1055.

14. *Journal of the Missouri State Convention . . . 1865*, 90, 109, 247. Rural delegates refused to follow Drake in his attempt to change the basis of representation for the House of Representatives from the counties to one hundred districts of equal population. This would have reduced rural strength in the House.

15. Drake, *Autobiography*, 1054-1055.

16. *Journal of the Missouri State Convention . . . 1865*, 15, 19, 224, 244.

17. *St. Louis Daily Missouri Democrat*, 24 February 1865; *St. Louis Tri-Weekly Missouri Democrat*, 17 March 1865.

18. *St. Louis Daily Dispatch*, 4 March 1865.

19. *Journal of the Missouri State Convention . . . 1865*, 26.

20. Ibid., 28, 131.

21. Ibid., 25.

22. *St. Louis Daily Missouri Democrat*, 13 January 1865.

23. *Proceedings of the Missouri State Convention . . . 1863*, 20.

24. *St. Louis Daily Missouri Democrat*, 13 January 1865.

25. *Journal of the Missouri State Convention . . . 1865*, 25, 27-28, 282.

26. *St. Louis Daily Missouri Democrat*, 18 January 1865; *Constitution of the State of Missouri, as Revised, Amended, and Adopted in Convention, Begun and Held at the City of St. Louis On the Sixth Day of January, One Thousand Eight Hundred and Sixty-five* (Jefferson City, 1865), art. IV, sec. 29.

27. *Columbia Missouri Statesman*, 5 May 1865.

28. *Gallatin North Missourian*, 1 December 1864; 16 March 1865; Drake, *Autobiography*, 1048.

29. *Journal of the Missouri State Convention . . . 1865*, 89.

30. Ibid., 14.

31. Drake, *Autobiography*, 1061.

32. *Journal of the Missouri State Convention . . . 1865*, 30-39.

33. *Constitution of the State of Missouri . . . 1865*, art. XIII, sec. 6.

34. The office of sheriff was added before the ordinance was adopted. *Journal of the Missouri State Convention . . . 1865*, 109, 159.

35. *St. Louis Tri-Weekly Missouri Democrat*, 20 January 1865.

36. *Constitution of the State of Missouri . . . 1865*, art. XII.

37. Ibid., art. IV, sec. 27.

38. Ibid., art. VIII, sec. 4.

39. Ibid., art. IV, sec. 23-25, 32.

40. Ibid., art. XI, sec. 13-16.

41. *Journal of the Missouri State Convention . . . 1865*, 31.

42. Quoted in *St. Louis Tri-Weekly Missouri Republican*, 1 February 1865.

43. *Constitution of the State of Missouri . . . 1865*, art. I, clause 9.

44. *St. Louis Tri-Weekly Missouri Republican*, 27 March 1865; *St. Louis Tri-Weekly Missouri Democrat*, 27 March 1865.

45. Drake, *Autobiography*, 1061; Chauncey I. Filley to Mrs. Nettie Harney Beauregard, 20 November 1917, Chauncey I. Filley Papers, Missouri Historical Society, St. Louis.

46. *Journal of the Missouri State Convention . . . 1865*, 89.

47. Ibid., 90.

48. *St. Louis Tri-Weekly Missouri Democrat*, 1 March 1865.

49. Ibid., 20 February 1865.

50. *Journal of the Missouri State Convention . . . 1865*, 146.

51. Ibid., 142-143.

52. Ibid., 203; *St. Louis Tri-Weekly Missouri Democrat*, 31 March 1865.

53. The term "Drake's bitters" was appropriated from the name of a tonic advertised by P. H. Drake & Co. Charles D. Drake was not connected with the firm.

54. *St. Louis Tri-Weekly Missouri Democrat*, 31 March 1865.

55. *Journal of the Missouri State Convention . . . 1865*, 30.

56. Ibid., 198; *St. Louis Tri-Weekly Missouri Republican*, 27 February 1865; *Constitution of the State of Missouri . . . 1865*, art. I, clause 3.

57. *St. Louis Daily Missouri Democrat*, 8 February 1865. Drake wished to leave the matter to future action by the people, first in 1870 and again in 1876. After that, if Negroes were still forbidden to vote, the General Assembly could enfranchise them.

58. *Gallatin North Missourian*, 15 December 1864; *Jefferson City Missouri State Times*, 3 December 1864; *St. Louis Daily Missouri Democrat*, 28 November 1864.

59. *St. Louis Tri-Weekly Missouri Republican*, 18, 30 January 1865.

60. *Constitution of the State of Missouri . . . 1865*, art. II, sec. 3, 6, 8, 9, 11. Drake opposed including clergymen and religious teachers among those required to take the oath. *St. Louis Tri-Weekly Missouri Democrat*, 3 April 1865.

61. *St. Louis Tri-Weekly Missouri Democrat*, 30 January, 3 February 1865; *St. Louis Daily Missouri Democrat*, 6 February 1865.

62. *Constitution of the State of Missouri . . . 1865*, art. II, sec. 4, 5.

63. *Journal of the Missouri State Convention . . . 1865*, 40.

64. *Constitution of the State of Missouri . . . 1865*, art. I, sec. 25, 26; *St. Louis Tri-Weekly Missouri Democrat*, 25, 27 January 1865.

65. *Constitution of the State of Missouri . . . 1865*, art. XI, sec. 12.

66. Ibid., art. XI, sec. 4.

67. *St. Louis Tri-Weekly Missouri Democrat*, 10 April 1865.

68. Drake, *Autobiography*, 1065.

69. Ibid., 1066.

Missouri and the American Civil War Novel

LARRY OLPIN

Henry Adams, in his *Education*, says that "he could plainly discern in history, that man from the beginning has found his chief amusement in bloodshed."[1] In all probability he is right, especially if love is excluded. No doubt Americans have been mightily "amused" by their own war. As a subject for literature, the American Civil War has been the source for countless poems, stories, and plays. But above all else, it has provided a source for novels. To date, the count reaches well over one thousand, and a new novel appears at the rate of almost one a month. If the amusing elements include vivid battles, blood and gore, the trials of good people sorely wronged, and heroic and villainous doings, then it would be difficult to imagine a better setting for the Civil War novel than Missouri.

With its divided loyalties, attempts to be a slave state and remain in the Union, and lengthy border wars between such mythic hero-villains as the jayhawkers, James Lane and Charles Jennison, or the bushwhackers, William Quantrill and Bloody Bill Anderson, Missouri has provided a setting for a wide variety of Civil War novels. Between 1863 and 1988, no fewer than sixty-two appeared in print.[2] Included are realistic and psychological stories, westerns, juvenile fiction, historical romances, and novels of unadulterated propaganda; though each is inherently interesting, they range from excellent to awful.

In their diversity and concern with a single period in history, these novels, centered on a common theme, make a good group to study. Many questions arise that involve both history and fiction. How does a novelist use history? Should there be a close adherence to historical fact? Or should the author

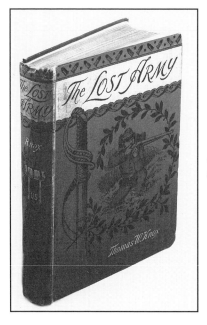

Many authors have used Missouri as the setting for Civil War novels.

freely use imagination to create a subjective world in dialogue and penetrate the minds of the characters? Also pertinent is the treatment of well-known historical figures. What does the writer do with such persons as John Brown or the colorful Frémonts, John and Jessie? The most popular historical personality for the Missouri novelists, Quantrill, appears in so many different guises he becomes unrecognizable between one novel and the next. And what about personal biases in the North-versus-South partisanship that so marks the period? These Civil War authors have their answers. However varied their perceptions or however well realized in literary terms, each novelist approached the subject convinced that the period and its strife made good fiction. Though the novels rarely result in great literature, they provide no lack of excitement in their struggle to capture an intense and dramatic moment in the history of Missouri and the nation.

The publication of several novels during the 1860s indicates writers of fiction immediately saw the war as good material. The first, which appeared at the early date of 1862, is J. H. Robinson's *Mountain Max, or, Nick Whiffles on the Border, A Tale of the Bushwhackers in Missouri.*[3] This short novel with romances, battles, melodrama, and polemic Unionism is a harbinger of many novels that follow. The novel's hero has a manner of speaking and a philosophy replete with the sentiments of other fictional characters of his time and place: "I can't fight for cotton and niggers, but I can fight for freedom and the Union as hearty and faithful as any man that lives."[4]

Robinson's novel, a short, cheaply bound paperback obviously written for a mass audience, is typical of others which are surely lost. Those available lack any claim to lasting literary merit but provide historical interest and can delight the reader with audacious assertions and bold melodrama. Their long, descriptive titles, a fashion of the time, contain no little sense of the tone and contents. Lieutenant Colonel Harry Hazelton, reputedly a member of General John C. Frémont's personal bodyguard, wrote *The Border Spy, or, The Beautiful Captive of the Rebel Camp: A Story of the War* (1863)[5] and *The Prisoner of the Mill, or, Captain Hayward's "Body Guard"* (1864).[6] Stephen Holmes Jr. wrote *The Guerrillas of the Osage, or, The Price of Loyalty on the Border* (1864).[7] One title to beat them all is Sergeant J. Winston's *Cora O'Kane; or, The Doom of the Rebel Guard. A Story of the Great Rebellion. Containing Incidents of the Campaign in Missouri under Generals Fremont and Sigel, and the Thrilling Exploits of the Unionists under Major Zagonyi.*[8] A somewhat later short paperback of the same type is *Fremont the Pathfinder, or, Bullet and Bayonet on Missouri Battlefields* (1887) by Mark Wilton.[9]

These and other early novels were written to tell an exciting story, but equally as important, each writer believed that fiction can and should influence public sentiment and the course of events. For the early Missouri writers, this meant propaganda for the Union cause. After all, most of the presses operated in the Northeast states. Despite a wide variety of public feeling and areas of intense sympathy for the South, the state remained under Union control for most of the war.

An example of a novel written solely for propaganda's sake is Jessie Benton Frémont's *The Story of the Guard: A Chronicle of the War* (1863).[10] A very assertive woman dubbed "General Jessie" by her detractors, she rarely appeared at loss for words or uncertain about her position. In fact the title itself indicates the temperament of the author; not a story of the guard, it remains *the* story. The Home Guard, organized to protect Union interests in the state, and the author's husband, General John C. Frémont, who for a short time directed the Union war effort in the West, both achieve heroic stature. The book claims to be fact and includes letters and military reports. However, the use of dialect and the free-ranging mind of the author give it an air of fiction and no strong sense of historical reality. In the end, nothing really matters to the author except the reputation of her husband. The effort results in a poor novel or, if the reader prefers, poor history.

Jessie Frémont appears later in two fictional accounts—both chapters appropriately entitled "General Jessie"—which precisely reflect the divergent

Jessie Benton Frémont sought to bolster her husband's reputation with her 1863 publication.

feelings that surround the Frémonts in the Missouri war. Popular historical novelist Irving Stone's *Immortal Wife, the Biographical Novel of Jessie Benton Frémont* (1944) presents simple hagiography.[11] The Frémonts can do no wrong and are defeated by enemies and circumstances beyond their control. In a large and ambitious novel, *Freedom* (1987), William Safire gives a rather negative view of the troubles caused for President [Abraham] Lincoln by the "two generals" and their premature emancipation of the slaves in Missouri.[12]

The best—used advisedly in this context—of the early novels is Isaac Kelso's *The Stars and Bars, or, The Reign of Terror in Missouri* (1863).[13] Kelso's setting shifts back and forth between the Arkansas-Missouri and the Kansas-Missouri borders. Thus he makes use of the two most dramatic trouble spots during the war. For him, the cause of these troubles becomes clear: the Confederacy embodies evil, while the Union personifies everything pure and decent.

For his largely propagandistic purpose, Kelso begins his novel by telling the reader he is writing "truth" not fiction. No question about it, however, a novel emerges, not history. Scenes, characters, dialogues, and inner thoughts are freely imagined and, in his partisanship, take on a shrill and unbelievable aura. His Union heroes become walking saints. Young Malvin on the Arkansas-Missouri border is typical:

> Vice in every form prevailed around him, and scenes of cruelty and injustice were constantly before his eyes; yet he maintained an upright

walk and spotless reputation, and unfolded his faculties, moral and intellectual, in rare harmony, beauty, and purity.[14]

Kelso does little better with his Confederate characters. He cannot decide whether to vent his spleen or laugh, whether to make his "secesh" characters crafty and villainous or bumpkins of low comedy. These characters, who burn, rape, pillage, and threaten the existence of the Union, sport such names as Dr. Puff and Mr. Skedaddle. One inept guerrilla-ruffian attempts an ignominious retreat facing the wrong way on his horse. With the horse's tail serving as his bridle, he mistakenly charges into the oncoming troops. Such names and antics render the characters and situations ridiculous rather than threatening and undercut the novel's purpose of exposing the horrible truth about the demon rebels.

Despite Kelso's inability to see except in black and white and his constantly preaching the Union cause—his mouthpiece, named the Reverend Mr. Southdown, gives long harangues filled with rectitude and piety that wear out the reader—Kelso shows literary ability. In some ways, his strengths become his weaknesses. His novel has the force of a writer confident he is right, and his characters exhibit a kind of robust vitality.

One other early novel of some interest to the Missouri Civil War scene is Mary S. Robinson's *A Household Story of the American Conflict: The Brother Soldiers* (1868).[15] This novel consists of letters home from various Union soldier brothers. One brother, in strong partisan terms, reports on the war situation from Missouri, his "adopted state."

In 1884, Henry Oldham introduced the distinct genre of the western to the Missouri Civil War setting with *The Man from Texas: A Western Romance*.[16] Highly pro-Confederate, the novel, excluding the likes of such border ruffians as Quantrill, portrays the guerrillas as chivalric knights and the pro-Union Missourians as lowbred "scum of the earth."[17] From the highborn, sensitive, refined ladies to the hard-riding, straight-shooting, whiskey-drinking heroes, this novel contains the earmarks of the cheap western.

While Oldham's novel represents the first western, its type became more common. Typical of the genre, most lack literary or historical merit. Adela E. Orpen's *The Jay-hawkers; a Story of Free Soil and Border Ruffian Days* (1900) remains of interest mostly for its melodrama.[18] The novel spins a tale of a pretty maid who will not "marry" a ruffian leader—presumably Quantrill—thus causing Lawrence to be sacked. Hal Borland, in *The Amulet* (1957), writes with a clear, effective style.[19] He handles action scenes well, but when he waxes philosophical, the quality drops sharply. Three-fourths of the novel involves a trip to Missouri and features the Battle of Wilson's Creek.

Alan LeMay's *By Dim and Flaring Lamps* (1962), another routine western, is set in central and southern Missouri.[20] A better than average western is Daniel Woodrell's *Woe to Live On* (1987).[21] Set in west central Missouri, the novel is replete with blood, gore, and some explicit sex. The first person narration, while good at times, does not always ring true. The latest of the genre, a paperback original, *The Exiles* (1988) by Greg Hunt, is basically a pulp western set near Kansas City.[22]

The aura of the western pervades the novels focusing on Confederate bushwhackers and their enigmatic leader, William Clarke Quantrill. They describe his character from hero of the oppressed Missourians to bloodthirsty killer. W. R. Burnett's *The Dark Command: A Kansas Iliad* (1938) names him Cantrell and effectively presents him as a flawed but romantic figure.[23] He becomes a man to pursue and kill in George C. Appell's *The Man Who Shot Quantrill* (1957)[24] and Frank Gruber's *Quantrell's Raiders* (1953).[25] In the latter, the hero infiltrates Quantrill's gang and, in defiance of history but in compliance with melodrama, kills George Todd, Bloody Bill Anderson and Quantrill himself. Among the best of the novels that focus on Quantrill is William Goede's *Quantrill* (1982).[26] Goede proves especially effective in rendering the famous bushwhacker raid on Lawrence through the double perspective of Quantrill and a ruffian who, against his better judgment, joins a friend in raping and murdering during the raid.

Novelists remain divided over William Clarke Quantrill—hero or villain?

A number of novels use Quantrill as a major figure in juxtaposition to Captain John Brown. Contrasting these two of course suggests political or social concerns, and as a group, these novels tend toward the fiercely partisan. Although uneven, perhaps the most interesting of these is the privately printed *A Union Forever* (1949) by Muriel Culp Barbe.[27] The first half of this long novel focuses on Brown, rendered the hero, while the second and more successful half focuses on Quantrill. Quantrill, in his own way, represents the worst and most wicked of them all, but Barbe's Missourians, on the whole, appear a rather pathetic lot. A newspaperman in the novel puts it this way:

> They're decided characters these Missouri "Pukes." They estimate a man by the amount of whiskey he can guzzle. . . . Hairy faces, yes. Red eyes, that's too much whiskey. Teeth the color of walnuts, that's from tobacco. Dirty shirts, wicked knives and handsome boots. Well-cleaned rifles and unclean tongues. That's your border ruffians.[28]

A novel even more polemic in its portrayal of the two characters is *A Wall of Men* (1912) by Kansas novelist Margaret Hill McCarter.[29] She likens Brown to Alexander, Caesar, and Moses, among others, and presents Quantrill basically through animal imagery, with repeated emphasis on his "yellow green tiger" eyes, ironically famous for their brilliant blue color.

Author Laurel O. Ringler presents the other side of the Brown versus Quantrill controversy in *Dark Grows the Night* (1961).[30] Ringler's Brown appears a raving madman while Quantrill follows a trail of justified vengeance. A gentle, scholarly soul, the latter might have been a poet had fate decreed otherwise. Underlying the writer's portrayal of Quantrill is sympathy for the Confederate cause. It seems somewhat ironic that such a bitterly partisan novel should appear as late as 1961, but no mistake about it, Ringler consistently directs his anger toward Kansas and his sympathy to Missouri:

> The one great difference between Jayhawkers and Missourians was the Jayhawker enthusiasm for this war. They were the trumpeters; the walls of Jericho would fall before them. Lawrence was an island in a sea of iniquity. Singing and praying, they set forth to destroy their enemies.
> Missourians entered into the fray reluctantly. They fought with dogged determination attempting to protect their homes and loved ones. With each passing day as the crimes committed against them increased in violence, they fought more bitterly.[31]

Three novels which have a western flavor and serve as a footnote to the war in Missouri recount the adventures of General Joseph O. Shelby and his men who refused to accept a Union victory and fled to Mexico. Competently written, Eugene P. Lyle's *The Missourian* (1905) blended realism and romance.[32] *Angel with Spurs, a Novel* (1942) by the popular novelist Paul I. Wellman followed, with its several flashbacks to wartime in Missouri.[33] Finally, Harley Duncan—a pseudonym for a group of writers—in *West of Appomattox* (1961) presented a typical western adventure story.[34]

The years of the 1890s and the early twentieth century were particularly productive for the Missouri Civil War novel. Both the numbers and types of fiction increased dramatically, with a complex blend of realism and romance, history and melodrama, and a new tendency to view the war in nonpartisan terms.

The period began with a melodramatic potboiler. John Bowles's *The Stormy Petrel: An Historical Romance* (1892) features a plot to take the breath away.[35] The hero catches a baby thrown from a slave boat on the Missouri River near its confluence with the Mississippi. The baby turns out to be the child of an extremely white slave woman. Through various manipulations of the plot the mother ends up the baby girl's slave and caretaker. The child does not know she carries the blood of a "despised race," but when she prepares to

Jacqueline, a French noblewoman, and John Dinwiddie Driscoll, the Missourian, are the main characters in Eugene Lyle's 1905 story set in Mexico.

marry an aristocratic Italian, the hero feels honor bound to let him know the girl's background. The Italian man will marry her anyway. As it turns out, her mother was not black but an aristocratic Italian, stolen into slavery. All would be all right, but the girl, "stormy petrel," already has thrown herself into the river. Not a bad writer, Bowles can be subtle at times, but melodrama and a constant desire for one more turn of plot do him in.

Among the weakest and silliest in its melodrama of all these novels is Robert Eggert's privately printed *The Log House Club* (1911).[36] Some idealistic young men set up a utopian household in a log cabin in St. Louis. The war sends them all out of the cabin in defense of the Union and in search of personal honor. Many sentimental and contrived episodes result.

Of particular historical interest in this period is Frank Sosey's *Robert Devoy: A Tale of the Palmyra Massacre* (1903).[37] Decidedly pro-Confederate, it tells the story of the Palmyra "massacre" where Union forces shot ten Confederate prisoners to protest a Union man's supposed abduction. Sosey handles the history well and writes movingly of the executions, but he adds a parallel plot of villains, heroes, and a melodramatic love entanglement that undoes the good writing found elsewhere in the novel.

J. G. Woerner's *The Rebel's Daughter: A Story of Love, Politics and War* (1899) never mentions the state by name, but the setting obviously is

J. Gabriel Woerner served as a St. Louis probate court judge for twenty-four years and wrote legal works and German-language dramas in addition to his Civil War novel.

Missouri.[38]   Greene County becomes Vernal County, Springfield becomes Brookfield, St. Louis is the metropolis, and Rolla is Rollaville.

Written in the style of the times, the novel portrays a pure hero, filled with rectitude and pride, and a heroine who is beautiful, pure, and a little feisty. The platitudinous dialogue often seems stiff and artificial. Yet the novel has strengths. Basically accurate historically, the novel creates especial interest with the slave girl, Cressie, a "beautiful Octoroon of voluptuous beauty and graceful presence," who clearly attracts the romantic interests of a Union soldier.[39]   In the end, she denies her suitor and stays "faithful" to her mistress after the war. However, Woerner's portrayal of Cressie suggests the strong sexual attraction between the races that so marked Southern fiction and fiction about the war, a subject that never became a topic of importance in the Missouri Civil War novel.

One of the strangest novels of the period is *The MacGregors* (1901) by Virginia McCanne, written under the pseudonym Marshall Home.[40]   Set in the hills just south of Springfield, the story features a bewildering array of characters adept at finding parallels between their own situations and those in the romances of Sir Walter Scott. Heavily pro-Confederate, the book presents a sentimental ending about the "lost cause."

Two novels of the early twentieth century stand out both for historical importance and literary merit: Winston Churchill's *The Crisis* (1901)[41] and Caroline Abbot Stanley's *Order No. 11: A Tale of the Border* (1904).[42]   Indeed, more than any other, Stanley's novel represents the prototypical Missouri Civil War novel.

To describe this typical novel: It would be set on the Kansas-Missouri border somewhere near Kansas City. A good mix of people would support each side, with the predominant group of wealthy, important characters backing the Confederacy. Trouble would develop for the innocent and good people at the hands of both Kansas jayhawkers and Missouri bushwhackers. A few well-known historical figures would make cameo appearances. Finally, the novel's love affairs would dominate the story.

Alas, the love affairs—many of them cause the novels to go astray in both characterization and plot. Often the major romance represents a split between North and South. The pro-Union male comes from a professional family, the son of a doctor or lawyer. The pro-Confederate female, from a slaveholding family, is a veritable Southern belle, raised with aristocratic pretensions and the special pampering that comes from having a personal slave. Even her name can be predicted: Virginia—no less than five have this name—an emblem of family ties with the "Old Dominion." She appears beautiful, feisty and, finally, in fictional terms, totally lovable. In short, she represents the type from which the heroines of the historical romance are made. To finalize the love theme, after many turns and twists in the plot, the lovers marry in a symbolic gesture uniting North and South.

Stanley's *Order No. 11* supplies all of the stereotypes with elaborate love themes that end in a unifying marriage. It portrays a young, wounded Jesse James and attempts to balance the interests of the Union and the Confederacy. It also includes a lot more. Order No. 11, from which the novel takes its name, was issued by the Union commander and required all rural people living in the counties of Cass, Jackson, Bates, and half of Vernon to vacate their homes and farms in fifteen days. Those able or willing to "prove" their loyalty to the Union could move to a military station; others were ordered to leave. Probably the worst aspect of the situation for the people—and the best for novelists in search of dramatic fare—was its enforcement by unruly Kansas military forces. Abuses ranged from burnings to indiscriminate hangings. Many people left their homes in makeshift wagons pulled by old, worn-out animals—the decent ones already appropriated by soldiers and guerrillas—with a view of their burning houses in the background. Such accounts appear often in the novels and seem to strain both the novelists' emotions and their prose. Stanley's description is typical:

> As the days went by the roads were filled with the wretched exiles, going they knew not where. Barefooted women and children, stripped of all but a scant covering for their bodies, struggled on through the dust and heat of an August sun. Behind them were their smoking homes; before them, the world was so big![43]

Order No. 11 gives both a typical and a better than average literary rendering of the Missouri Civil War scene. It covers the war in its most intensive and dramatic setting, from its beginning to the end. Even its virtues and flaws are representative of other novels of the time.

Without doubt, the best-known Civil War novel set in the state remains Winston Churchill's *The Crisis*. The novel, which enjoys the status of a minor classic about the war, deserves its reputation, but it often has been praised for the wrong reasons. For example, Lincoln plays a major part in the novel and received praise as the main character and a well-conceived literary personality. But he appears so overdone in his legendary greatness and so much in the guise of the tragic jokester that he becomes rather a cliché. In fact, Churchill's handling of major characters ranges from mediocre to bad. His main character, Stephen Price, appears a hopelessly noble prig, and his counterpart in the battle of love, the Southern belle, Virginia Carvel, is not much better in her

"Wretched Exiles, Going They Knew Not Where"

stereotypical splendor. Nor is Churchill skillful with plot, for which he also has been praised. The woes of courtship and love in the portrayal of Stephen and Virginia are enough to exhaust all but the most devoted of readers. The lovers are brought together and married by no less a distinguished go-between than Abe Lincoln.

While Churchill has difficulty drawing his major characters and placing their actions into a significant plot, he adroitly creates minor characters, settings, and vivid scenes. In *The Crisis* Churchill's claim to fame lies in his portrayal of wartime St. Louis and the city's conflict between the pro-Union immigrant (mostly German) forces and the older, slaveholding aristocrats. In his rendering of this conflict, he came near to writing the classic many of his contemporaries thought he had. In a passage that mirrors Stanley's description of people fleeing the ravages of Order No. 11 on the other side of the state, Churchill marshals his strongest, though somewhat old-fashioned, rhetoric to depict the confusion as panic-stricken people attempt to flee St. Louis because of rumors of imminent battle:

> Down on the levee wheels rattled over the white stones washed clean by the driving rain. The drops pelted the chocolate water into froth, and

a blue veil hid the distant bluffs beyond the Illinois bottom-lands. Down on the levee rich and poor battled for places on the landing-stages, and would have thrown themselves into the flood had there been no boats to save them from the dreaded Dutch. Attila and his Huns were not more feared. Oh, the mystery of that foreign city! What might its Barbarians do when roused? The rich and poor struggled together; but money was power that day, and many were pitilessly turned off because they did not have the high price to carry them—who knew where?[44]

Despite the melodrama of the passage and excesses in the language, the passage works effectively in its context. If Churchill is read with pleasure today, it is for scenes such as this, rather than for his hackneyed plots and his contrived love stories.

Churchill's skill in depicting the St. Louis war scene becomes apparent when compared to others. Although St. Louis appears in several Civil War novels, none of them equals *The Crisis*. Perhaps *Civil War Dragoon* (1965) by W. C. Fordyce Jr. comes the closest.[45] The most successful part of this novel portrays a double agent in St. Louis during the early part of the war. Although the characters are wooden and the plot somewhat contrived, Fordyce's history proves accurate, and the story moves quickly and with some interest.

The 1890s also saw the advent of the juvenile novel, which like the western, later became a staple form of the genre. Perhaps the surest literary

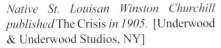

Native St. Louisan Winston Churchill published The Crisis *in 1905.* [Underwood & Underwood Studios, NY]

success has been in this area. First came *The Lost Army* (1894) by Thomas W. Knox, a long novel full of advice for young boys about war and life in general but lacking significant literary value.[46]

Of greater interest, the more ambitious "Young Missourian Series" (1910-1914) includes five novels by Byron Archibald Dunn. Written in the tradition of adventure and romantic literature for youth, Dunn's series traces the activities of a young Union soldier and his friends. The author manages to place them at virtually every important event in the state's war history. The range of the series and the author's enthusiasm partially make up for a lack of literary merit and an overbearing Union partisanship.[47] In this same period, another juvenile novel, *The Hoosier Volunteer* (1914) by Kate and Virgil D. Boyles, recounts the adventures of some earnest young hoosiers among the backwoods people and guerrillas of central Missouri.[48]

After Dunn's series, almost thirty years lapsed before the publication of other juvenile novels about the war. Since that time they have appeared at a steady rate. The first, and one of the most successful, is Ada Claire Darby's *Look Away, Dixie Land* (1941).[49] Set in Lexington, the novel features a girl who becomes a nurse and supports the Union cause while most of her friends, those from the "better families," favor the South. Enid LaMonte Meadowcroft portrays a negative view of the state in *By Secret Railway* (1948), a juvenile novel set in Chicago and eastern and northern Missouri.[50] The dark, wicked side can be found in slave-ridden Missouri from which the youthful hero rescues his young black friend who has been sold "down there." Manly Wade Wellman wrote a fast-moving story for the beginning reader, *Rebel Mail Runner* (1954), set in eastern Missouri and northern Arkansas.[51] Probably the best juvenile novel, Harold Keith's *Rifles for Watie* (1957) won the 1958 Newbery Award.[52] Set mostly in Kansas and the Oklahoma Cherokee Indian territory, the story, however, includes scenes in Kansas City and at the Battle of Wilson's Creek. This well-written novel has all the ingredients of the good juvenile adventure story. It features a Melvillian villain after the manner of Claggert and a young hero of the Stephen Crane type who muses about the romance of war versus realism.

The Island on the Border, A Civil War Story (1963) by Trella Lamson Dick is an adventure story set in the Mississippi River area of Missouri and Tennessee and on an island between the two states.[53] It presents such stock characters as a very superstitious free Negro and a shadowy Quantrill, whose raids cause many problems and fears for the young hero and his family. Gertrude Bell wrote two juvenile novels, *First Crop* (1973)[54] and *Where Runs the River* (1976).[55] Both novels are set in western Missouri. *Where Runs the River*, written in a rather beguiling but at times confusing style, focuses on the

Melodramatic situations abound in Civil War novels set in Missouri.

mind of a young girl. Two images of escape flicker through her mind—floating down the river to New Orleans and fleeing to Texas in a rickety wagon loaded with a poor family and their belongings. Both images suggest in different ways the horrors of the Missouri war scene. *First Crop*, a 1974 Mark Twain Award nominee, features a boy who, much against his own interests and wishes, helps people unable to flee the area. In *Save Weeping for the Night* (1975), Loula Grace Erdman presents a juvenile, fictional biography of Bettie Shelby, the wife of General Jo Shelby from Waverly, Missouri.[56] The novel suffers from sentimentality and wooden characters. Bettie Shelby appears a regular Penelope, and the general remains a man of honor at all times. In their overwrought goodness, neither of them becomes a believable character.

Several Civil War novels using the Missouri setting were published during the 1930s, '40s and '50s. Many of these works reflect the changing trends in fiction at the turn of the century, coupling realism in dialogue and descriptive detail with a rigorous attempt at historical accuracy. Infused with this is a new seriousness and literary ambition. This high time of achievement for the Civil War novel exemplifies the national trend of the thirties with the appearance of novels by William Faulkner, Allen Tate, Caroline Gordon, Margaret Mitchell, and others.

A Missouri novel of large pretense, written with the hope of it taking its place alongside the serious novels, is Dagmar Doneghy's *The Border: A Missouri Saga* (1931).[57] A young boy tells the story and focuses on the problems of a woman left with six sons to care for while her husband fights for the Confederacy. The novel has some good writing, but the quality is uneven and the epic scope somewhat out of the novelist's reach.

Much less successful novels include *First the Blade* (1938) by May Miller[58] and *Bound Girl* (1949) by Everett and Olga Webber.[59] The early part of the first novel is set near St. Louis, where the war disrupts the normal life of a young girl. Only about a third of the novel takes place in Civil War Missouri, the rest in postwar California. The Webber novel is a rather shrill romance occurring on the Missouri-Kansas border. Lots of stock villains appear, with the real villains on the Confederate side. The Webbers provide some melodramatic touches with historical figures: the heroine has a revered poet cousin named "Walt," and young Jesse James gets an unfortunate girl pregnant and will not pay the consequences.

Three novels and two novelists stand above the others for their achievement during this period: Jane Hutchens's *John Brown's Cousin* (1940)[60] and *Timothy Larkin* (1942)[61] and John Burress's *Bugle in the Wilderness* (1958).[62] By concentrating on the telling of her stories and on giving the details that fill the world of her characters, Hutchens manages to avoid both propaganda and lifeless, wooden personalities. In *John Brown's Cousin*, the protagonist, Henry Brown, appears in ironic contrast to his famous cousin and many other Civil War heroes. A nonviolent person, he would today be called a conscientious objector. Like his modern counterparts, he even flees to Canada for the duration of the war. He defines his creed in the homey idiom of the western Missouri frontier when he explains to his mother why he cannot fight: "I can't do it Ma. . . . Even animals don't go around killin' each other. Even hogs."[63] *Timothy Larkin*, probably a better novel than *John Brown's Cousin*, ranges from the Kansas-Missouri border to the east and southeastern parts of the state. The main character has trouble with a wandering heart in matters of love, as did his father. He serves as a Union scout during the war and, with backwoods guile, manages to escape from some difficult situations. Hutchens successfully handles elements of traditional realistic fiction. Her characters, both major and minor, appear well conceived and her plots effective. She is worth reading because she tells a story so well.

The single most successful Missouri Civil War novel, John Burress's *Bugle in the Wilderness*, is told in the first-person narrative of a twelve-year-old boy. Set in the Missouri Bootheel in Dunklin County, the novel places the problems brought on by the war against the personal tragedy of a rural family. The boy, who harbors a sense of guilt about his insane mother, focuses his attention on a not-so-heroic father. The father, a philanderer with a severe drinking problem, breaks some important promises to the boy and is not heroic in war. When soldiers approach the family cabin from time to time, the boy says, "Sometimes they wore gray and sometimes blue, and sometimes they was so muddy and their uniforms so faded it was hard to tell which they was. Pap didn't take any chances and had us go in the brush any time they was movements of soldiers from either side."[64] Yet, the boy tells the story in such a way that this flawed and brooding father becomes something of a hero to both the boy and the reader. In the boy's vernacular idiom, the novel takes on a lyric quality that effectively weaves personal guilt with the community guilt engendered by the war.

Published in 1966, Loula Grace Erdman's *Another Spring* revisits the territory of Order No. 11 and depicts a hidden settlement set up by a group of people to wait out the horrors of the war.[65] The novel covers all classes and types of people from slave to aristocrat, from noble soul to downright villain. A better than average novel, it convincingly highlights the difficulties generated by Order No. 11.

A successful novel set just outside the state is *Elkhorn Tavern* (1980) by Douglas C. Jones.[66] The Battle of Elkhorn Tavern, perhaps better known as the Battle of Pea Ridge and fought only four miles from the Missouri border, was of central importance to the war in the West. *Elkhorn Tavern* deals with the struggles of a family left behind by a Confederate soldier. The family survives the battle, its two armies, the jayhawkers and bushwhackers, and most of all, local people who try to use the chaotic situation to their own advantage. An old-fashioned storyteller, Jones deals well with characters and plot.

Aside from *Elkhorn Tavern* and another novel or two, novels written about the war during the past two decades have produced an increase in formula-type westerns and historical romances. This indicates the taste of the modern reading public and, perhaps, the economics pushing the market. A recent novel of the type includes Rebecca Brandewyne's *The Outlaw Hearts* (1986).[67] A standard historical romance set in the Missouri Ozarks, the novel, despite moments of competent writing, fails because of its focus on a lurid and unbelievable romance between a "plain" girl and a dashing, handsome outlaw with a good and decent heart. Jan McKee in *By Love Divided* (1988) covers fairly well the history near Kansas City but emphasizes a conventional romance.[68] Even less effective as works of literature are some of the recent paperback westerns with stereotypical characters and plot situations.

Despite the current negative trends, with only a fair number of good novels dealing with the Missouri war scene, there is no reason for despair. Other writers, as did their predecessors, will turn to this dramatic material and, with depth and freedom of the imagination, offer a great novel. Though a *Red*

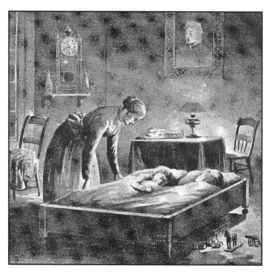

The Family Left Behind

Badge of Courage or even a *Raintree County* is unlikely, the possibility remains.

Yet waiting for the future would be a mistake. What has been accomplished remains significant, and one can get a solid sense of the Missouri Civil War novel and an enlightening look at history through the careful selection of a few novels. One should choose an early novel, probably Kelso's *The Stars and Bars*, Stanley's *Order No. 11*, Churchill's *The Crisis*, either Hutchens's *John Brown's Cousin* or *Timothy Larkin*, John Burress's *Bugle in the Wilderness*, and finally one of the novels about the jayhawkers and bushwhackers. After this, the only restraints are preference and time.

History comes more quickly and usually more accurately from historians, but many agree with Samuel Taylor Coleridge who said, if his words can be twisted a little: "Who would take away the liberty of the novelist and fetter his feet in the shackles of an historian?"[69] It has been said that history which reads like a novel is the best kind of history. The only thing better is a good novel itself.

NOTES

1. *The Education of Henry Adams: An Autobiography* (Boston: Houghton Mifflin, 1918), 128.

2. Although it has some errors and gaps, by far the most useful resource for this study has been Albert J. Menendez, *Civil War Novels: An Annotated Bibliography* (New York: Garland, 1986). Also of value is the Wilmer Collection of Civil War novels at the University of North Carolina at Chapel Hill. Many of the novels also are available in libraries in Missouri and Kansas. Every attempt has been made to find and read all the Civil War novels set in the state, and each of the novels is mentioned at least once in the essay or the notes.

3. (New York: F. A. Brady, 1862).

4. Ibid., 16.

5. (New York: Beadle, 1863).

6. (New York: Beadle, 1864).

7. (New York: Beadle, 1864).

8. (Claremont, NH: Association of Disabled Soldiers, 1868).

9. (New York: Novelist Publishing, 1887).

10. (Boston: Ticknor & Fields, 1863).

11. (Garden City, NY: Doubleday, Doran, 1944).

12. (Garden City, NY: Doubleday, 1987).

13. (Boston: A. Williams, 1863).

14. Ibid., 9.

15. (New York: N. Tibbals, 1868).

16. (Philadelphia: T. B. Peterson & Bros., 1884).

17. Ibid., 242.

18. (New York: D. Appleton, 1900).

19. (Philadelphia: Lippincott, 1957).

20. (New York: Harper, 1962).

21. (New York: Holt, 1987).

22. (New York: PaperJacks, 1988). This novel is a sequel to Hunt's *Borderland* (New York: PaperJacks, 1987), which deals with John Brown and the trouble in Kansas before the war.

23. (New York: A. A. Knopf, 1938).

24. (New York: Doubleday, 1957).

25. (New York: Ace Books, 1953). Although both novels are set mostly in Kansas and their major action takes place after the war, two other novels by Gruber have some bearing on the war in Missouri: *Buffalo Grass: A Novel of Kansas* (1956) and *The Bushwhackers* (1959), both published in New York by Rinehart.

26. (Montreal, Quebec: Quadrant Editions, 1982).

27. (Glendale, CA: Barbe Associates, 1949).

28. Ibid., 37-38.

29. (New York: A. L. Burt, 1912).

30. (New York: Pageant Press, 1961).

31. Ibid., 334. The wars in Kansas during the 1850s with Brown and his family at the center were a prelude to the war in Missouri, and they too have generated a surprising number of novels. The best among these include Margaret Lynn, *Free Soil* (New York: Macmillan, 1920); Leonard Ehrlich, *God's Angry Man* (New York: Simon & Schuster, 1932); and Truman Nelson, *The Surveyor* (Garden City, NY: Doubleday, 1960).

32. (New York: Doubleday, Page, 1905).

33. (New York: J. B. Lippincott, 1942).

34. (New York: Appleton-Century-Crofts, 1961).

35. (New York: A. Lovell, 1892).

36. (Philadelphia: John Winston, 1911).

37. (Palmyra, MO: Press of Sosey Bros., 1903).

38. (Boston: Little, Brown, 1899). For an interesting look at history behind the novel, see William F. Woerner's *J. Gabriel Woerner: A Biographical Sketch* (St. Louis: Nixon-Jones, 1912), 15, 102-103.

39. Woerner, *Rebel's Daughter*, 71.

40. (Chicago: Scroll, 1901).

41. (New York: Macmillan, 1901).

42. (New York: A. L. Burt, 1904).

43. Ibid., 293.

44. Churchill, *The Crisis*, 317-318.

45. (New York: Exposition Press, 1965).

46. (New York: Merriam, 1894).

47. The novels in the series in order of their appearance are *With Lyon in Missouri* (1910), *The Scout of Pea Ridge* (1911), *The Courier of the Ozarks* (1912), *Storming Vicksburg* (1913), and *The Last Raid* (1914). All five volumes were published in Chicago by A. C. McClurg.

48. (Chicago: A. C. McClurg, 1914).

49. (New York: Frederick A. Stokes, 1941).

50. (New York: Crowell, 1948).

51. (New York: Holiday House, 1954).

52. (New York: Crowell, 1957).

53. (New York: Abelard Schuman, 1963).

54. (Independence, MO: Independence Press, 1973).

55. (Independence, MO: Independence Press, 1976).

56. (New York: Dodd, Mead, 1975).

57. (New York: W. Morrow, 1931).

58. (New York: A. A. Knopf, 1938).

59. (New York: Dutton, 1949).

60. (New York: Doubleday, Doran, 1940).

61. (Garden City, NY: Doubleday, Doran, 1942).

62. (New York: Vanguard Press, 1958).

63. Hutchens, *John Brown's Cousin*, 68.

64. Burress, *Bugle in the Wilderness*, 159.

65. (New York: Dodd, Mead, 1966).

66. (New York: Holt, Rinehart and Winston, 1980).

67. (New York: Warner Books, 1986).

68. (New York: Pocket Books, 1988).

69. Samuel Taylor Coleridge, *The Collected Works of Samuel Taylor Coleridge*, vol. 7, *Biographia Literaria or Biographical Sketches of My Literary Life and Opinions*, ed. James Engell and W. Jackson Bate (Princeton, NJ: Princeton University Press, 1983), 127. Coleridge's original reads ". . . who takes away the liberty of the poet, and fetter his feet in the shackles of an historian."

Contributors

Robert Patrick Bender is a history instructor at Eastern New Mexico University-Roswell. He received a PhD degree from the University of Arkansas.

John W. Blassingame retired as a professor of history at Yale University. He received a PhD degree from Yale. (Deceased 2000)

Albert Castel retired as professor of history at Western Michigan University in Kalamazoo. He received a PhD degree from the University of Chicago.

Lawrence O. Christensen is a Curators' Teaching Professor Emeritus at the University of Missouri-Rolla. He received a PhD degree from the University of Missouri-Columbia.

William B. Hesseltine retired as Vilas Professor of History at the University of Wisconsin-Madison. He received a PhD degree from Ohio State University. (Deceased 1963)

Arthur Roy Kirkpatrick retired as a history professor at Bethany College, Bethany, WV. He received a PhD degree from the University of Missouri-Columbia. (Deceased 1980)

Susan A. Arnold McCausland, a resident of Lexington, Missouri, once described herself as a "nonreconstructable, unsurrenderable Confederate." (Deceased 1925)

David D. March retired as professor emeritus of history at Truman State University, Kirksville. He received a PhD degree from the University of Missouri-Columbia. (Deceased 2005)

Larry Olpin is professor emeritus of English at Central Missouri State University, Warrensburg. He received a PhD degree from the University of Massachusetts.

William E. Parrish is professor emeritus of history at Mississippi State University. He received a PhD degree from the University of Missouri-Columbia.

William Garrett Piston is a professor of history at Missouri State University, Springfield. He received a PhD degree from the University of South Carolina.

Marguerite Potter retired as a professor of history at Texas Christian University, Fort Worth. She received a PhD degree from the University of Texas. (Deceased 1981)

Index